SEARCH FOR THE UNKNOWN

Search for the Unknown

Canada's UFO Files and the Rise of Conspiracy Theory

MATTHEW HAYES

McGill-Queen's University Press
Montreal & Kingston • London • Chicago

ISBN 978-0-2280-1074-6 (cloth)
ISBN 978-0-2280-1229-0 (ePDF)
ISBN 978-0-2280-1230-6 (ePUB)

Legal deposit second quarter 2022
Bibliothèque nationale du Québec

Printed in Canada on acid-free paper that is 100% ancient forest free (100% post-consumer recycled), processed chlorine free

This book has been published with the help of a grant from the Canadian Federation for the Humanities and Social Sciences, through the Awards to Scholarly Publications Program, using funds provided by the Social Sciences and Humanities Research Council of Canada.

Funded by the Government of Canada | Financé par le gouvernement du Canada | Canada

Canada Council for the Arts | Conseil des arts du Canada

We acknowledge the support of the Canada Council for the Arts.
Nous remercions le Conseil des arts du Canada de son soutien.

Library and Archives Canada Cataloguing in Publication

Title: Search for the unknown : Canada's UFO files and the rise of conspiracy theory / Matthew Hayes.
Names: Hayes, Matthew (Historian), author.
Description: Includes bibliographical references and index.
Identifiers: Canadiana (print) 2021036355X | Canadiana (ebook) 20210363649 | ISBN 9780228010746 (cloth) | ISBN 9780228012290 (ePDF) | ISBN 9780228012306 (ePUB)
Subjects: LCSH: Unidentified flying objects—Sightings and encounters—Canada—History—20th century. | LCSH: Unidentified flying objects—Government policy—Canada—History—20th century. | LCSH: Government information—Canada—History—20th century. | LCSH: Conspiracy theories—Canada—History—20th century.
Classification: LCC TL789.6.C3 H39 2022 | DDC 001.9420971—dc23

This book was typeset in 10.5/13 Sabon.

Contents

Figures and Plates vii

Acknowledgments xi

Abbreviations xiii

Introduction 3

1 Wilbert Smith and Project Magnet, 1950–54 18

2 Project Second Storey, 1952–54 49

3 Very Persistent Men, 1954–67 71

4 Three Cases of High Strangeness, 1967 106

5 The End, 1967–95 125

Conclusion 162

Notes 169

Index 207

Figures and Plates

FIGURES

0.1 UFO types. Library and Archives Canada, RG 77, vol. 308, file UAR/N76 051-090, microfilm reel T-1742. 7

1.1 Portrait of Wilbert Smith, Department of Transport engineer. Archives of the University of Ottawa, CA ON0034 30-003-S1-SS3-F1, Wilbert Smith: Biographical Material. 20

1.2 Wilbert Smith balloon experiment. Archives of the University of Ottawa, CA ON0034 30-003-S1-SS2-F3, Project Second Storey: Department of Transport Weather Balloon Experiment. 28

1.3 Wilbert Smith's UFO observatory at Shirley's Bay, near Ottawa. Archives of the University of Ottawa, CA ON0034 30-003-S1-SS1-F8, Project Magnet: Photographs. 36

1.4 Interior of Smith's UFO observatory. Archives of the University of Ottawa, CA ON0034 30-003-S1-SS1-F8, Project Magnet: Photographs. 38

3.1 CERVIS-MERINT reporting procedure poster. Library and Archives Canada, RG 12, acc. 1980–81/303, box 14, file 700 20, pt. 2. 88

4.1 Sketch of UFO by Stephan Michalak. Library and Archives Canada, RG 77, vol. 311, file DND/UAR (1967) 200, microfilm reel T-1744. 111

4.2 Drawing of crop circles near Camrose, Alberta, by Captain Walker, Royal Canadian Army Service Corps. Library and Archives Canada, RG 77, vol. 310, file DND/UAR (1967) 91–100, microfilm reel T-1744. 117

4.3 "Dark Object" telex report detailing Shag Harbour incident. Library and Archives Canada, RG 77, vol. 310, file DND/UAR (1967) 116–25, microfilm reel T-1744. 120

5.1 CAPIC citizen UFO investigation budget. Library and Archives Canada, RG 24-G-1 BAN 2003-00412-2, box 1, file 2000-4. 133

5.2 Last sighting report of the NRC's UFO sightings program. Library and Archives Canada, RG 77, acc. 1997–98/046, box 1, file N95, 1–54. 158

PLATES

1 UFO drawing: "What I saw in the sky on July 2, at night." Library and Archives Canada, RG 77, vol. 307, file UAR/N74 001-062, microfilm reel T-1742.

2 Drawing of UFO on Royal Canadian whisky pad paper. Library and Archives Canada, RG 77, vol. 309, file UAR/N80 151-200, microfilm reel T-1743.

3–4 Rudimentary UFO sketches. Library and Archives Canada, RG 77, vol. 306, file UAR/N69 050-100, microfilm T-1741.

5 "Electron" UFO drawing, July 1992. Library and Archives Canada, RG 77, acc. 1992–93/308, vol. 1, file N92, 1–83.

6 "Wavy" UFO drawing. Library and Archives Canada, RG 18, vol. 3779, file HQ-400-Q-5, pt. 2.

7 Drawing of UFO with flaming tail. Library and Archives Canada, RG 97, vol. 182, file 5010-4, pt. 1.

8 Drawing of UFO with foggy light and truck. Library and Archives Canada, RG 77, acc. 1986–87/377, box 1, file N86, 61–87.

9 UFO drawing with map. Library and Archives Canada, RG 77, acc. 1985–86/179, file N84, 1–29.

10 Drawing of UFO with road, couple on porch, and barking dog. Library and Archives Canada, RG 77, acc. 1986–7/377, box 1, file N85, 1–75.

11 Drawing of "very low" UFO. Library and Archives Canada, RG 77, vol. 307, file UAR/N3 001-054, microfilm reel T-1741.

12 Street map from Yellowknife, Northwest Territories, indicating UFO sighting. Library and Archives Canada, RG 18, vol. 3779, file HQ-400-Q-5, pt. 5.

13 Pilot's cockpit diagram of UFO sighting. Library and Archives Canada, RG 77, acc. 1992–93/016, box 1, file N91, 70–115.
14 Drawing of rolling/spinning UFO. Library and Archives Canada, RG 77, vol. 309, file UAR/N80 001-050, microfilm reel T-1743.
15 UFO report from Strasbourg, Ontario, with small drawing. Library and Archives Canada, RG 18, vol. 3779, file HQ-400-Q-5, pt. 2.
16 Three-witness UFO sighting with drawings. Library and Archives Canada, RG 97, vol. 182, file 5010-4 pt. 1.
17 UFO drawing with cobras and other creatures. Library and Archives Canada, RG 77, vol. 308, file UAR/N77 101-130, microfilm reel T-1743.
18 Drawing of flying saucers with electricity transmission line. Library and Archives Canada, RG 77, vol. 308, file UAR/N77 101-130, microfilm reel T-1743.
19 "Dipper" UFO drawing. Library and Archives Canada, RG 18, vol. 3779, file HQ-400-Q-5, pt. 5.
20 Drawing of striped UFO with blue tail flame. Library and Archives Canada, RG 77, vol. 310, file DND/UAR (1967) 41–50, microfilm reel T-1743.
21 Glowing white UFO resting atop four pillars. Library and Archives Canada, RG 77, vol. 311, file UAR/N81 1–68, microfilm reel T-1744.

Acknowledgments

This book began its life as a PhD dissertation in the School for the Study of Canada at Trent University. I owe thanks to a number of people there, who provided patient and encouraging guidance, foremost among them: my supervisor Christopher Dummitt, my committee members Peter Hodgins and Edward Jones-Imhotep, and the school's administrators Cathy Schoel and Jeannine Crowe. I benefitted greatly from the chance to speak about my project on the CBC program *Ideas*, which helped me make sense of what I was trying to say. Thank you to Nicola Luksic and Tom Howell for the opportunity. One day, out of the blue, Kyla Madden from McGill-Queen's University Press reached out to me to talk about a possible book. I am grateful that she did so. I cannot thank Kyla enough for her patience and expert editorial guidance on turning my dissertation into this book. Thanks also go to a number of other people who have provided invaluable assistance along the way: Christopher Ryan, Leah Weiner, Veronique Paris, Wendy Robicheau, Laura Thursby, and Noah Morritt. Lastly, I want to thank all the civil servants and ufologists who have worked to understand what this whole UFO phenomenon amounts to. They have often disagreed with one another (and probably still do), yet their interactions are the reason I was able to do this project at all. Whatever UFOs turn out to be, I am grateful for their efforts.

Abbreviations

CAPIC	Canadian Aerial Phenomena Investigations Committee
CAPRO	Canadian Aerial Phenomena Research Organization
CFB	Canadian Forces Base
CFHQ	Canadian Forces Headquarters
CUFOR	Canadian UFO Research
DND	Department of National Defence
DoT	Department of Transport
DRB	Defence Research Board
JIC	Joint Intelligence Committee
LAC	Library and Archives Canada
NICAP	National Investigations Committee on Aerial Phenomena
NRC	National Research Council
PM	Project Magnet
PSS	Project Second Storey
RCAF	Royal Canadian Air Force
RCMP	Royal Canadian Mounted Police
UOA	University of Ottawa Archives
UFO	unidentified flying object

Plate 1 | Drawing of UFO typical of the sort that accompany many sighting reports. This example depicts a classic-type domed flying saucer, described simply as "shiny" and "metallic," with a "tail-light." There is no sense of scale or position, other than a crescent moon. The note at the top – "What I saw in the sky on July 2, at night" – provides no information that would help identify the object. Investigators found it difficult to make use of such drawings, and generally did not take them seriously.

Plate 2 | Sometimes witnesses felt the need to draw what they saw immediately, before the details slipped away. And sometimes in such moments, all the paper they had to hand was stationary from a hotel or bar – in this case, a pad advertising Royal Canadian whisky.

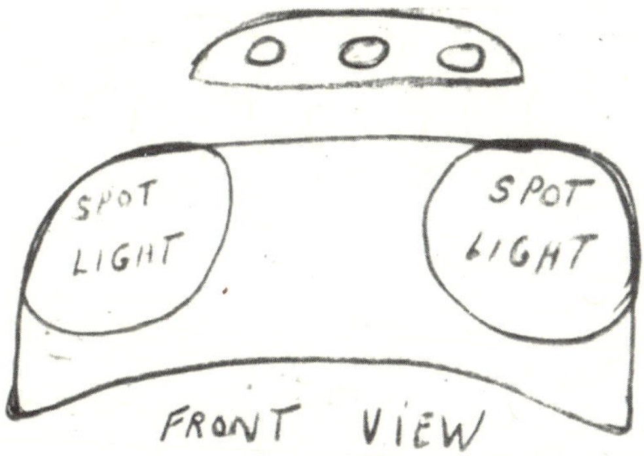

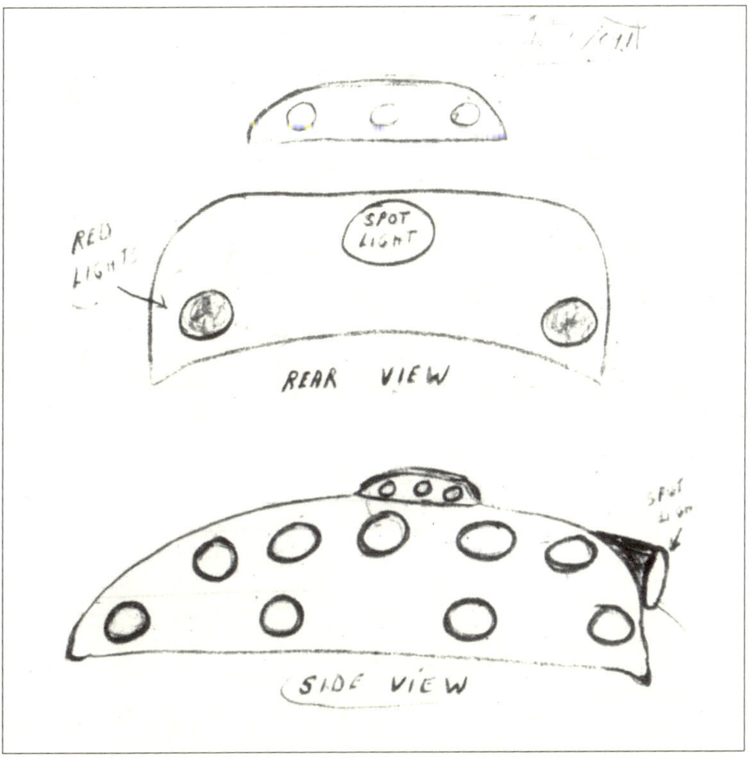

Plates 3–4 | More often than not, UFO drawings by citizens looked like these: rudimentary, with scant detail and little or no sense of scale or setting. It is hard to glean much from drawings like these, posing a problem for investigators: what to do with them?

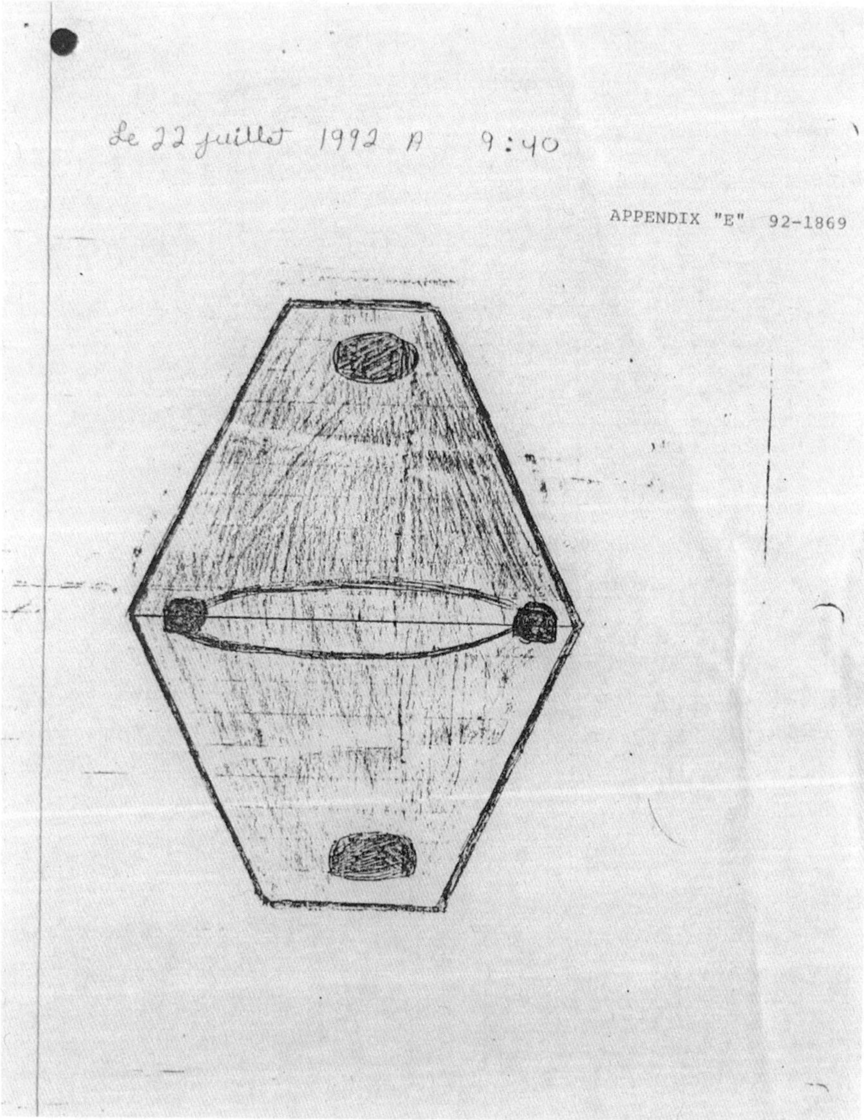

Plate 5 | "Electron" UFO. The centre portion of this drawing, from July 1992, resembles two electrons orbiting one another. That is likely not what the witness intended, but we tend to project our imaginations onto drawings such as this, which are ambiguous enough to invite multiple readings. In this case, at least, the artist gave the object shading to indicate texture.

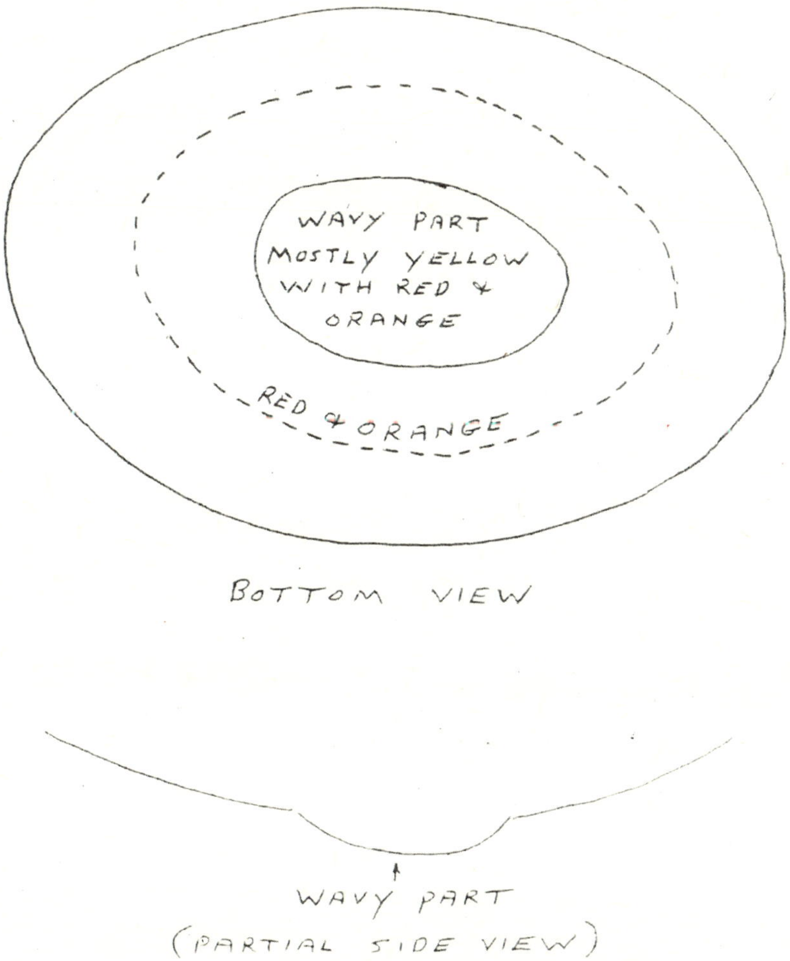

Plate 6 | "Wavy" UFO. This drawing is typical as the hues indicated – red, yellow, and orange – were the most commonly reported colours of UFO lights. In fact, often reported sightings were simply sightings of lights, without any craft. This UFO appears to have a domed top, another characteristic feature of many drawings.

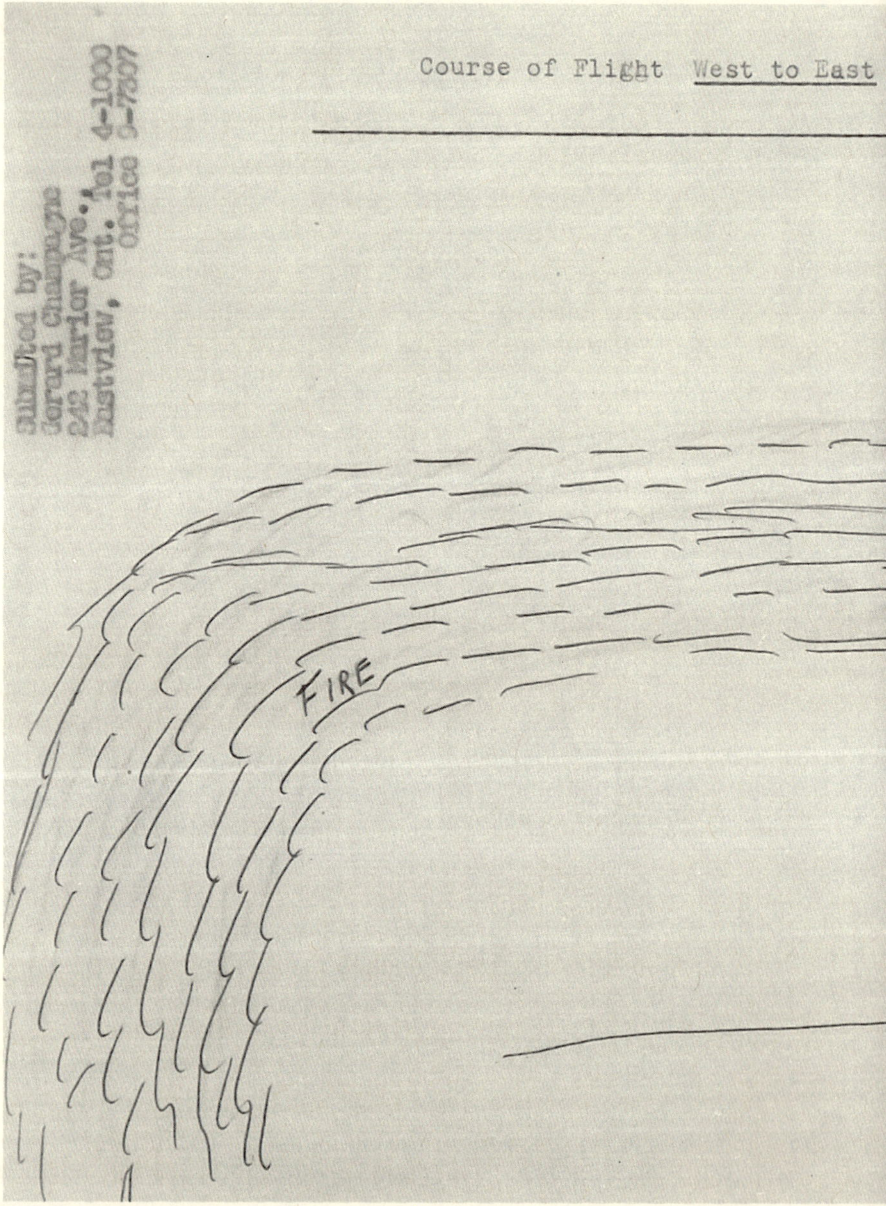

Plate 7 | This drawing is unusual because witnesses do not often report UFOs with tails of flame, which are more characteristic of conventional aircraft.

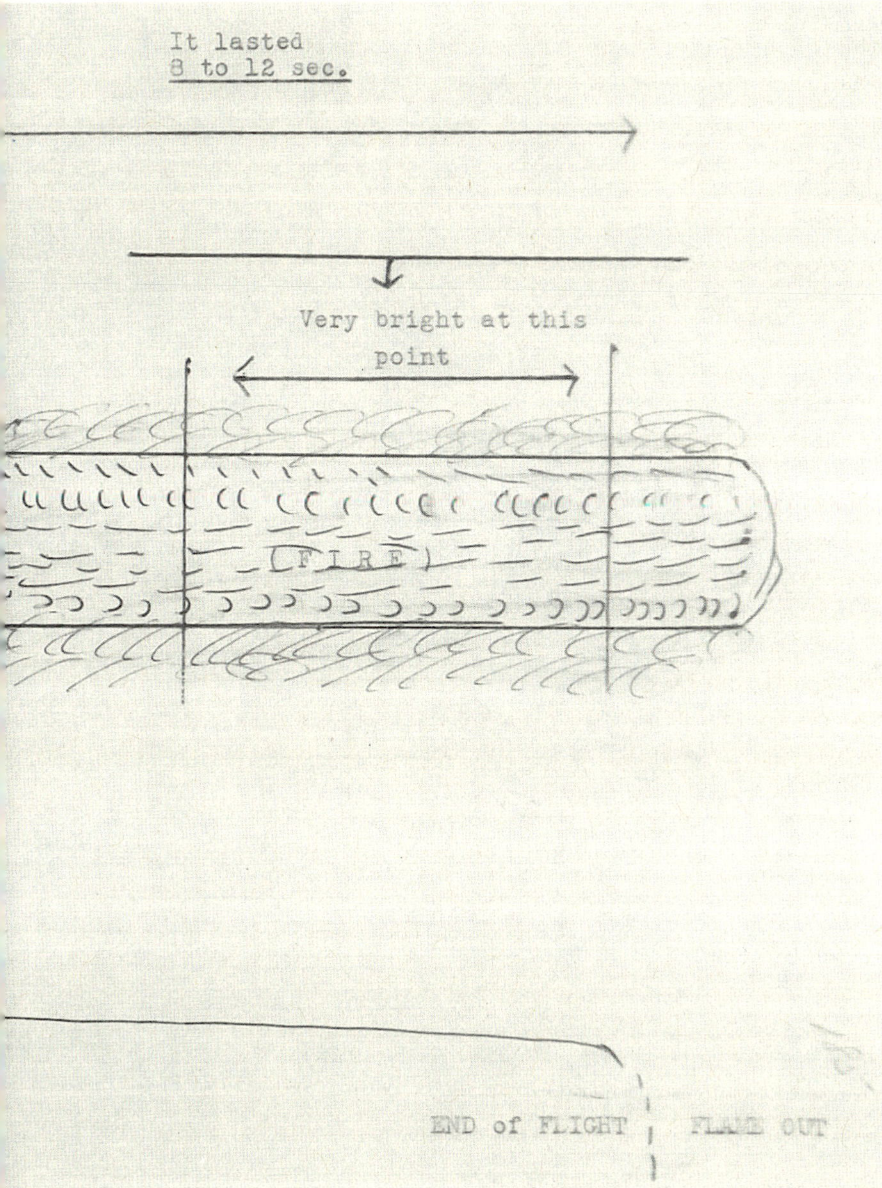
It lasted
8 to 12 sec.
Very bright at this point
(FIRE)
END of FLIGHT
FLAME OUT

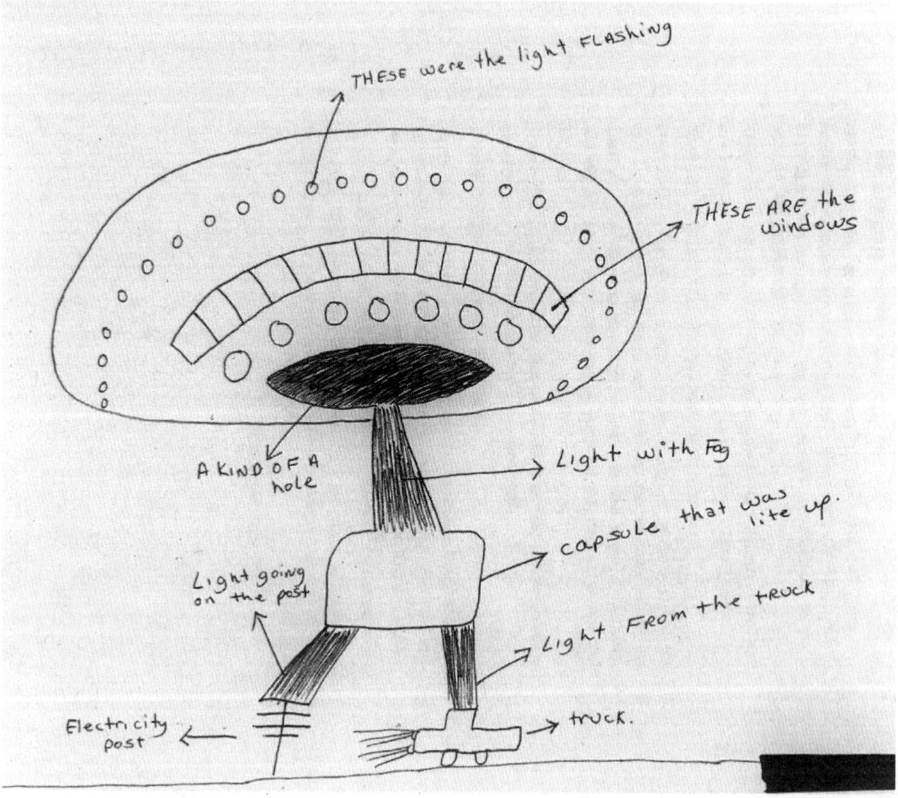

Plate 8 | This UFO drawing may please fans of the 1977 film *Close Encounters of the Third Kind,* as it recalls the famous scene in which the spacecraft envelops a truck with light.

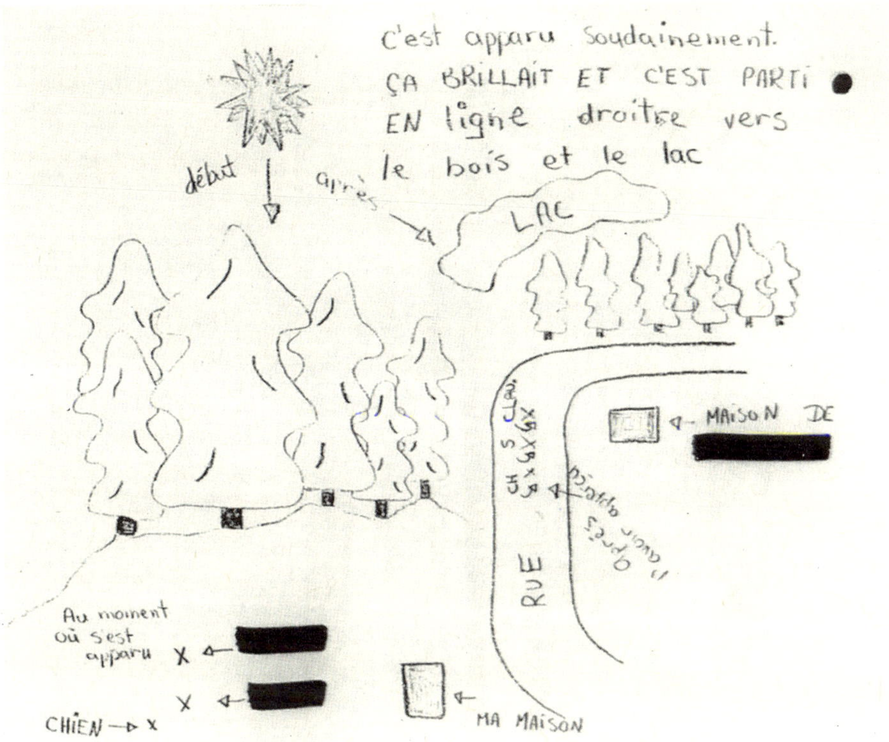

Plate 9 | "C'est apparu soudainement." Some UFO drawings provide better scale and detail than others. This image, with a small map of the scene, provides a sense of direction and position that others lack.

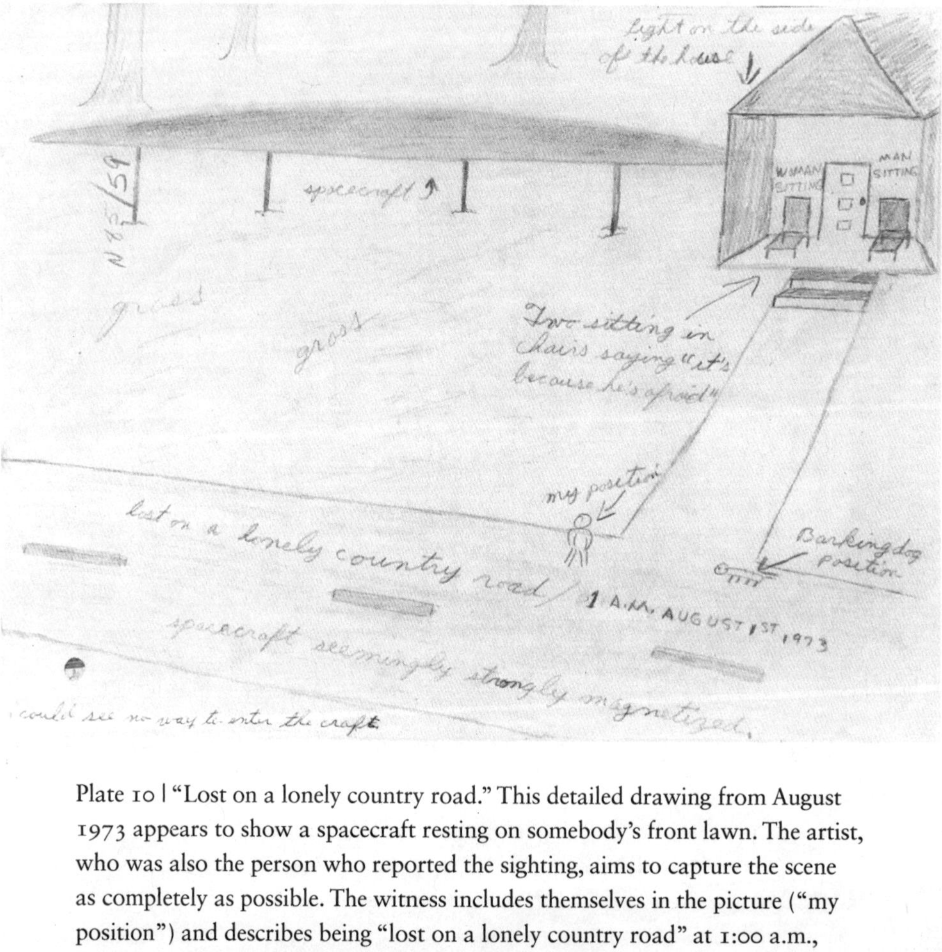

Plate 10 | "Lost on a lonely country road." This detailed drawing from August 1973 appears to show a spacecraft resting on somebody's front lawn. The artist, who was also the person who reported the sighting, aims to capture the scene as completely as possible. The witness includes themselves in the picture ("my position") and describes being "lost on a lonely country road" at 1:00 a.m., when the sighting took place. The picture shows the chairs of two people – a man and a woman – sitting on their front porch (though only their chairs are depicted) with a barking dog on the sidewalk. A written detail indicates the couple explaining that the dog was barking "because he's afraid." Were they?

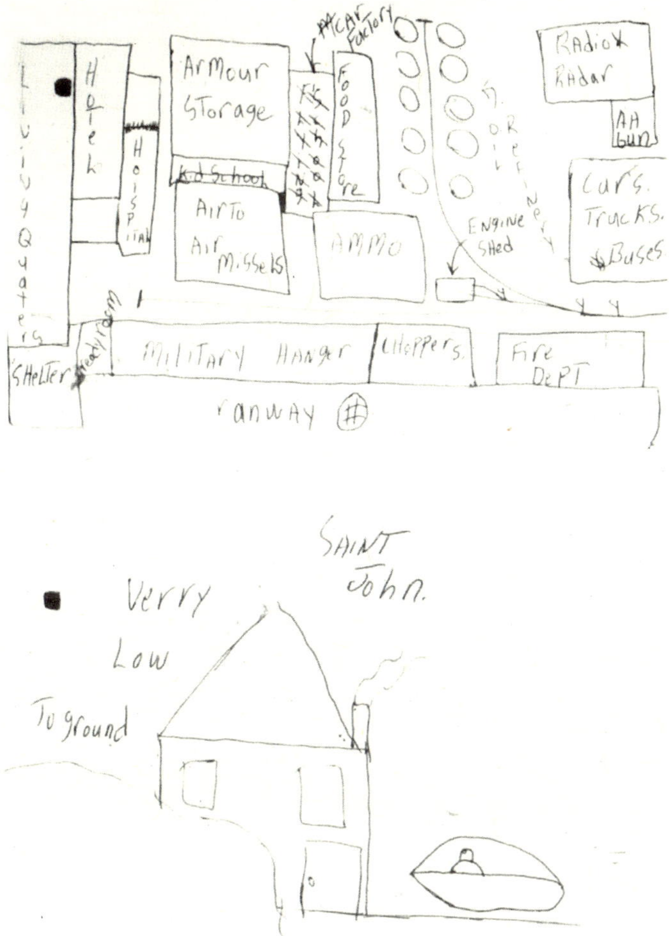

Plate 11 | "Very low" UFO. What at first appears, in the upper drawing, to be a map of a military base becomes a bit confusing: it is not clear why a base would have a hotel. This map was perhaps drawn from memory, and so might contain some inaccuracies. Some investigators took it upon themselves to surveil military bases because these areas tended to see higher numbers of sightings; in fact, this is the premise of the second episode of the television series *The X-Files*. The lower drawing shows a UFO hovering just above the ground, next to a house. It is one of only a few drawings to depict an occupant of the craft.

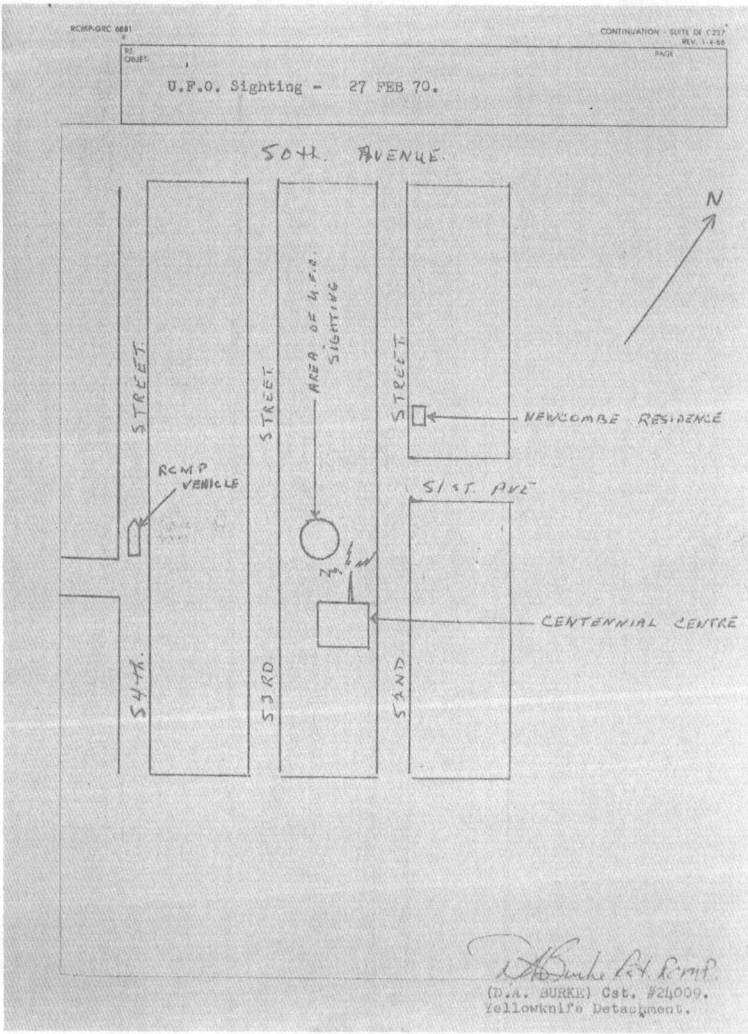

Plate 12 | This drawn map of a residential section of Yellowknife, Northwest Territories, is quite precise, perhaps because it was prepared by an RCMP officer. The map clearly indicates the location of an RCMP vehicle and the area of the UFO sighting, next to a building marked "Centennial Centre," with a transmitting antenna.

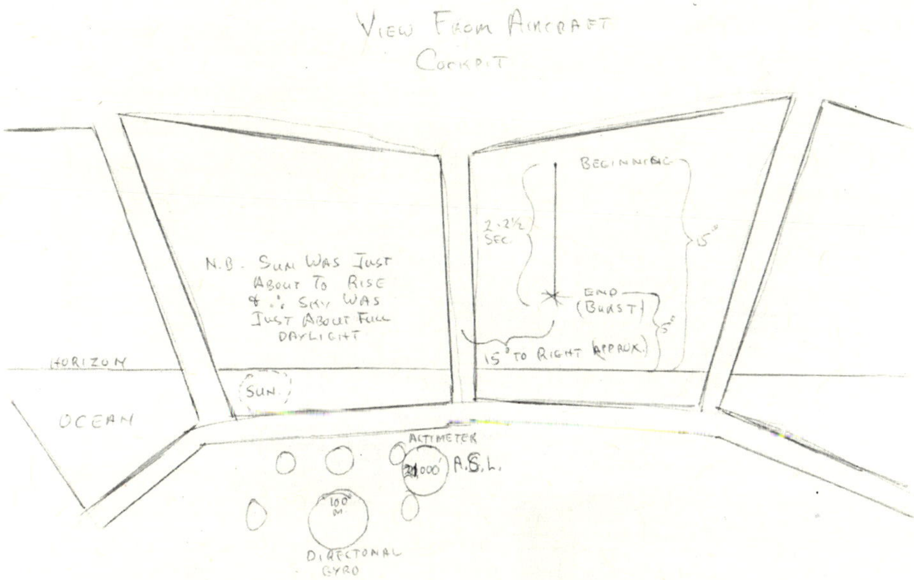

Plate 13 | Officials generally considered reports by pilots to be more reliable than those of citizen witnesses because of their "sky training." This drawing of the cockpit of the pilot's aircraft contains technical details that most citizen drawings lack.

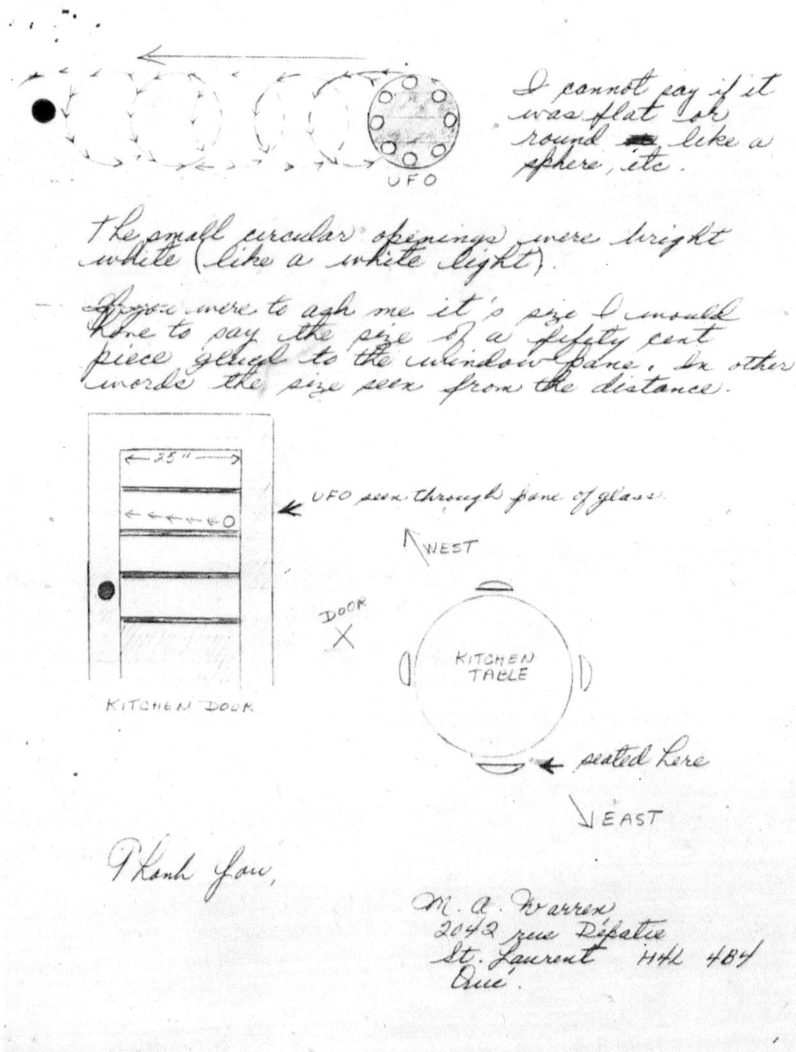

Plate 14 | This drawing shows a UFO, seen through a kitchen window, spinning through the air in a rolling motion. The illustration indicates the object's direction of motion, a detail most drawings lacked.

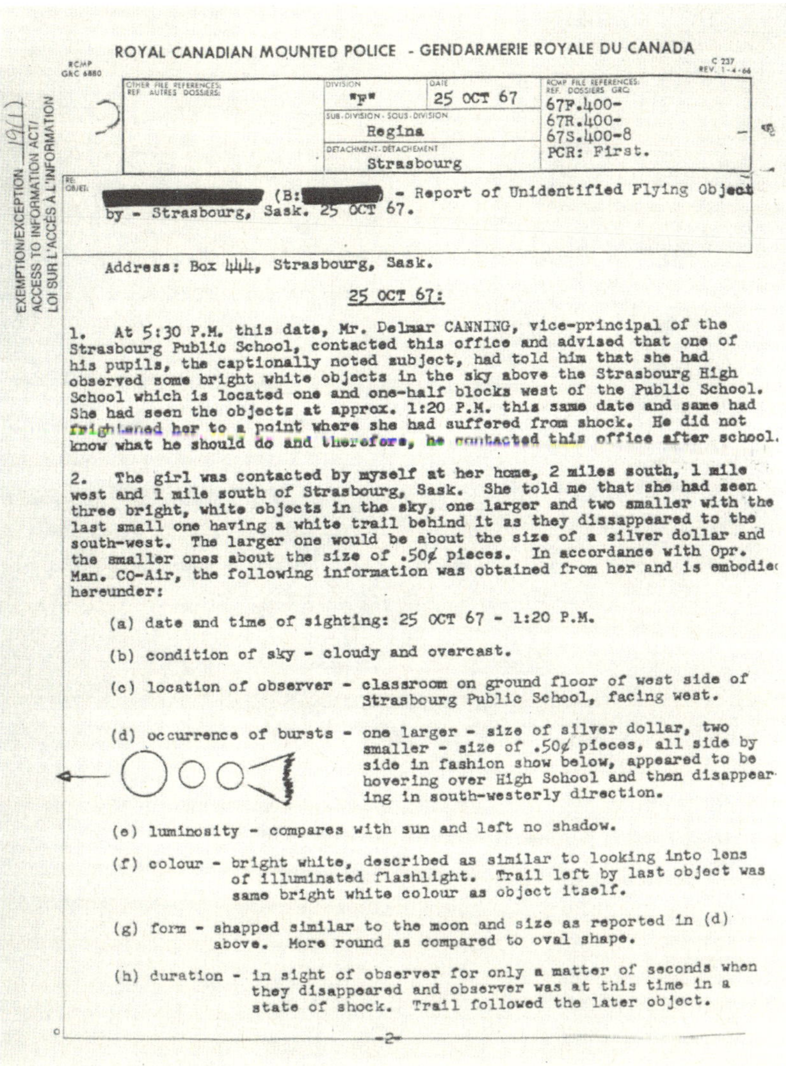

ROYAL CANADIAN MOUNTED POLICE - GENDARMERIE ROYALE DU CANADA

RCMP GRC 6880 | C 237 REV. 1-4-66

EXEMPTION/EXCEPTION 19(1)
ACCESS TO INFORMATION ACT/
LOI SUR L'ACCÈS À L'INFORMATION

OTHER FILE REFERENCES: REF. AUTRES DOSSIERS:	DIVISION: "F"	DATE: 25 OCT 67	RCMP FILE REFERENCES: REF. DOSSIERS GRC: 67F.400- 67R.400- 67S.400-8 PCR: First.
	SUB-DIVISION - SOUS-DIVISION: Regina		
	DETACHMENT - DÉTACHEMENT: Strasbourg		

RE: OBJET: ██████████ (B: ██████) - Report of Unidentified Flying Object by - Strasbourg, Sask. 25 OCT 67.

Address: Box 444, Strasbourg, Sask.

25 OCT 67:

1. At 5:30 P.M. this date, Mr. Delmar CANNING, vice-principal of the Strasbourg Public School, contacted this office and advised that one of his pupils, the captionally noted subject, had told him that she had observed some bright white objects in the sky above the Strasbourg High School which is located one and one-half blocks west of the Public School. She had seen the objects at approx. 1:20 P.M. this same date and same had frightened her to a point where she had suffered from shock. He did not know what he should do and therefore, he contacted this office after school.

2. The girl was contacted by myself at her home, 2 miles south, 1 mile west and 1 mile south of Strasbourg, Sask. She told me that she had seen three bright, white objects in the sky, one larger and two smaller with the last small one having a white trail behind it as they dissappeared to the south-west. The larger one would be about the size of a silver dollar and the smaller ones about the size of .50¢ pieces. In accordance with Opr. Man. CO-Air, the following information was obtained from her and is embodied hereunder:

(a) date and time of sighting: 25 OCT 67 - 1:20 P.M.

(b) condition of sky - cloudy and overcast.

(c) location of observer - classroom on ground floor of west side of Strasbourg Public School, facing west.

(d) occurrence of bursts - one larger - size of silver dollar, two smaller - size of .50¢ pieces, all side by side in fashion show below, appeared to be hovering over High School and then disappearing in south-westerly direction.

(e) luminosity - compares with sun and left no shadow.

(f) colour - bright white, described as similar to looking into lens of illuminated flashlight. Trail left by last object was same bright white colour as object itself.

(g) form - shapped similar to the moon and size as reported in (d) above. More round as compared to oval shape.

(h) duration - in sight of observer for only a matter of seconds when they disappeared and observer was at this time in a state of shock. Trail followed the later object.

-2-

Plate 15 | This UFO report, from Strasbourg, Ontario, is quite typical of those from the RCMP in terms of format, length, and style. It is accompanied by a small drawing, integrated directly into the report, though it is not clear who drew it – the RCMP officer or the witness. In this case, the modest drawing serves as a quick visual aid.

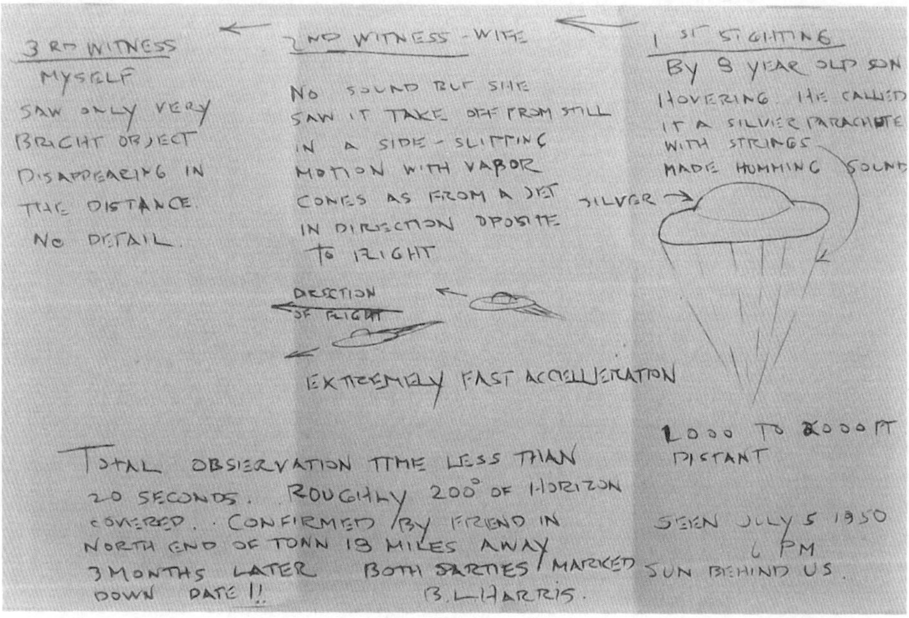

Plate 16 | What is unique about this drawing is that it contains the reports of three different witnesses (albeit all from the same family). Reports that included corroboration from more than one witness were quite unusual and often led investigators to conclude that the account of the incident was more reliable.

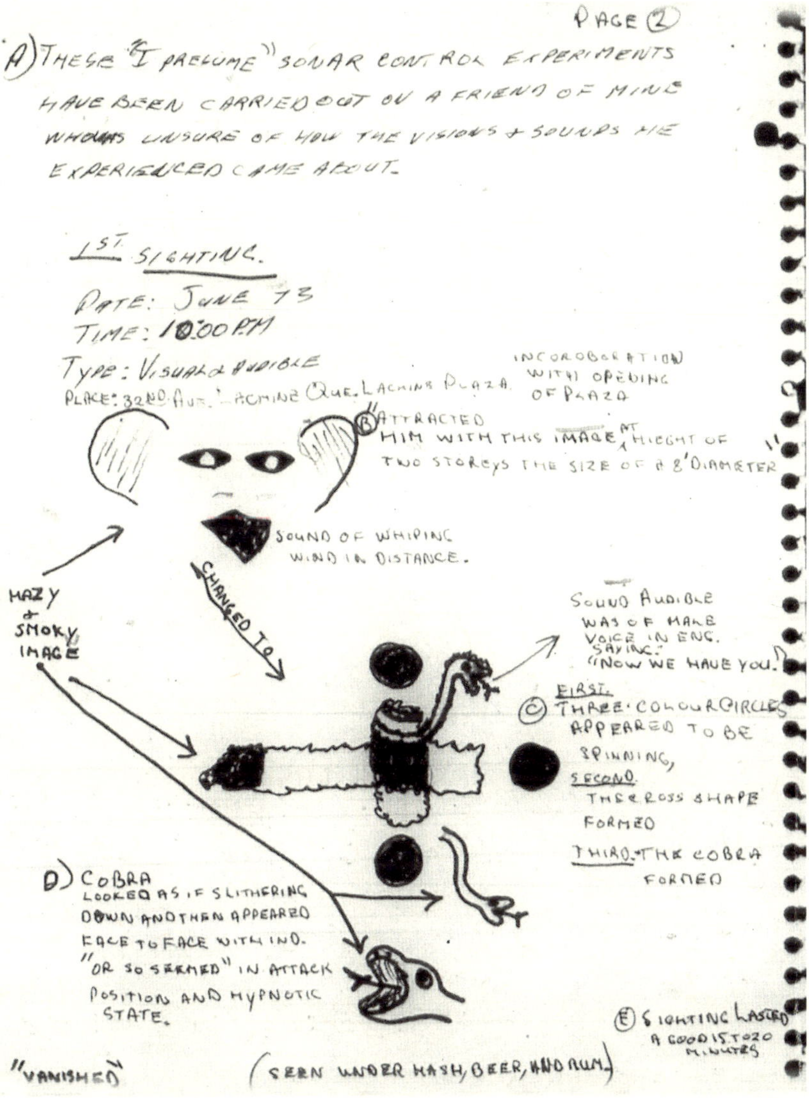

Plate 17 | "Now we have you." Perhaps the oddest drawing in the Canadian UFO files, this one seems to depict a series of strange creatures who spoke to the witness and hypnotized them for a time. Most unfortunate for the credibility of this witness, the document notes that they were under the influence of "hash, beer, and rum."

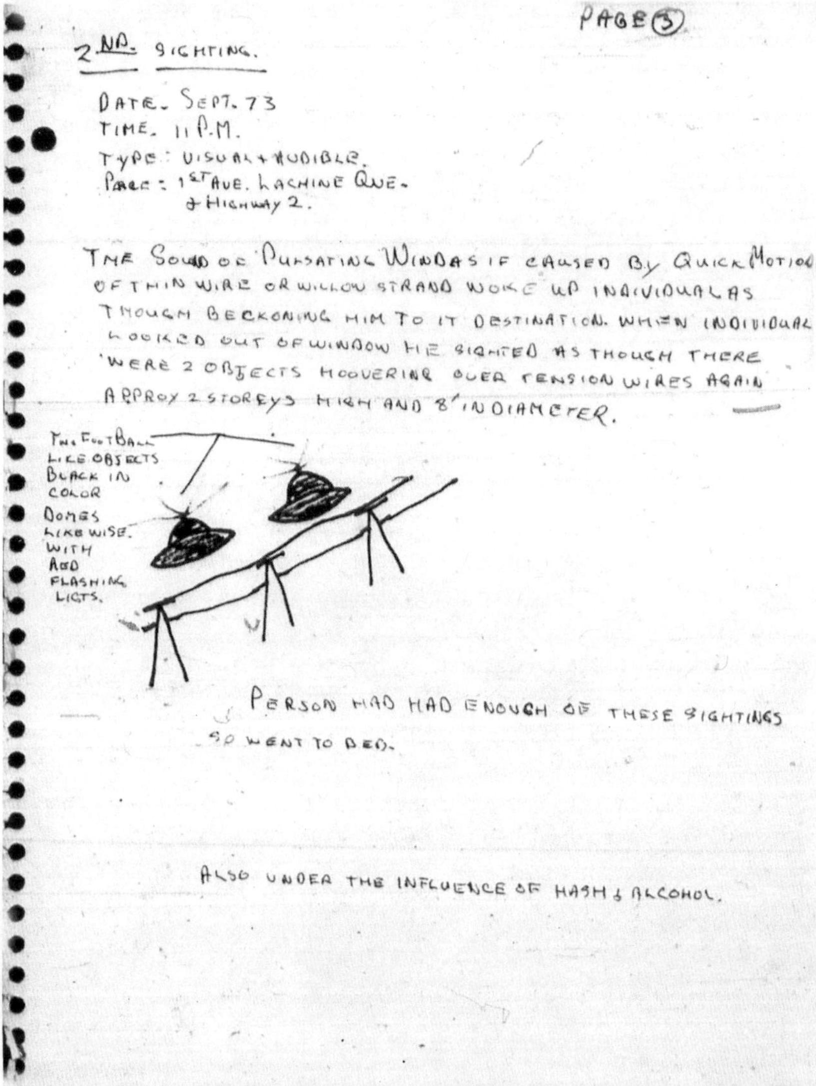

PAGE (3)

2ND. SIGHTING.

DATE. SEPT. 73
TIME. 11 P.M.
TYPE: VISUAL + AUDIBLE.
PLACE: 1ST AVE. LACHINE QUE. & HIGHWAY 2.

THE SOUND OF PULSATING WIND AS IF CAUSED BY QUICK MOTION OF THIN WIRE OR WILLOW STRAND WOKE UP INDIVIDUAL AS THOUGH BECKONING HIM TO IT DESTINATION. WHEN INDIVIDUAL LOOKED OUT OF WINDOW HE SIGHTED AS THOUGH THERE WERE 2 OBJECTS HOOVERING OVER TENSION WIRES AGAIN APPROX 2 STOREYS HIGH AND 8' IN DIAMETER.

PERSON HAD HAD ENOUGH OF THESE SIGHTINGS SO WENT TO BED.

ALSO UNDER THE INFLUENCE OF HASH & ALCOHOL.

Plate 18 | Part of the same report as the image in Plate 17, this drawing seems to depict two flying saucers hovering above an electricity transmission line. Although not common in the UFO files, behaviour of the sort exhibited by this spacecraft is not unheard of. The witness again made sure to declare the substances they had imbibed.

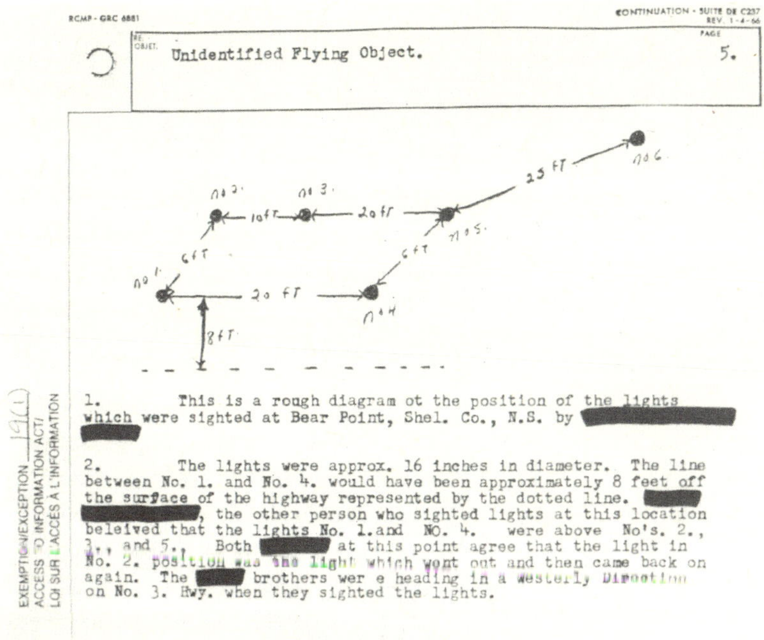

RCMP - GRC 6881

CONTINUATION - SUITE DE C237
REV. 1-4-66

RE: OBJET. Unidentified Flying Object.

PAGE 5.

1. This is a rough diagram ot the position of the lights which were sighted at Bear Point, Shel. Co., N.S. by [redacted]

2. The lights were approx. 16 inches in diameter. The line between No. 1. and No. 4. would have been approximately 8 feet off the surface of the highway represented by the dotted line. [redacted], the other person who sighted lights at this location beleived that the lights No. 1.and NO. 4. were above No's. 2., 3., and 5., Both [redacted] at this point agree that the light in No. 2. position was the light which went out and then came back on again. The [redacted] brothers wer e heading in a westerly Direction on No. 3. Hwy. when they sighted the lights.

EXEMPTION/EXCEPTION 19(1)
ACCESS TO INFORMATION ACT/
LOI SUR L'ACCÈS À L'INFORMATION

Plate 19 | This RCMP report features a drawing of what appears to be a dipper-type constellation, although it is not described as such. Although it is unclear what the witness saw, the drawing strongly suggests a constellation of stars. Misidentifications of natural phenomena account for a large portion of UFO sightings.

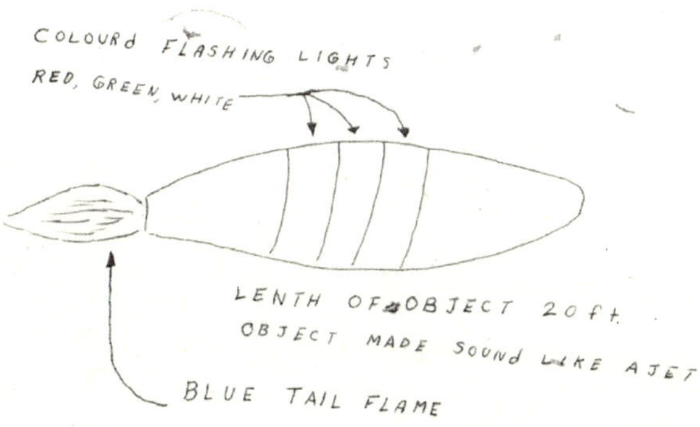

Plate 20 | Perhaps a misidentification of a conventional aircraft, this drawing depicts a classic cigar-shaped UFO. However, witness reports of a tail flame or jet-like sounds are rare.

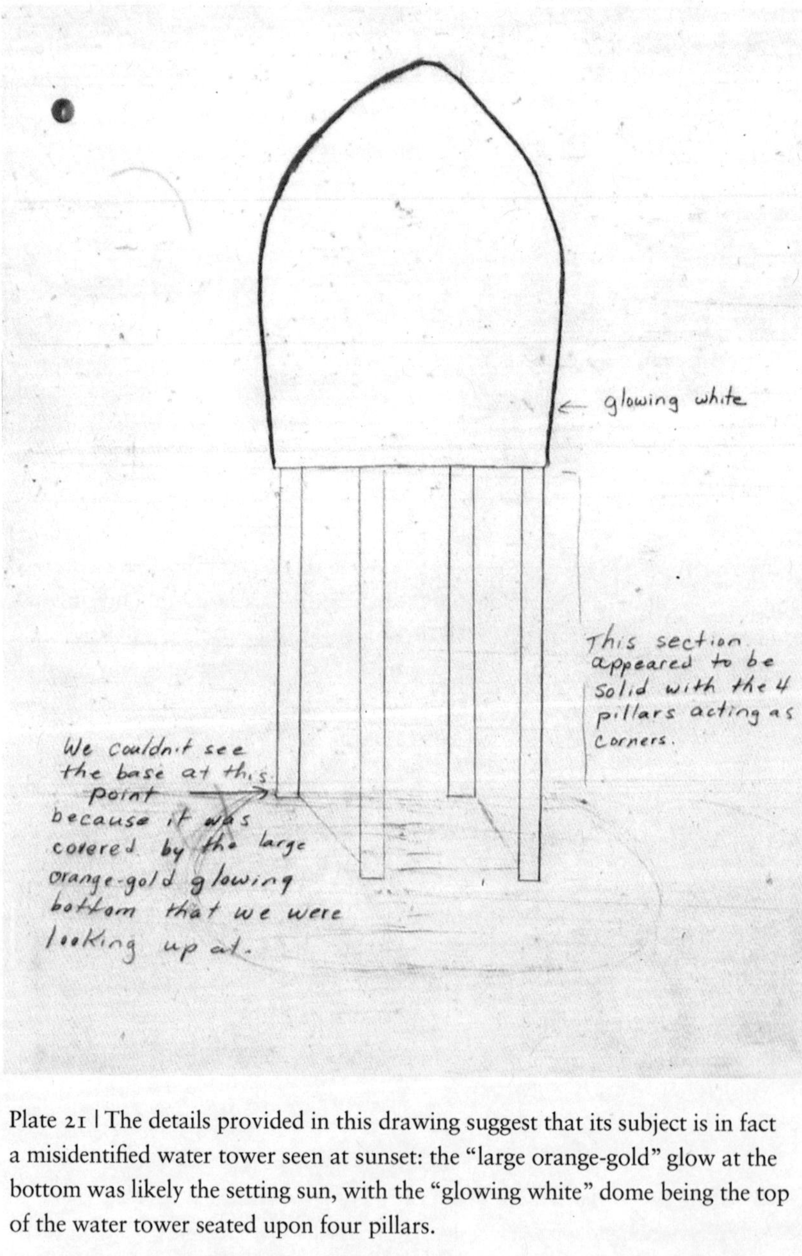

Plate 21 | The details provided in this drawing suggest that its subject is in fact a misidentified water tower seen at sunset: the "large orange-gold" glow at the bottom was likely the setting sun, with the "glowing white" dome being the top of the water tower seated upon four pillars.

SEARCH FOR THE UNKNOWN

Introduction

In July 1960, Vancouver resident Ken Kaasen wrote a letter to the Defence Research Board, Canada's postwar military science agency. "It is a fact that Canada and the United States are not in complete control of their skies ... As bad as it sounds, North America, and many other countries, are wide open for inspection by these unknown flying objects. Can you honestly deny that?" Kaasen was referring to UFOs. He was convinced that they existed, and that the government knew this, but chose to cover it up and stay silent. Kaasen closed his letter with a prayer: "I only hope the UFOs prove to be harmless."[1]

The next month, a publicity officer responded to Kaasen, refuting his claim. "You may be interested to learn that the vast majority of reported sightings have been explained by known phenomena. The remainder have not supplied evidence that any threat to our country exists."[2] Kaasen wrote back that proof that UFOs were piloted by extraterrestrial beings would be forthcoming imminently, though he did not say where this proof would come from. The publicity officer did not respond, and so Kaasen moved on and began writing to other departments, hoping to find a sympathetic ear.

For two years, Ken Kaasen pursued correspondence with various government departments about unidentified flying objects, seeking answers about their origins, their purpose, and their risk to Canadians. He even wrote directly to the minister of national defence. None of the replies that Kaasen received seemed to satisfy his curiosity or alleviate his concerns, and the government officials involved admitted internally that they did not know how to handle his letters.

Kaasen's letters are but one of many exchanges between Canadian citizens and Canadian government officials on the subject of UFOs.

Often, UFO enthusiasts were bold in their assertions and demands for government intervention. In response, government officials usually attempted either to ignore such appeals altogether, or when they did engage, to debunk claims of UFO sightings as nothing other than normal atmospheric phenomena. These exchanges could become heated and convoluted, and could carry on for months or even years.

This book presents a history of the Canadian government's investigations into reports of UFOs, and how these were handled, handed off, and defended from 1950 to the 1990s. In the early part of this period, the Departments of National Defence and Transport, the National Research Council, and the RCMP attempted to understand what UFO sightings were, and whether they posed a security threat or presented an opportunity for scientific inquiry. When they determined by the mid-1950s that there was neither, the challenge became one of responding to claims of UFO sightings and quelling public anxieties. Over the course of the next four decades, these government agencies received approximately 4,500 unique UFO sighting reports and accumulated more than fifteen thousand pages of related documentation. Most of these reports came from, or were initiated by, concerned citizens such as Ken Kaasen, who were not happy with the government's assumption – which citizens gleaned from their correspondence with government officials – that UFOs posed no threat. These citizens wrote thousands of letters to the government campaigning for the disclosure of information about UFOs. When they received what they thought were inadequate responses, they turned, in some cases, to conspiracy theories, and otherwise tried to solve the mystery themselves by starting UFO clubs and citizen investigation groups. Despite these efforts, Canadians know little more about the UFO phenomenon than they did in the late 1940s.[3]

I do not seek to confirm or deny the existence of UFOs, nor do I attempt to explain, or explain away, UFO sightings. Rather, my aim is to understand the history of Canada's responses to the suggestion of the existence of UFOs, which ranged from puzzlement and condescension on the part of the government and law enforcement to suspicion, anxiety, and the dogged pursuit of answers by dedicated citizen UFO enthusiasts.[4] This is a story about what some Canadians expected from their government, how these expectations changed over time, how the government responded, and what this tells us about the state's evolving relationship with its citizens.[5] The actors in this story include scientific and military personnel from various government departments, RCMP officers in detachments around the country, and a wide variety of citizens from every province and major city, and seemingly every small town.

THE MODERN ERA OF UFOS

To date, there has been very little writing on Canada's involvement with the UFO phenomenon. Several books have explored aspects of the investigation, focusing on specific events or surveying sightings over the years, but no work has provided a systematic history of the investigation from start to finish.[6] To get a sense of how Canada came to be involved with the UFO phenomenon at all, a brief history of the American investigation is necessary. As Greg Eghigian has stated, America was the clear "vector" in the UFO story[7] and, given Canada's proximity to the US, there was bound to be some spillover.[8] Canada's UFO history is also simultaneously a history of increasing American influence over Canadian affairs, especially in the cultural and political domains.

The year 1947 was pivotal to the UFO phenomenon; it was the beginning of the "modern era of UFOs."[9] On 24 June 1947, a businessman and private pilot named Kenneth Arnold was flying over Washington state when he witnessed nine shiny discs flying in formation past Mount Rainier. According to Arnold, the discs moved like rocks skipping across water. Arnold's sighting gave rise to the moniker "flying saucer," which an anonymous Associated Press journalist coined in the days after Arnold reported his sighting.[10] Several weeks later, a second event was reported: an alleged crash in the desert outside of Roswell, New Mexico. This event, perhaps the most infamous of the entire phenomenon, is largely responsible for many of the familiar images now associated with UFOs. The standard story is that a technologically advanced craft piloted by extraterrestrial beings malfunctioned and crashed in the desert, only to be found by a local rancher in the early hours of the morning. The US army soon arrived and cleared the scene completely, leaving no traces behind. The next day, an army press release announced that a flying disc had crashed and was recovered. However, this story was quickly retracted and the army instead claimed that what was really recovered was the remains of a balloon that had crashed. This correction was confirmed decades later by an investigation that revealed the details of Project Mogul, a US operation that used balloons to test for nuclear explosions in the upper atmosphere.[11]

The reason for these tests was, of course, the Cold War, which was in full swing by this point. The Cold War – that "competition of ideas" between America and the Soviet Union[12] – impacted the UFO phenomenon in a significant way in its early days, during the 1950s and into the 1960s. As explored in Chapters 1 and 2, fear of advanced Soviet technology and invasion was, at first, the obvious explanation for UFOs, at least for military and government officials. Some citizens, too, were explicitly concerned about Soviet intrusions, as expressed in their letters to the government. It certainly played a role in initiating Canada's own investigations into UFOs, fearing that the Soviets might invade remote northern Canada as a means of gaining access to the US. This is one example of the increasing influence of American concerns on Canadian policy.

Perhaps unexpectedly, however, and quite abruptly, the Cold War fades from the picture after the mid-1960s. By this point, the American and Canadian governments had concluded that UFOs were not connected to the Soviet Union and, in fact, no nation on the planet seemed capable of producing such physics-defying craft. As such, the impact of the Cold War plays a relatively minor role in this story.

In the late 1940s, though, nobody knew quite what to think. Those with a conspiracist mindset pounced on the 1947 Roswell UFO crash story, accusing the US government of a cover-up. This idea has only grown in scope and imagination since, and serves as a founding myth of the phenomenon.[13] The contemporary "disclosure" movement is predicated on the idea that the US government is hiding the "Truth" about Roswell and associated crashes and sightings, and that one day this information will finally be revealed to the public.[14] Part of what fuelled this longstanding interest were the investigations that the US government conducted. After Kenneth Arnold's sighting, which gained significant press attention, UFO sightings began to pour in.[15] Even smaller newspapers, such as the *Charlottetown Guardian* in Prince Edward Island, commented on how widespread the sightings had become: "stories about the discs from many parts of Canada and the United States continued to swirl just as rapidly as the objects themselves."[16] While the American government presumed that UFOs were misidentified natural phenomena, the fear that they were a foreign intrusion, or a top-secret domestic project unknown even to the Air Force, forced the US government to take action.

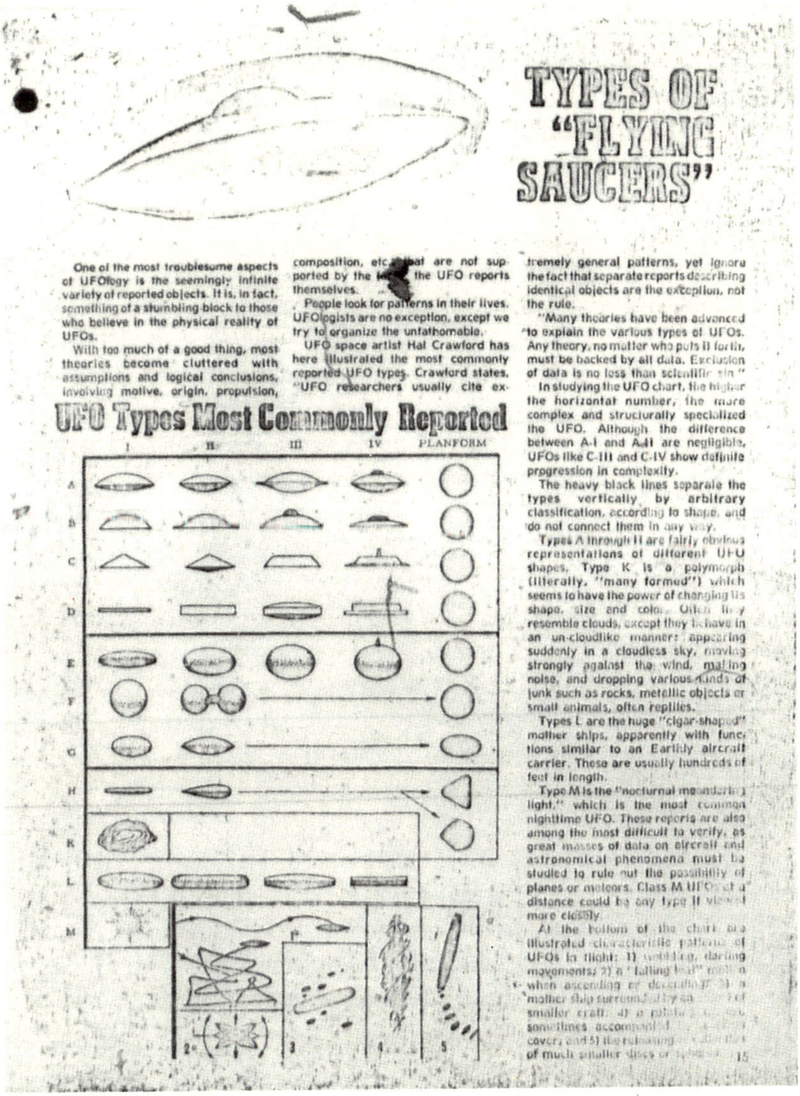

TYPES OF "FLYING SAUCERS"

One of the most troublesome aspects of UFOlogy is the seemingly infinite variety of reported objects. It is, in fact, something of a stumbling block to those who believe in the physical reality of UFOs.

With too much of a good thing, most theories become cluttered with assumptions and logical conclusions, involving motive, origin, propulsion, composition, etc. [illegible] are not supported by the [illegible] the UFO reports themselves.

People look for patterns in their lives. UFOlogists are no exception, except we try to organize the unfathomable.

UFO space artist Hal Crawford has here illustrated the most commonly reported UFO types. Crawford states, "UFO researchers usually cite extremely general patterns, yet ignore the fact that separate reports describing identical objects are the exception, not the rule.

"Many theories have been advanced to explain the various types of UFOs. Any theory, no matter who puts it forth, must be backed by all data. Exclusion of data is no less than scientific sin."

In studying the UFO chart, the higher the horizontal number, the more complex and structurally specialized the UFO. Although the difference between A-I and A-II are negligible, UFOs like C-III and C-IV show definite progression in complexity.

The heavy black lines separate the types vertically by arbitrary classification, according to shape, and do not connect them in any way.

Types A through H are fairly obvious representations of different UFO shapes. Type K is a polymorph (literally, "many formed") which seems to have the power of changing its shape, size and color. Often they resemble clouds, except they behave in an un-cloudlike manner: appearing suddenly in a cloudless sky, moving strongly against the wind, making noise, and dropping various kinds of junk such as rocks, metallic objects or small animals, often reptiles.

Types L are the huge "cigar-shaped" mother ships, apparently with functions similar to an Earthly aircraft carrier. These are usually hundreds of feet in length.

Type M is the "nocturnal meandering light," which is the most common nighttime UFO. These reports are also among the most difficult to verify, as great masses of data on aircraft and astronomical phenomena must be studied to rule out the possibility of planes or meteors. Class M UFOs at a distance could be any type if viewed more closely.

At the bottom of the chart are illustrated characteristic patterns of UFOs in flight: 1) [illegible], darting movements; 2) a "falling leaf" [illegible] when ascending or descending; 3) a mother ship surrounded by [illegible] smaller craft; 4) a [illegible] sometimes accompanied [illegible] cover; and 5) [illegible] of much smaller discs or [illegible]

15

Figure 0.1 | The sheer variety of UFO shapes and sizes bedevilled investigators, as this chart of UFO types admits: it calls the variety "troublesome" and "a stumbling block." The difficulty in finding a clear pattern in turn made it difficult for scientists to engage with the issue.

Beginning in 1948, two projects – Project Sign and Project Grudge – were established to investigate the phenomenon.[17] The projects came to very different conclusions about UFOs: the former concluded that extraterrestrials could be behind the sightings, whereas the latter concluded that all sightings were due to common, natural events. The difference between the two reports has certainly contributed to the idea that some kind of a cover-up was taking place.

To the public, it seemed that the Air Force had stopped investigating UFO reports altogether by the end of 1949. They no longer made any public pronouncements about the subject and did their best to curb their correspondence with civilians. The US government did not like the publicity the studies were attracting, and there was always the fear that someone would divulge legitimate secrets. It is clear from the Air Force's actions that they simply wanted the problem to go away as quickly as possible.[18] But behind closed doors, the US Air Force investigation continued, albeit at a much more minimal level. Project Blue Book, the new investigation launched in 1952, "became largely a public relations effort to convince the American people that UFOs were explainable in prosaic terms."[19] This effort culminated in 1966, when the Air Force commissioned Edward Condon, a physicist at the University of Colorado, to assemble a team of scientists who would analyze the sighting reports that Project Blue Book had compiled. The result was the Condon Report, issued in January 1969, which concluded that the previous twenty-one years of UFO studies had yielded nothing of scientific value and that all efforts into the matter should be discontinued. It also reiterated the official stance that all sightings had mundane origins and that any unexplained cases were simply lacking information.[20] On the report's recommendation, the Air Force terminated Project Blue Book, ending the US government's investigations, at least for the time being.[21]

THE CANADIAN UFO FILES

There is no single Canadian UFO archive. The approximately fifteen thousand pages of documentation that I used for this study are drawn from multiple government departmental archives and collections – and were mostly located with a keyword search. They come from the files of the Department of National Defence, the Department of Transport, the Department of Communications, the RCMP, and the National Research Council.[22] Rarely did departments communicate or collaborate with one another on UFO investigations – a dynamic that will be explored in the following chapters – and so the documents usually remained with the originating department. This reluctance to communicate interdepartmentally became especially obvious when citizens began writing to various departments demanding answers to their questions and receiving different (stock) responses that were sometimes contradictory.

The vast majority of the documents are UFO sighting reports, either formal reports written by government officials, or handwritten or typed letters that citizens sent to the government. In addition, a small selection comprises minutes and associated correspondence from Project Second Storey, one of Canada's two UFO investigations, which ran from 1952 to 1954, and is the subject of Chapter 2. A number of newspaper clippings of UFO stories are found throughout the various files, along with the occasional document from the US government. There are also letters that citizens wrote to various departments, distinct from the sighting reports; these are covered in detail in Chapters 3 and 5. Nearly all sighting reports originated with a citizen who informed authorities – for instance, the local RCMP detachment. From there, the RCMP investigator or government official would type up and file the report with their department. However, many of the letters that citizens sent in were much more than just a report of an observation. They often contained detailed speculations about the origins of the UFOs and asked many questions of the government about its understanding of the phenomena. There are inevitably some letters from citizens who, convinced that the Canadian government was covering up the truth, demanded some kind of disclosure.

The bulk of the documents were conventional sighting reports.[23] These were often RCMP reports, although some originated through other bodies such as the Department of National Defence and, in some cases, air traffic control centres. In total, I counted nearly 4,500 unique UFO sightings in Canada from 1949 to 1995.[24] Most sightings came from Ontario, Alberta, Quebec, and British Columbia. There was a very large spike in sightings in 1967. Sighting reports slowly increased over the years, reaching their highest point in 1969 with 283 sightings. The 1970s was the decade with the most sightings;[25] these were distributed approximately 75 per cent rurally and 25 per cent in urban centres.[26] This is easily explained by such simple factors as the level of light pollution in urban centres, which made it difficult to make out aerial or celestial objects. The overall increase in sighting reports over time reflects several factors: a growing awareness among the public about UFOs; a willingness to report sightings; and the standardization of reporting mechanisms within the government.

While 4,500 sightings sounds like an impressive number, spread over forty-five years it amounted to an average of one or two sightings per week nationwide.[27] In some weeks there were several sightings, with none being reported in other weeks. Considered from this angle, it is perhaps unsurprising that the media paid little attention. From 1947 until 1995, only about a dozen articles on the topic were published in national newspapers or magazines. Local newspapers, especially in rural areas, published about UFOs more regularly, however. And since they were usually reporting on local sightings by people known within the community, they tended to take a less skeptical position and described in detail what had been told to them. This difference in media reporting will be highlighted by the inclusion of local articles that countered the "official" or national view.

In addition, other kinds of media are explored throughout the chapters, namely: films, TV series, and books that played a pivotal role in disseminating information about UFOs to the public. The role of (American) pop culture and entertainment on the UFO phenomenon was significant, certainly helping to drive up sightings over the years. Newspaper reports served to highlight the many sightings reported from around the country, but it was the films of Hollywood, along with television shows and books, predominantly from American producers, that helped solidify the UFO and extraterrestrial tropes with which we are now familiar. These included, notably, the alien abduction theme and even the physical look of the typical almond-eyed extraterrestrial, made famous by the cover of *Communion*, Whitley Strieber's best-selling account of alien abduction.[28]

Overall, the UFO reports registered as a persistent low-level hum, a phenomenon constantly in the background of RCMP, National Research Council, and Department of National Defence activities, among other departments. This history of UFO investigation focuses mostly on the peak periods of activity – on both the government side and the citizen side. Yet it is important to keep in mind that throughout this nearly fifty-year period, there was a continuous flow of sightings all across the country.

THEORETICAL FRAMEWORK

This book is a history of how the Canadian state and some Canadian citizens understood and responded to the idea of UFOs. More specifically, it is about the kinds of "work" – political, psychological, social – that UFOs performed for these two groups.[29] The state and its citizens *used* UFOs in specific ways and toward certain ends. For citizens, the UFO phenomenon inspired them to mobilize and organize to demand greater transparency from a state that appeared inaccessible and even untrustworthy. For the state, the UFO investigations were an opportunity to convince Canadians of the value of scientific knowledge and expertise, and even to make this an expectation of citizenship; in so doing, the state enhanced its own authority as the arbiter of expertise.

The postwar era was one of significant change. The horrors of the world wars shook public confidence in technical expertise and the state's ability to ensure the safety and well-being of its citizenry. It became common to hear Canadians express distrust of their government and even opposition to its authority. Ian Milligan argues that "a new culture of defiant anti-authoritarianism and self-expression" animated youth during the 1960s.[30] Lara Campbell and Dominique Clément argue that when we talk about "the sixties," we should not be talking strictly about a single decade but rather an *idea* – that of questioning established and hierarchical authority.[31] Neil Nevitte, writing about the 1980s specifically, has called this change a "decline of deference."[32] As the UFO documents explored here will show, however, this shift began decades earlier.

Canadians were also grappling with increasing Americanization of their culture and politics at this time. Whereas prior to the Second World War, Canada's allegiances fell squarely with Britain, this allegiance shifted to the US in the postwar period.[33] Canadians began seeing themselves not as British subjects, but as North Americans.[34] This meant, for instance, that Canada's military and political agendas came more in line with America's. In the case of Canada's UFO investigation, this is clearly seen in the laissez faire attitude many Canadian government officials adopted, preferring to wait for the Americans to make pronouncements about UFOs rather than to do so themselves. Canadians also began to notice an ever-increasing amount of American culture and entertainment filling their lives, from the films and TV shows they watched, to the magazines and news stories they consumed. Canadians were able to consume a steady diet of UFO content from American filmmakers and writers. These influences will be highlighted throughout the book, especially in the case of the decline of deference to authority, an already well-established political position in the US.[35]

Sometimes, this decline of deference transformed into conspiracy theory. A number of Canadians were convinced that UFOs existed, that they were piloted by extraterrestrial beings, and that the government at the time knew this but chose to hide the truth. Conspiracy theories are about power: who has it and who does not. Whether economic, social, or political, conspiracy theory is a means of accounting for the uneven distribution of power in society, and is most commonly used as a tactic by those who do not possess any significant power or authority. Conspiracy theories are a weapon of the weak, a means of making sense of a rapidly changing world.[36]

On the other hand, recent psychological investigations have found that conspiracy theory is a normal function of our cognition. Humans seem to be hard-wired to look for patterns even when they do not exist, to look for people or institutions to blame for unfortunate events, and to disregard evidence that contradicts our beliefs (otherwise known as confirmation bias).[37] In other words, conspiracy theory does real work for us – social, political, and psychological work. Belief in conspiracy theory can build social networks and community. It can provide an opportunity to engage with the political process, and it can satisfy psychological needs for certainty. So, while Canadian state officials assumed that UFO enthusiasts were simply "delusional" or ill-informed – in other words, exceptions to the rule – these citizens' efforts to find out information about UFOs could be interpreted as a cognitively normal response.

Moreover, from the perspective of their proponents, conspiracy theories are an alternative form of "knowledge." However spurious the evidence, ideas, and methodology on which these theories rested, they were attempts to respond to the state's arguments against the existence of UFOs with retaliatory "knowledge" – in the form of arguments of their own, sometimes with complex reasoning and evidence. Many UFO enthusiasts believed that the state should not – and did not – have a monopoly on what was considered legitimate knowledge. Through their correspondence with the government, these citizens worked to undermine the state's authority by presenting their own interpretations of the UFO phenomenon.

While most of the scholarly literature has used political and psychological explanations for conspiracy theory, I will take a historical approach, arguing that conspiracy theory also arose out of the countercultural movement of the postwar period. The UFO documents show what Greg Eghigian has called a "mutual mistrust" between state and citizens, a mistrust that hardened over the course of Canada's investigations and in the decades that followed.[38] It was not simply the case that the government and certain citizens held different views on the matter. The back-and-forth was more dynamic, with each side's attempts to convince the other simply reinforcing already entrenched views. Joseph Uscinski describes this situation as a battle of ideas: "It isn't just that conspiracy theorists have a different set of explanations, it is that their explanations call into question our knowledge-generating and knowledge-disseminating institutions."[39] In a sense, the UFO issue in Canada represents a failure for both sides: citizens were mostly unable to convince the state of the reality of UFOs and the need to release information; and the state was unable to convince citizens of what it considered the irrationality of the whole pursuit.[40]

But what is the Canadian state? Where is it? How does it operate? This book adopts Margot Canaday's vision of a "social history of the state." For Canaday, we "see the state through its practices; the state is 'what officials do.' And by officials, I mean not only top decision-makers but bureaucrats at all levels. This is, moreover, not only a 'people' but a 'places' approach to the state."[41] The state is visible in many different places and at different times, and manifests in the actions of its officials as the events described in this book will show.[42] In the case of Canada, E.A. Heaman goes further: "There is no such thing as the state in Canada." Rather, what we think of as the Canadian state is "a chained series of institutions, across the various territories constituting contemporary Canada, that people recognized as the state at any given time."[43] And what the state *does* is exactly those actions by officials working within this chained series of institutions. It is these officials with whom Canadian citizens interacted when they wrote letters to the government. In this respect, I also aim to follow Tina Loo's recent work by "attach[ing] faces and names to 'the state,' to render a picture of its agents."[44]

This history is rife with instances when a Canadian civil servant responded to a letter about UFO information, whether from the publicity office of the Department of National Defence in Ottawa or a small RCMP detachment in Barrington, Nova Scotia. As Mike Larsen and Kevin Walby argue, referring to citizens' access-to-information requests: "There is no 'state' as such; a quick scroll down the list of departments to which one can submit an ATI request at the federal level alone suggests that we are dealing with a multitude of networked government agencies, each with specific missions, which also have a degree of autonomy from one another."[45] The history of the Canadian state explored here bears out this argument, as it shows various instances of departmental autonomy and subsequent miscommunication and confusion when it comes to UFO information and responsibility for investigation. There is no one Canadian state, but a plethora of departments and individuals working within them, all attempting to make sense of UFOs and citizen requests for information, often in isolation.

Nevertheless, I refer to the Canadian state as a shorthand, with the understanding that it is multifarious, and the history told here shows the disconnection between its parts. Thinking about the Canadian state this way makes it easier to identify the broader priorities it explored during the postwar years.

One such priority was the citizen itself. Zygmunt Bauman argues that beginning in the mid-eighteenth century, a shift occurred in (especially) French statecraft. Whereas the state's initial goal had once been to control the masses and maintain order, it turned then to civilizing them, to "lifting fellow human beings to a new level of existence."[46] Society became a school, the state the teacher. The state would educate citizens in order to rid them of ignorance and superstition, and replace these outdated ideas with reason, thus producing a better quality of citizen.[47] This task would be achieved by drawing on the authority of the scientist, whose trusted voice of reason dispelled ignorance and replaced it with objective knowledge that could be applied across time and space.[48] Dipesh Chakrabarty describes this as the two-fold task of "the supposed triumph of humankind over nature" and "the triumph of humankind over itself."[49]

Scientific knowledge became the privileged means of producing more effective social control, bringing the state and scientists closely together.[50] As Edward Jones-Imhotep and Tina Adcock argue, "science and technology have been the unacknowledged legislators of modern Canada."[51] They have been enrolled at various times and places in the service of the state, in order to shore up its authority, even if these attempts inadvertently revealed "cracks in the nation's façade."[52]

What this history of Canada's UFO investigation shows is an attempt to educate citizens about the value of a scientific production of knowledge, which was simultaneously an attempt to produce a better kind of citizen who thought rationally and fit into an orderly society.[53] Belief in UFOs and conspiracy theory was, in Bauman's words, nothing but ignorance and superstition that the state needed to clear away in order to lift citizens up to a new level of existence. However, the state's efforts did not go according to plan. The rise of conspiracy theory and resistance to established authority, including specifically a "declining public trust in the political and cultural role of scientists,"[54] in the 1950s and 1960s began producing a new kind of citizen activism in competition with the state's vision of an orderly, rational public. The following chapters detail the conflict that resulted between these two visions.

OVERVIEW OF CHAPTERS

The book proceeds chronologically, covering the span 1950–95. Chapter 1 tells the story of Wilbert Smith, an electrical engineer employed with the Department of Transport. In 1950, Smith established "Project Magnet," the first Canadian investigation into UFOs. On the surface, Magnet was a study on the nature of geomagnetic phenomena and their potential for energy and propulsion, a legitimate research activity that fit within Transport's mandate. Below the surface, Smith actually wanted to determine how UFOs were propelled, hypothesizing that they operated using magnetic energy of some kind. Smith did not immediately inform his superiors about his real aim for the project. However, as the months and years passed, and it became obvious that Smith believed UFOs were extraterrestrial in nature, his supervisors within DOT began to have second thoughts. In 1954, claiming that it was receiving too much adverse publicity, and that Smith's work had ventured outside the bounds of its mandate, the department terminated Project Magnet. Chapter 1 examines the Canadian state's first real glimpse at the lengths to which a dedicated ufologist would go to reveal the truth. State officials were unprepared. This was the first volley in this clash of ideas, and it set the tone for what followed.

Chapter 2 traces the history of Canada's second UFO investigation, "Project Second Storey," which ran from 1952 to 1954 and was based within the Defence Research Board. Unlike Project Magnet, which was essentially conducted by one man, Project Second Storey comprised an advisory committee of scientists and military officials, which would comment on reported sightings and answer queries from other government departments when requested. The goal of Project Magnet had been to do a proper scientific study of UFOs that took them very seriously. Project Second Storey proceeded from a more skeptical position. The minutes from the committee's final meetings make it clear that its members felt they had sufficiently debunked the whole subject and that no further investigation was necessary. The committee concluded that the UFO phenomenon did not "lend itself to a scientific method of investigation." Project Second Storey represents the state's attempt to fight back against what it saw as the irrationality of otherwise reliable people, such as Wilbert Smith, and to reassert control over the situation.

Chapter 3 covers the period 1954–67, a time seemingly in between major events in the UFO investigation. With Projects Magnet and Second Storey terminated, the government settled into a passive role that included only the collection of UFO sighting reports, with no investigations. However, citizens around the country attempted to fill the investigative gap by forming UFO clubs and writing to various departments and agencies, demanding answers to the mystery. This chapter shows a growing unrest and mistrust of government "doublespeak," as citizens felt that they were either being directly lied to or were outsiders encountering sinister secrecy. Some citizens were bold enough to accuse the government of conspiracy, and so the chapter approaches conspiracy theory as a historical phenomenon very much tied to the broader cultural and political changes taking place after the war. The chapter also traces changes in the way the government, following several years of inactivity, began collecting and writing up UFO reports in the mid-1960s, reflecting what appeared to be a renewed interest in the phenomenon.

Chapter 4 provides a detailed look at three UFO incidents from the year 1967. Canada's centennial year was a strange one. In addition to the celebrations, there was also a spike in UFO sightings, and other related phenomena, across North America. There was no single cause for the spike, but the three incidents explored in this chapter show that the Canadian government *was* interested in some UFO incidents. The difference was that these three incidents – the "Falcon Lake Incident" in Manitoba, a series of crop circles in Duhamel, Alberta, and the Shag Harbour UFO crash in Nova Scotia – left behind physical evidence for government scientists to collect and analyze. This chapter represents the height of the government's interest in UFOs and the point at which UFOs seemed most tangible.

Chapter 5 traces the history of the investigation from the late 1960s until its end in 1995. This may seem like an unwieldly span of time to cover in a single chapter, but very little activity was recorded after 1980. Citizen UFO investigators saw their role changing. Whereas the citizens writing to the government featured in Chapter 3 were concerned with answers to the extraterrestrial question and the conspiracies presumed to surround it, many investigators featured in this last chapter began to put UFOs to a different use: to critique and expose government secrecy more generally, as part of a growing interest in government "transparency" and the move toward access-to-information legislation.

The book's conclusion provides a summary of the narrative and returns to the broader argument about the clash of ideas and the different purposes to which UFOs were put. In the early days of this study, I quickly came to the conclusion that this research was not really about UFOs at all. At first, this seemed somewhat disappointing. Why write at length about UFOs if the work is not actually about UFOs? I realized, though, that UFOs were just the surface of a much deeper and, I think, more interesting story about the significant changes taking place in Canada in the postwar years.

1

Wilbert Smith and Project Magnet, 1950–54

Canada's UFO investigation began in 1950 with the work of Wilbert Smith, an electrical engineer employed at the Department of Transport. Hypothesizing that UFOs somehow used the power of the Earth's magnetic fields as a source of propulsion, Smith thought he could make this technology available to the Canadian government. Perhaps surprisingly, the department granted Smith permission to carry out his research, and Smith initiated Project Magnet.

Why did the Department of Transport agree to Wilbert Smith's proposal, and what did Smith achieve with Project Magnet? The government became involved in the phenomenon because Smith was able to frame research into UFOs as part of the department's existing research program on ionospheric and magnetic phenomena. In effect, Smith shoehorned the investigation into existence. The events and press of 1947 – the Kenneth Arnold UFO sighting and the alleged Roswell crash – forced the US government into action. There was no similarly clear hinge point for the Canadian government. If not for Smith's personal interest, it is conceivable that the Canadian government might never have engaged with the phenomenon. Indeed, by the time of Project Magnet's termination in 1954, the Department of Transport wished it never had.

Project Magnet laid the groundwork for subsequent Canadian investigations. The dynamic between the Department of Transport and Wilbert Smith, revolving around differing ideas about the nature of UFOs, was a point of origin for the mutual mistrust that developed between state and citizen. Smith attempted to use UFOs to show the reticence of the state to engage with unorthodox ideas, while the state used Smith's work as an example of the kind of irrationality it wanted to eliminate.

In other words, Smith's work became the first case in which state and citizen disagreed about UFOs, and put them to work in conflicting ways.

THE SARBACHER MEMO

The "curious and sincere" Wilbert Brockhouse Smith was born in Lethbridge, Alberta, in 1910.[1] Smith received his bachelor's and master's degrees in electrical engineering from the University of British Columbia, in 1933 and 1934 respectively. After working for a time as the chief engineer at CJOR,[2] a Vancouver radio station, in 1939 Smith found employment with the Department of Transport (DoT) in Ottawa. According to a DoT obituary, Smith "was engaged in engineering Canada's wartime monitoring service during World War II and in 1947 was in charge of establishing a network of ionospheric measurement stations, several of which were in isolated parts of the North."[3] He contributed to a number of cross-border radio initiatives, including the 1947 Canada-US FM Broadcasting Agreement and the 1952 TV Allocation Agreement, and attended conferences like the 1949 North American Regional Broadcasting Conference in Montreal, and the same in Washington in 1950. When the Soviet satellite Sputnik was launched in 1957, Smith was among those in charge of receiving and analyzing radio transmission reports.[4] He died of cancer on 27 December 1962.

Paul Hellyer, who became the minister of transport in 1967, recalled that Smith's reputation was still very high in the department at that time.[5] Smith was a senior engineer with the DoT by the time he became involved with the UFO phenomenon. He became interested in UFOs in the late 1940s, after reading several newspaper reports. These were the years immediately after the 1947 Roswell crash and the increasing publicity surrounding the US projects Sign and Grudge. Everything changed for Smith when he travelled to the US and met with an American scientist.

In 1950, Smith attended a radio broadcasting conference in Washington, DC. While there, he met with Dr Robert I. Sarbacher, an American physicist and defence consultant. Sarbacher allegedly told Smith that flying saucers were indeed real and that the "matter is the

Figure 1.1 | Portrait of Wilbert Smith, Department of Transport engineer.

most highly classified subject in the United States Government, rating higher even than the H-bomb."[6] He also told Smith that the flying saucers most certainly did not originate on Earth and that they were of such advanced technology that the US government had been unable to duplicate them. The details of this meeting are very unclear, and it is unknown why Smith even met with Sarbacher in the first place. But it is clear that the meeting was a catalyst for Smith.

Evidence regarding this meeting comprises two documents, both written by Smith. The first, a handwritten document dated 15 September 1950, outlines a series of questions and answers between Smith and Sarbacher, reproduced here:

WBS: I am doing some work on the collapse of the earth's magnetic field as a source of energy, and I think our work may have a bearing on the flying saucers.
RIS: What do you want to know[?]
WBS: I have read [Frank] Scully's book [*Behind the Flying Saucers*, published in 1950 by Henry Holt] on the saucers and would like to know how much of it is true.
RIS: The facts reported in the book are substantially correct.
WBS: Then the saucers do exist?
RIS: Yes, they exist.
WBS: Do they operate as Scully suggests, on magnetic principles?
RIS: We have not been able to duplicate their performance.
WBS: Do they come from some other planet?
RIS: All we know is, we didn't make them, and it's pretty certain they didn't originate on the earth.
WBS: I understand the whole subject of saucers is classified.
RIS: Yes, it is classified two points higher even than the H-bomb. In fact it is the most highly classified subject in the U.S. government at the present time.
WBS: May I ask the reason for the classification?
RIS: You may ask, but I can't tell you.
WBS: Is there any way in which I can get more information, particularly as it might fit in with our own work?
RIS: I suppose you could be cleared through your own Defense Department and I am pretty sure arrangements could be made to exchange information. If you have anything to contribute we should be glad to talk it over, but I can't give you any more at the present time.

Note:The above is written from memory following the interview. I have tried to keep it as nearly verbatim as possible.[7]

This document is seemingly a recollection of Smith's interview, written after the fact. It is not an official document; it is not part of Canada's national archives but rather may be found in the archives at the University of Ottawa, in the Arthur Bray fonds. Bray was an independent UFO investigator active mostly in the 1960s and 1970s who took an interest in Smith's story after the engineer's death. Bray self-published two books, *Science, the Public and the* UFO and *The* UFO *Connection*, both of which mention Smith and his work.[8] Bray wrote that he obtained Smith's personal papers, many of which contained copies of official DOT documents or their first drafts, from Smith's widow. Bray eventually donated his collection of materials on Smith to the University of Ottawa. For those interested in studying Smith's work, this collection is actually more complete and better organized than the one at Library and Archives Canada.

What makes the matter of Smith's meeting with Sarbacher more unclear is that the handwritten interview notes are prefaced with the line: "Notes on interview through Lt/C. Bremner with Dr. Robert Sarbacher." Bremner was a defence attaché at the Canadian embassy in Washington, and it is unclear whether Smith spoke to Sarbacher in person or simply passed on questions to the scientist through Bremner. While this document is not found in the national archives, there exists in that location another, similar document. A memo of 21 November 1950 on DOT letterhead, from Smith to the department's telecommunications controller, outlines Smith's thoughts about flying saucers and mentions that he had met with a prominent American scientist. This meeting, Smith explains, he arranged by making "discreet enquiries through the Canadian embassy staff in Washington." The meeting yielded the following information:

a The matter is the most highly classified subject in the United States Government, rating higher even than the H-bomb.
b Flying saucers exist.
c Their modus operandi is unknown but concentrated effort is being made by a small group headed by Doctor Vannevar Bush.[9]
d The entire matter is considered by the United States authorities to be of tremendous significance.[10]

The official memo did not mention Sarbacher's claim that UFOs were definitely extraterrestrial, but did allude to the idea by referencing two books published in the same year that had popularized the idea. Smith instead emphasized the need to research the saucers for scientific purposes. Specifically, Smith noted that he was interested in UFOs for their potential to convert geomagnetic energy into electrical energy. He thought that they might be operating "on some hitherto unknown magnetic principles" that manipulate the planet's gravitational fields. He requested permission to set up what he called Project Magnet to pursue this theory.

Smith's request represents Canada's entry into UFO investigation. There is a key difference between Smith's request and the kind of analysis that the US projects undertook. The latter focused on analyzing UFO sighting reports in an attempt to ascertain their credibility and explain them away as misidentifications or hallucinations. The effort was a scientific one – but one that was intent on seeing through the fog of untrained eyes. Most of those working on the US projects shared the assumption that UFOs were not real and were simply mistaken observations. Smith's efforts, on the other hand, focused on reverse-engineering a technology that existed only theoretically. There was no physical evidence of UFOs that he could use to make conclusions. Smith set out to remedy this situation. He tried to solve an engineering problem inspired by accounts he had only read, but which he nevertheless believed were legitimate.

PROJECT MAGNET

In the official memo to his superior, Smith requested permission to start Project Magnet and to use DOT equipment to do so. Commander C.P. Edwards, the deputy minister of transport for air services, granted this permission and, in December 1950, Smith began his investigations.[11] At first, Smith was the only DOT employee working on the project, and then only on a part-time basis. This quickly changed as Magnet acquired the assistance of three engineers and two technicians by the end of 1950 – still meagre resources by Smith's reckoning.[12] The physical resources available to the team were basic. Smith had at his disposal, for instance, a galvanometer, a gamma-ray detector, a radio receiver, and a gravimeter, all spare technologies that the DOT had on hand.[13] The project received a "Secret" security rating, due to its use of potentially profitable technologies.[14] This classification would become a sore point for the DOT and one of the main reasons the department would later shut the project down.

In Magnet's early days, Smith worked quietly on what he called "small and very crude" experiments. He had actually carried out his first experiment into "geomagnetics" about a year before requesting permission to start the project. Spurred by reports of UFOs in the late 1940s, Smith had already begun trying to puzzle it out. A preliminary report on the results of this experiment provided details on Smith's attempt to induce the collapse of the Earth's magnetic fields and thereby capture the released electrical energy through a system of coils wound around "a core of ferro-magnetic material." Smith concluded that the experiment was successful, in that the captured energy was able to register a reading on a voltmeter, but that "the apparatus was extremely crude and very difficult of precise measurement" and so "the observations were purely qualitative in nature."[15] Thus, the object of pursuing Project Magnet eight months later was to construct more adequate equipment and test his hypotheses in a more rigorous and quantitative manner. Smith believed that if these more advanced experiments were successful, they would prove that he could harness energy from the induced collapse of the Earth's gravitational fields and use it as a method of propulsion. UFOs might operate using the same principle, Smith proposed, and so it was necessary to continue the study to determine exactly what kind of technology the flying saucers represented.[16]

Judging from later correspondence, officials within the government did not believe that the flying saucers were of extraterrestrial origin. In fact, the DOT likely did not have any interest in UFOs at all, except for the potential (however small) of uncovering new technology that might assist with aviation. What made the proposal palatable to the DOT was that Smith's ideas fell in line with research that the department was already carrying out. In the late 1940s and early 1950s, the Canadian government was intensely interested in the study of aurorae and their effect on radio waves. Edward Jones-Imhotep has written that scientists in Ottawa struggled to understand the unique conditions of the ionosphere and the possibilities they might present for the extension of reliable communications throughout the Canadian North. In fact, the technology these government scientists used to produce and read ionograms – the visual images of the ionosphere that "furnished the working objects of the discipline" – regularly failed, and this technological failure was used to help define a certain idea of "nordicity" and the Canadian nation. The ionosphere scientists pointed to the apparent uniqueness of Canada's ionosphere and claimed an expertise for Canadian science distinct from America's expertise, which might help bolster the nation's sovereignty during a time of "national redefinition. It was hoped that this unique understanding of far-North communications would help Canada articulate its own vision of national security and international relations."[17]

Smith wrote that Project Magnet was a way to delve more deeply into "the study of various aspects of radio wave propagation," such as "the fields of aurora, cosmic radiation, atmospheric radio-activity and geo-magnetism," and contextualizing the proposal in these terms made it plausible. Conveniently for Smith, the DOT already had a hand in ionospheric research. In fact, one of Smith's responsibilities during this time was to assist in the establishment of a network of ionosphere stations throughout the North, with the explicit goal of researching communication issues. As a result, the DOT viewed Smith's proposed work on UFOs as a logical extension, given that he articulated it primarily as a study of geomagnetic phenomena, within the same category of ionosphere research.

In 1951, Smith wrote several reports on observations arising from his experiments. The papers are all short, usually two to three pages, and contain text and sometimes equations in which he puzzles out results that sometimes do and sometimes do not accord with pre-existing frameworks in the study of electrical engineering. His main preoccupation was an attempt to determine the relationship between the propagation of a magnetic field and the electric current used to "excite" that field.[18] Smith did not address these short papers to any specific person; likely he produced them for the Magnet team's internal use, or just for his own reference. It was not until 1952 that Smith began regularly reporting to his superiors on Magnet's progress.

The introduction to a draft report from March 1952 summarized why Magnet had been established and reiterated that the "large number of sightings of unidentified objects, generally called 'flying saucers,' raised the question as to whether such objects could be emissaries of some other civilization having a technology somewhat different than ours, and possibly more advanced in magnetics."[19] Smith's speculations reflected a growing awareness among the public about possible extraterrestrial life and technology. Hollywood was already churning out alien contact and invasion films by this point, having released *The Day the Earth Stood Still* only the previous year, a film in which Klaatu, an alien emissary, lands in Washington, DC, and attempts to make peace with the Americans. An anxious soldier shoots Klaatu and destroys a piece of advanced technology that the emissary intended to offer as a gift to the president.[20] The trope of extraterrestrials offering technology would soon become commonplace within the UFO community.

In Smith's original project proposal, his mention of the extraterrestrial possibility was more of a footnote, but increasingly his correspondence with superiors foregrounded this idea. It was likely at this point, if not earlier, that his superiors began to suspect that Smith's understanding of his research differed from theirs. To be frank, Smith's interest in UFOs was becoming a problem for the DoT. His 1952 report marked the beginning of a cycle of mutually reinforced mistrust between Smith and the DoT that, in his particular case, ended in the project's termination, but which also broadened out to affect the relationship between the government and inquisitive Canadian citizens. Around this time, certain citizens began to express their frustration with the government's response to UFO reports and especially the stigma which tended to attach to those who reported them. These complaints were usually published in local newspapers, which provided a counterpoint to government responses. In one such example, a resident of Didsbury, Alberta, complained that the fear of ridicule made her hesitant to speak out. Overall, however, the article was sympathetic, stating that "many of these [UFO] reports are from reliable people" and that other recent editorials had also acknowledged that UFOs might be real.[21]

The remainder of Smith's report outlined various experiments that the Magnet team undertook to determine if Maxwell's equations – which describe the behaviour of electrical and magnetic fields – are inviolate or are instead "a special case of a more general set of equations." In effect, Smith and his team were working to confirm experimentally equations that had been dominant in the field since James Clerk Maxwell introduced them in 1861, all because of UFO sightings and hypotheses made about their flight. Smith's efforts on these more prosaic and fundamental scientific questions, as noted above, were one of the main reasons why the DoT granted permission for Magnet in the first place: when contextualized within the existing paradigm, the study of UFO technology did not appear so absurd.

Smith concluded the report by writing that the results of the project "to date have hardly been spectacular and may even be claimed to confirm only what could be expected in the behaviour of fields." In other words, by simply replicating longstanding results, Smith was unable to produce any novel conclusions and make any headway toward explaining the UFO phenomenon. He also noted in the report's conclusion that while Magnet "was quite small to start with," it "was further depleted during the [previous] year by two resignations in favour of more lucrative positions elsewhere."[22] Smith and the Magnet team were doing this work on a part-time, even casual basis. Their main priorities were their regular DOT duties, and so the time they could commit to Magnet was extremely limited. As a result, after only a year of operations, Project Magnet was floundering.

Smith's next official report was even less optimistic. Titled "Project Magnet Thinking as of July, 1952," it posed the problem of UFOs in the form of two questions: first, "their origin and purpose"; and second, "their technology." Smith quickly acknowledged that the answer to the first question was beyond the team's ability to explain and so skipped over it. The answer to the second question took up the rest of the fourteen-page report. Smith dismissed, each in turn, the possibility that UFOs were powered by chemical fuels, nuclear energy, and electricity and magnetism. In the case of the latter – the very sources of energy which Smith had spent the previous two years investigating – the reason was the fact that his experiments found no useful variation in Maxwell's equations and that they were unable to reliably harness the energy produced from a gravitational field collapse.

Smith concluded that flying saucers operated either by way of a technology unknown to scientists on Earth, or by using known principles that their extraterrestrial makers had extended beyond current human understanding. In the end, the report was highly theoretical and concluded by stating that if the project – and science generally – is to understand UFOs and their underlying physical principles, then the only option left was to continue tinkering and await the discovery of new results and formulas. He left unsaid the idea that the extraterrestrials which Smith believed to exist might gift this new knowledge to the human race. As such, Smith explicitly asked for continued support and funding (however meagre) for Magnet despite having no concrete results to show for the previous years of work.

Perhaps in an attempt to provide some results, Smith proposed an experiment. He had noticed by this point that in interviews with those who had seen UFOs, the witnesses displayed "a certain amount of malobservation and faulty memory." In an attempt

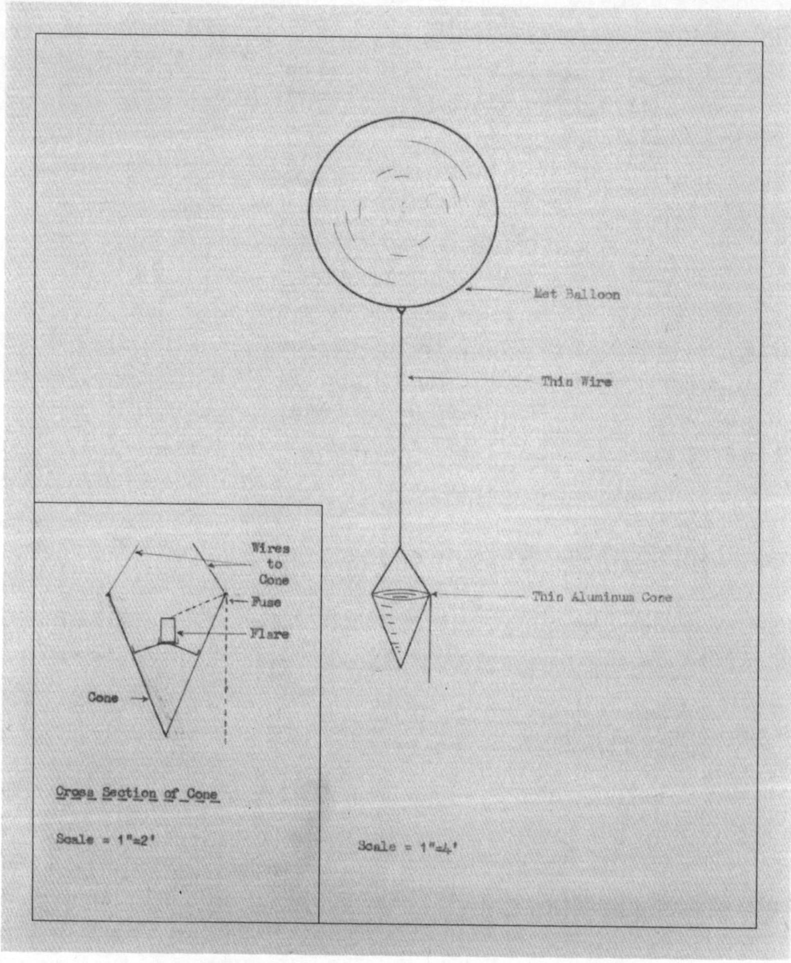

Figure 1.2 | Balloon experiment. Wilbert Smith's diagram of his proposed balloon experiment, which he carried out in Ottawa on 8 September 1952. The experiment proved inconclusive.

to test this in a more controlled setting, he outlined a plan that would "check the general characteristics of public observational capacity." Smith proposed to inflate a meteorological balloon controlled by bursts from a magnesium flare, suspended underneath, which would lift it into the air. The balloon would be "brilliantly illuminated" and provide "a suitable object for observation." The plan was to release the balloon into the skies above Ottawa without any advance notice and wait to see if anyone reported it as a UFO, either to the newspapers or the government. Smith and his team could then interview witnesses and measure their accounts against the known facts of the experiment.[23]

Smith's superiors approved the experiment, but he was unable to acquire the necessary equipment until nearly three months later. Finally, on 8 September 1952, at 9:45 p.m., they released the balloon. They timed the magnesium flare to burn for one minute. The balloon successfully floated "over the Rideau Canal near Dow's Lake at an elevation of 1.1 miles." Smith and a colleague made two simultaneous observations at different locations, to obtain bearings that would corroborate one another. To Smith and his colleagues, the first phase of the experiment was a success: "The flare was clearly visible from Ottawa and did not resemble a meteor or northern lights. It could not be mistaken for a star and could not be associated with the moon which was on the eastern horizon. It could not be mistaken for a plane, since it was soundless and flashed only for a short time from an almost stationary position." Once the one-minute flare ended, the anticipation began.

Alas, Smith was to be disappointed. His summary of the experiment concluded anticlimactically: "There was no mention made of this object in the newspapers."[24] Perhaps there had been some Ottawa residents pondering the heavens during the exact one-minute duration of the experiment. If they were out there, though, they neglected to report the incident. The experiment was inconclusive.

By the end of 1952, Smith had also compiled twenty-five sighting reports from that year which, to his mind, defied conventional explanation. He included his analysis of these sightings as an appendix to another progress report on Project Magnet. The appendix noted that a "few other sightings were reported [to the DoT during 1952] but were obviously of conventional objects and [so were] omitted from analysis."[25] The report also concluded that despite the small sample of data used, "the Department of Transport sightings are quite representative of the sightings reported throughout the world."[26]

Even as early as 1952, sighting reports were coming in from around the country. Specifically, for Smith's analysis, six were from Ottawa, four more from small Ontario towns, three from Halifax, four from Regina, three from British Columbia, and one each from Calgary,

Newfoundland, New Brunswick, Manitoba, and the Northwest Territories. Aspects of all the sightings defied full and satisfactory explanation despite Smith's attempts to make them fit into predetermined categories. As a result, he wrote: "We are forced to the conclusion that the vehicles are probably extra-terrestrial, in spite of our prejudices to the contrary" and "regardless of whether or not they fit into our scheme of things." The only thing left to do was to mount "a substantial effort towards the acquisition of as much as possible of this technology, which would without doubt be of great value to us."[27] Smith's report put all his cards on the table. What began for Smith in early 1951 as an effort to understand the relationship between magnetic and electrical fields transformed, over the span of three years, into a full-fledged belief in the existence of extraterrestrials and the urgent need to make contact and acquire their knowledge.

BAD PUBLICITY

Despite Project Magnet's "Secret" classification, Smith's efforts did not stay classified for long. American interest in the UFO phenomenon was steadily growing, and word of an obscure Canadian scientist working on the issue – and with government sanction – eventually got out. Magnet's classification became a sore point for the DOT. Smith's work should have remained secret. It was to the DOT's chagrin that it had got out at all and, especially, that it was Smith himself who had communicated the work to others. Officials at the DOT were beginning to feel that Smith and those interested in his work were antagonizing them, and that withdrawing from the whole subject might be the only sensible solution.

In the early 1950s, a number of bestselling American books and alien invasion films helped shape the foundations of the UFO stories still told today.[28] As Mark O'Connell writes: "With so little being done officially to address the questions and anxieties of the public where UFOs were concerned, Hollywood sensed the country's mood and provided the necessary nightmare, in the shape of the 1951 film *The Thing from Another World* … [which] terrified moviegoers across the country and single-handedly created the template for the alien invasion movie."[29] The public consumed these books and films amid the paranoia of the Cold War and the threat of a Soviet invasion of North America.[30] Alien invasions from Mars and flying saucers piloted by extraterrestrials represented the violent intrusion of the unknown and expressed the fear, thinly veiled, that North Americans felt at the prospect of the Soviet Union creeping ever closer. International communism was on the rise and one could never tell where it might spring up. The trope of the body snatcher clearly played on this theme: one could not know if such a menace was in fact one's own neighbour, or even a family member, whom the "Others" had silently converted.[31]

For many, this fear was made more acute by outrage. Americans were angry that the government might be covering up its knowledge of UFOs and thereby putting citizens in danger: "the alien invasion movies did their best to convince the public that aliens from other worlds were ready to attack and destroy us at any time, while UFO books and magazine articles did their best to convince the public that the government already knew all about the aliens' nefarious plans and was keeping them a secret."[32] National security concerns have always been at the forefront of UFO disclosure rhetoric.[33] However, as Whitaker and Marcuse write in *Cold War Canada*, the primary target of Canadian government surveillance was its own citizens rather than spies abroad.[34] In the early Cold War period, fear of dissension and subversion was sufficiently acute to justify a number of secretive and invasive actions. Dennis Molinaro, for instance, has written about the existence of an extensive Cold War wiretapping program in Canada. These wiretaps were government-sanctioned and executed without the need for any warrant.[35] Additionally, the RCMP was authorized to carry out security clearance investigations on civil servants whom the service believed might constitute a risk.[36] These investigations were not simply a matter of screening for security risks but an active form of moral regulation.[37]

Against this backdrop of paranoia, a number of American writers began releasing books that accused the government of a UFO cover-up. Perhaps the most prominent among these was Donald Keyhoe, a retired Air Force major. Keyhoe was injured in an airplane crash while on duty in the early 1920s. During his convalescence, he began writing short science fiction stories for various pulp magazines.[38] By the time he retired from the Air Force not long thereafter, Keyhoe had established himself as a writer of "weird tales" – a position perfect for an entry into the world of UFOs.

In January 1950, Keyhoe published an article in *True* magazine titled "Flying Saucers Are Real." The article was so popular that even local newspapers in Canada reported on its publication, remarking on the thoroughness of Keyhoe's research and the confusion over official government responses.[39] Shortly afterward, Keyhoe expanded the article into his first UFO book, *The Flying Saucers Are Real*. In this book, he claimed to have used his military contacts to unearth previously unknown details about the US government's knowledge of the matter. He wrote that the government did indeed know about flying saucers, that they were of extraterrestrial origin, and that the government was covering it all up in the interest of public safety, lest a panic break out. In a later book, he described this secrecy as "dangerous."[40] He concluded that the extraterrestrials must have been surveilling Earth for hundreds of years already, but that they had increased their attention beginning in 1945 because of the atom bomb detonations.[41]

It is no surprise that Keyhoe located his expose within the context of the atom bomb. Joseph Masco argues that the first atomic detonation in the New Mexico desert "can only be narrated as a moment of historical rupture and transformation."[42] While the atom bomb served as a symbol of American technological superiority and the end of the Second World War, its legacy is much more unclear. The Manhattan Project, Masco writes, inaugurated a new sense of American society as one defined by risk, "a new modernity in which dangers produced by the nation-state can no longer be controlled by it or be contained within its borders."[43] A direct analogue of this fear was to be found in the 1954 Hollywood film *Them!*, which depicted huge irradiated ants wreaking havoc near Alamogordo, the site of the first atomic bomb test.[44] The profound consequences of the Manhattan Project, and the secrecy that shrouded it, generated ambivalence and fear as much as pride, leading some to question the motivations behind the project, and behind the state and the scientific establishment more generally.

Like Keyhoe, other authors and producers also tapped into these fears, helping to establish the trope of the benevolent humanoid alien attempting to stop Earthlings from destroying themselves with nuclear weapons. Opposed to this image was that of the merciless extraterrestrial monster intent on colonizing the planet.[45] Writers like George Adamski fashioned themselves as "contactees" – and in his case, a specific type of contactee who had been taken up in alien crafts and spirited throughout the universe.[46] This kind of contactee invariably arrived back on Earth with messages of peace and the need to disarm.

Keyhoe's widely read books, however, focused specifically on the government's involvement with UFOs and extraterrestrials. In addition to *The Flying Saucers Are Real*, he also published such titles as *Flying Saucers from Outer Space* (1953), *The Flying Saucer Conspiracy* (1955), *Flying Saucers: Top Secret* (1960), and *Aliens from Space* (1973). With one of these later books, in which Keyhoe told the story of Wilbert Smith's work, news of the Canadian government's involvement began to spread in earnest. Smith and Keyhoe first began corresponding in 1950, when Smith wrote to Keyhoe expressing his interest in Keyhoe's first UFO book. In the 1950 memo to his superiors in which he asked for permission to establish Project Magnet, Smith specifically mentioned Keyhoe's book as being among those that advocated the extraterrestrial hypothesis. Smith also told Keyhoe about his own work on the conversion of energy through the collapse of magnetic fields.[47] They began to correspond regularly after this and Smith provided Keyhoe with more information about his experiments, in violation of Project Magnet's security classification. In his 1953 book, *Flying Saucers from Outer Space*, Keyhoe dedicated an entire chapter to "The Canadian Project." He described Smith as a "tall quiet-voiced man with close-cropped black hair, [who] had the cool detachment of a typical scientist." It is clear from the rest of the chapter, however, that Smith was anything but detached. Keyhoe's prose presented Smith as intelligent, articulate, and deeply dedicated to figuring out how flying saucers work. Keyhoe wrote that other "reputable groups" had previously suggested theories along the same lines as Smith but had ultimately dismissed them for fear of their reputations. Keyhoe quoted Smith extensively on the details of his theories of propulsion, which Keyhoe then used to confirm to his readers the truth of various sightings he had dug up. In Keyhoe's words, "Smith's earlier explanations seemed almost uncanny" in their ability to make sense of recent sighting reports.[48] *Flying Saucers from Outer Space* gave Smith his most widespread exposure, and the effect was significant.

Almost as soon as this book came out, Smith and the DOT began receiving telephone calls and letters from both Americans and Canadians wanting more information. For instance, a citizen in California wanted to know more about "certain experiments having been conducted by your government."[49] The DOT was concerned about the conflation of its work with Smith's, considering that Smith's work represented but a very small part of a single department of the government.

Another letter, from a citizen in Quebec, was slightly more specific. Writing to Smith, the author stated that he had read Keyhoe's book: "It is in this book that I have discovered YOU." They did not mention the government specifically but did ask for details about sightings made in Canada, as if in their mind Smith had become a clearinghouse for UFO information. In a way, Smith had. In the years following Magnet's termination, other officials regularly dumped letters about UFOs on Smith's desk.[50] As will be explored in more detail later, this goes to show how unorganized the government's UFO investigation was and how little communication existed between departments. It is also clear that the DOT did not strictly enforce the security restriction on Magnet. The letter writer from Quebec had indicated that they would understand if Smith could not divulge more information about his work because of security restrictions. This is ironic, given that Smith began telling others about his research almost immediately after the DOT approved Project Magnet.

The letters were not all as benign. With the arrival of a number of letters from writers whom Smith and his superiors began referring to as "cranks,"[51] they agreed to create a separate file for such letters, which they would ignore. Several of these crank letters contain, in nearly illegible handwriting, what seem to be streams of consciousness detailing religious and cosmic visions, verging on incoherent rambling.[52] An undated letter from a twenty-two-year-old man contained a request for a job with Smith's "private company" which, in his understanding, was in search of life on other planets. The writer also made sure to mention that they were "on a diet of cold Orange Juice and Cold Water, which a doctor told me I have to be on for the rest of my life."[53]

More difficult to dismiss were the letters from colleagues. A letter from the Washington, DC–based Westinghouse Broadcasting Company, for instance, began with the author reminding Smith of their acquaintance, as they had first encountered each other at a radio broadcasting conference in 1950 – the very one where Smith allegedly met with American physicist Robert Sarbacher. After reading Donald Keyhoe's book, the writer had discussed Smith's ideas with a colleague in the same field, and doubted the results: "This letter may be impertinent, but I would appreciate hearing from you and learn[ing] whether you substantiate within reason the statements made by Major Keyhoe."[54] Another letter came from a student at the Massachusetts Institute of Technology. The student was interested in knowing more about magnetic propulsion, but also expressed skepticism: "as far as I can learn this theory belongs in the realm of pseudo-scientific theories, and no one seems to know anything about it, except you."[55] Even Keyhoe himself was skeptical at first: "I'd checked [on the validity of the theory] with two or three engineers. But when several well-known scientists ridiculed the theory, I'd lost interest in it."[56] Nevertheless, Keyhoe included the material in his book, and the publicity Smith received generated excitement and interest among the public in the activities of the Canadian government. It also raised eyebrows among colleagues and cast doubt, if not on the facts in Keyhoe's book, then on Smith's reputation.

Officials at the DOT were not pleased. J.C. Lessard, the deputy minister for transport, explained to the minister that the publicity now pouring in was due entirely to Keyhoe's book. Lessard attempted to reassure the minister: "Mr. Smith informed the Press that the equipment used was entirely of the reclaimed type and that the activities of Project Magnet represent a very small outlay of funds."[57] It seems that despite the enthusiasm of Smith and other like-minded persons aware of his work, the project was almost unknown to higher officials, even within the same department. They only became aware of the project once Keyhoe's book generated adverse publicity, and this made it a problem.

A draft speech prepared by Lessard in 1953 makes this evident. The deputy minister wrote the speech for members of the House of Commons, who had obviously heard enough about Smith in the newspapers that they requested a report. The speech began by mentioning "the somewhat sensational articles appearing in the press as to some of the researches being carried out by the Department of Transport" and outlined the potential value of studying the small percentage of UFO sightings that remained unexplained. Lessard never explicitly mentioned the words "UFO" or "flying saucer" but referred to them rather euphemistically as "strange objects, lights or queer effects in the sky." The report made it clear to the House that the "small group" carrying out this work was using instruments "left over from a previous program of radio skywave recording" and that it "is in no sense unusual since most of the instruments are quite conventional." The report ended by reassuring the listeners that the small group was "not assigned exclusively to this work, and in fact much of the work has been done on their own time."[58] In an attempt to deflect attention, the DOT began using the same refrain:

Figure 1.3 | UFO Observatory 1. Exterior of a shack with antennae at Shirley's Bay, Ontario, near Ottawa, which Wilbert Smith repurposed to track atmospheric disturbances that he hypothesized were caused by UFOs.

that Project Magnet, while given official sanction, was a casual, spare-time activity that utilized dusty old equipment.

However, concern within the DoT escalated when word got out that Smith was not only doing part-time research into UFOs but was actively building a UFO observatory. Newspaper stories appeared in November 1953 ranging in tone from interested and curious to outright disparaging. The *Vancouver Daily Province* stated, "Canada has launched a highly-technical research program to learn whether the earth has had interplanatary [*sic*] visitors during the last few years."[59] The *Sudbury Daily Star* reported that the observatory was a joint effort of the DoT and the Defence Research Board (DRB) intended to "track down the truth of the flying saucer mystery – 'just in case.'"[60] A *Jerusalem Post* article ended thus: "Mr. Smith said that although scientists believed there was no real proof that flying saucers existed 'there is a high degree of probability that they do exist and are interplanetary.'"[61] The Canadian edition of *Time* described the laboratory as "a complicated jumble of electronic gear" that aided in Smith's study of "flying crockery."[62]

Perhaps the most scathing report appeared in the *Toronto Daily Star*, headlined "Maze of Instruments in Tiny Shack Hunts for Saucers." It began: "The world's first flying saucer sighting station, the unwanted, virtually disowned, child of the Canadian government, yesterday went into operation at Shirley's Bay, 10 miles northwest of here." The article referred to "sheepish government officials" who dismissed the station and its purpose, being "reluctant to confess that they regard stories of flying saucers as anything but utter nonsense." The article also quoted DRB chairman Omond Solandt as saying that the DRB had nothing to do with the project. The minister of transport, the *Daily Star* alleged, said that Smith was undertaking the project for the National Research Council, quoting him as saying that "the sighting station is ludicrously small and insignificant to be engaged in such a project."[63]

The reality of Smith's "makeshift" UFO observatory was very close to what the papers reported.[64] It was indeed a small shack located at Shirley's Bay, a restricted military site about fifteen kilometres west of Ottawa on the river. The site, previously part of the Army's firing range, had become home to a chemical laboratory and a telecommunications centre. Construction on the site was not finished until the mid-1960s and, prior to this, comprised a motley collection of buildings and equipment.[65] Smith's shack had a large antenna attached to

Figure 1.4 | Interior of Wilbert Smith's shack at Shirley's Bay, with unnamed man at work. Smith mentioned several part-time and casual Department of Transport employees who assisted with the work in the early 1950s.

it and a maze of equipment filling the interior. However, it had nothing to do with the National Research Council. Project Magnet did have a connection to the DRB, however, as the DOT had consulted Solandt before giving approval for the project, and the DRB had use of the Shirley's Bay site.[66] By late 1953, Magnet was winding down and it seems clear that Smith was once again the only DOT employee working on the project. The shack itself, being quite small, surely could not have accommodated more than one person. So how did Smith obtain these additional resources, given the lack of concrete results from his previous two years of study? Likely, Smith was able to stretch the bounds of the latitude initially granted to him, while bureaucratic inertia prevented his superiors from shutting him down earlier. By this point, also, Smith was a senior engineer, and so he likely had access to spare equipment – and the department's trust that he would not abuse it.

The press around the saucer station brought more letters to the DOT's doorstep. Bill Bantey, a "publicity counsellor" from Montreal, wrote to the department asking for more information and photographs of the Shirley's Bay shack. In an attempt to appease him and deflect attention from the issue, W.H. van Allen, the chief of the DOT's Information and Editorial Bureau, sent Bantey several photographs along with the remark, "You will see that [the observatory] does not lend itself to publicity and we are discouraging any attempt at further pictorialization."[67]

Van Allen's attempt failed considerably, as the following year brought further international press. Alexander Barrie, a Toronto-based writer with the UK Kemsley Newspapers group, contacted the DOT to arrange an interview with Smith. Van Allen granted access with the understanding "that there be no interview quotations, no levity and no comments which might hurt the project." Barrie enclosed a copy of the story to van Allen, in which he wrote that the topic "has been treated in a sober manner and the story makes it clear that investigation of UFO's is a small part of Wilbur [*sic*] Smith's work."[68] Barrie wrote that because the story had taken longer to finish than anticipated, he had already sent it to the publisher without DOT's final approval.[69] Van Allen responded with frustration: "I waited for considerable time to receive your copy in connection with the Shirley Bay development ... Despite the fact that your article may have been overdue in England, it was certainly most inadvisable to send it along before enabling us to see the copy. Frankly, I am disappointed with the sensationalism you have worked into it and must ask that you recall the copy." The remainder of the letter included seven objections and requested changes, including: "Eliminate reference to 'alien vehicle'" and "Reference to Mr. Smith's or any government office uncalled for."[70]

The DOT was clearly worried about the impact any article could have that referenced the extraterrestrial hypothesis in the same space as the Canadian government. Mark O'Connell similarly writes that the idea "caused a significant amount of concern in some quarters" of the US government[71] and so it is likely that the Canadian government was worried about receiving the same kind of attention. Just the year before, in 1952, two articles were published in national publications, one in *Time* and the other in *Saturday Night*, which likely helped fuel this concern. The *Time* article, at least, was entirely meant to debunk the phenomenon by focusing on the case of two men convicted of fraud for weaving a tale about flying saucers and little men landing on farmers' fields.[72] *Saturday Night*, however, took a different approach. Mentioning specific names in the article, like Omond Solandt and Peter Millman, an astronomer, the article claimed that Canadian scientists agreed "that the saucers are no laughing matter and must be closely investigated."[73] This was certainly an exaggeration and must have seemed like the same kind of story as the one that Alexander Barrie later wrote.

Unfortunately, for the DOT, they were too late to intervene in the latter case. Barrie wrote that the story was going ahead without the requested changes and that he was taken aback by the DOT's reaction: "Some of your comments surprise me. I cannot see that 'sensationalism' was 'worked in' – except in so far as flying saucers are by themselves inclined to be something of a sensation at any mention." Barrie went on to chastise van Allen about journalistic integrity by writing that "it puts a reporter in an extremely difficult position when a good and legitimate story of this sort is only to be half-told. It is not part of a newspaper's job to suppress facts except when such things as security regulations require it." Barrie's letter ended with an apology for the misunderstanding but also expressed the firm belief that the story did not contain anything harmful. Perhaps Barrie's letter convinced van Allen of this belief or perhaps the DOT simply resigned itself to its fate, as van Allen's response was short and to the point: "It would be regrettable if Kemsley Publications used the article as sent, but I do not think any great damage would be done."[74] At this point, DOT's public relations unit was attempting damage control, and not particularly successfully. One journalist later accused the DOT of placing an "iron curtain" around Smith in an attempt to stop the flow of information to the press.[75] Rather than try to put out individual fires, however, higher officials within the department sought to stamp out the source: termination of the project was in the works.

Though the end was in sight, a glimmer of hope emerged. One of the instruments in the shack at Shirley's Bay was a gravimeter, a device "designed to detect and record gamma rays, magnetic fluctuations, radio noises and gravity and mass changes in the atmosphere."[76] In the same way a polygraph records changes in a person's vitals, the gravimeter used a pen that reacted to atmospheric changes by scribbling lines "along a four-inch wide, 250-foot long strip of paper."[77] Since becoming operational in late 1953, the gravimeter had been recording these signals nonstop. The main source of fluctuations had been airplanes flying overhead, but even these registered only small blips on the paper. On 8 August 1954, however, at 3:01 p.m., the gravimeter registered something else. The detection was so large that it set off alarm bells in the shack. Smith came running, and later said: "The deflection in the line was vastly greater and much more pronounced than we had seen even when a large aircraft had passed close overhead." He ran outside to obtain visual confirmation of the unknown object only to find that the sky was so overcast that nothing was visible. Despite the care that astronomers take in their work, and their confidence in their calculations and refined equipment, the weather often thwarts their attempts to map the heavens. Something as innocuous as a cloud passing overhead can destroy years of preparation.[78]

Smith's moment of excitement and potential success quickly dissipated. While he noted that the reading might have indicated a flying saucer, it may also have been nothing more than equipment malfunction. Without confirmation of a clear visual sighting, Smith could not confidently say one way or the other. The press briefly reported on the incident, but it does not even register in any official documentation available today. This was likely because the termination of Project Magnet had already been set in motion. To Smith's superiors, an ambiguous reading on an obscure piece of instrumentation in a tiny, cluttered shack on the outskirts of Ottawa turned out to be less than convincing. For Project Magnet, the flying saucer observatory was the last gasp as the increased attention and a lack of results caught up to Smith, and the DOT shut the project down the very next year.

THE WRONG FIT

The DOT was not happy about the publicity surrounding Wilbert Smith's UFO observatory and Donald Keyhoe's book. In June 1954, DOT officials terminated Project Magnet. The memo reasoned that "no facts had emerged which would warrant making this a special government project" and that no other country – in particular the US or the UK – had any such project either. Of course, this was not entirely accurate. The US had continued its own investigations under Project Blue Book, although that project operated on a minimal level. It is possible that officials in the Canadian government were not yet aware of it or were simply ignoring it, the better to press their argument against Magnet.

In any case, the memo requested that "Mr. Smith should be told that so far as official work is concerned, this project must not be carried on in Departmental time, and that what he wishes to do in his own free time is purely a matter for himself." Smith could continue to use DOT equipment so long as it was not in use elsewhere, but, "in the event of Mr. Smith's name being coupled officially with the Department in any publicity, that might eventually develop through his spare time investigation, the Department would have to take the position publicly that there was no official Departmental sponsorship of Mr. Smith's activities."[79] Indeed, the DOT very quickly began disavowing all participation in the project. The department stated that while Magnet once had official sanction, this was no longer the case and any efforts Smith was making were entirely unrelated to government business. A form letter that van Allen began using in 1955 to respond to inquiries read: "It is regretted that we are unable to supply you with any information of the type requested in your letter, as the Government decided last year to discontinue official investigations along the lines previously carried out."[80]

Officials in other departments started using similar form letters to respond to inquiries about Smith, and continued to do so long after the DOT terminated Magnet and even years after Smith's death. Arthur Bray, the UFO investigator responsible for the collection of Smith's papers at the University of Ottawa, was one such recipient.

Bray wrote to the DOT in 1964 asking for information about Magnet. Bray noted that he had, "on many occasions, read conflicting reports concerning the activities of The Dept. of Transport in this field," and that because UFOs obviously did not pose a threat to national security, "there can be no reason to keep information from the tax-payer."[81] F.G. Nixon, the director of the DOT's Telecommunications and Electronics Branch, stated: "At no time has this Department carried out research in the field of unidentified flying objects. The late Mr. W.B. Smith, an employee of this Department, who died in December 1962, however, did study unidentified flying objects as a personal hobby. The Department did not take part in any of his research work nor did Mr. Smith provide the Department with any useful information arising out of his work."[82]

Another letter from 1964, this time from the RCAF's deputy public relations director to a correspondent in England, was even blunter: "I regret that we have been unable to provide you with all of the information you require. Every attempt was made to provide you with satisfactory answers, insofar as is permissible by security regulations. As you have been supplied with all the information permissible, it is suggested that further correspondence on this matter would be pointless."[83] By the late 1970s, the DOT had apparently clamped down entirely on the issue. An anonymous resident of Truro, Nova Scotia, wrote to the DOT in 1978 inquiring not about Project Magnet but about UFOs in the area. The Truro resident claimed to have been given the runaround and of having heard "the same excuse and explanation" so often that contacting the "Queen of England would be simpler."[84]

After Magnet's termination, the DOT's goal, especially by the 1960s, was to cease all communication with "cranks" as soon as possible. When the DOT terminated Magnet, Smith acknowledged that a "backlog of mail" had accumulated at the department that was "obviously in the 'crank' class."[85] The following September, the issue was still unresolved. Smith once again informed van Allen that the letters remained unanswered. Smith struggled with the difference between the crank letters and those "written to me in good faith," and therefore proposed to ignore the former but answer the latter politely.[86] He did not indicate in what way he distinguished between the two, perhaps assuming it was obvious to all involved. A clearer directive did not come until March 1955. Van Allen explained the situation to J.R. Baldwin, the deputy minister for transport: "Many of [the letters Smith has received] come under the 'crank' letter type and should be absolutely ignored, but others could be persons of some importance and can not be ignored."[87] Baldwin advised that the DOT proceed in one of three ways: first, entirely ignore all outdated correspondence (leaving the definition of "outdated" to van Allen's "reasonable discretion"); second, send a form reply to those who wrote in good faith that clearly states all investigations have ceased (this is the form letter quoted above); and third, leave it up to Smith to reply privately so long as he also indicates the same. For Baldwin, the most important objective was to avoid involving the DOT "in any correspondence with a lot of 'cranks.'"[88] Baldwin, and others at the department, clearly did not trust the judgment of citizens inquiring about Magnet. To the DOT, UFOs were not real and so any attempt to engage with the issue was bound to end in frustration.

Smith complied with Baldwin's directive and began using the form letter, if grudgingly, for he had not entirely given up hope of continuing with his investigations. Immediately after the DOT terminated Magnet, Smith wrote to C.M. Brant, the Superintendent of Radio Regulations, appealing for further support. Someone must have tipped off Smith that the department was going to terminate Magnet – or perhaps he simply felt the winds of change. In his letter to Brant, Smith firmly resolved to carry on with his studies, whether or not they would "continue within the purview of this Division." He acknowledged that "this subject can hardly be considered as a Telecommunications matter" and so suggested one of three potential courses of action: first, to re-establish Magnet within the DOT but in a separate division; second, for the DOT to provide "a nominal grant" so that he might continue Magnet as a part-time project; or third, for the DOT to "release the project entirely from this Department so that it may be carried on as a private effort."

The DOT chose the third option. The department wanted nothing more to do with Smith's studies, and it is not difficult to see why. Smith had prefaced the three options he presented with an unequivocal statement: "I am satisfied that there is a sufficient probability for the real existence of some Unidentified Flying Objects as Alien Vehicles, to warrant carrying on with the investigations and if possible, expanding them to include a more intensive study of the physics of the problem." If Smith had not made his views on the matter clear to the DOT before this point, then he certainly accomplished it here.

A handwritten note at the bottom of Smith's letter reads: "As you are aware I am not in agreement with para. 2." Superintendent Brant was the writer of this note and directed it to "C.T." – the department's controller of telecommunications – who issued Magnet's termination fifteen days later.[89]

Those within the DOT, and likely also other departments, were not happy that journalists and other citizens had conflated Smith's work with the Canadian government. In the government's view, this coupling did not reflect its true relationship with Smith and his research. What began for the DOT as a modest part-time project aimed at experimentally testing legitimate electric and magnetic principles related to ionosphere research had ballooned into a public relations fiasco. Those associated with the project were not quick to forget it. A.S. Shore, the DRB's liaison officer in London, England, wrote to the DRB chairman in 1957 asking for guidance about a student request for information on the project. "If my memory serves me aright," Shore wrote, "W.R. Smith [*sic*] is the Department of Transport employee who caused considerable embarrassment to the Board a year or two ago by disclosure to the Press of his private studies of flying saucers."[90]

Smith was equally unhappy about how things turned out. Responding to a citizen inquiry, he wrote: "You see, I put it straight to the Government that a half effort wasn't good enough, and it was an all out effort or drop it so that I could carry on in my own way. So I guess they felt they couldn't justify a big project in the face of the public reaction, so they dropped it."[91] It seems that Smith, at least in private correspondence, attempted to claim some ownership over the decision by framing it as the result of the ultimatum he delivered to his superiors. Smith had previously complained about the government's lacklustre attitude toward UFOs.[92] He felt that the phenomenon was more important than this and deserved the proper resources. Some of Smith's correspondents felt the same. One W.W. Stewart, for instance, expressed disappointment that the government had shut down the observatory and his concern for what this meant more generally: "I felt that the Canadians were going to lead the rest of the world in solving the mystery of the flying saucer phenomina [*sic*]."[93] Donald Keyhoe concluded that Project Magnet's termination was further evidence of a government cover-up.[94] Even as early as the mid-1950s, citizens interested in UFOs – much like Smith – were beginning to feel that the government was failing them.

In the end, the DOT justified the termination of Project Magnet by appealing to mandate. In the view of certain officials in the department, the goals and details of the project fell outside the scope of Transport affairs. In charitable terms, they felt that what Smith was attempting to accomplish was more akin to basic science, a subject that in the Canadian government of the early 1950s had no appropriate home. In less charitable terms, Smith's work was downright pseudoscience. The DOT's mandate is to do research into and develop policy related to making transportation systems in the country safer and more efficient. It is a very practical and, frankly, down-to-earth mandate, and one would be hard pressed to make a case that investigations into potentially extraterrestrial, gravitationally driven flying discs falls within its scope.

The death of Project Magnet was ultimately bureaucratic. There was no place for it within the Canadian government. It likely would not have fared any better even within a department that supported basic or less mainstream science, if one existed. For government officials, the study of UFOs was unscientific. The fact that Magnet produced no applicable results simply confirmed this for the DOT. The form letter which the DOT asked Smith to use in reply to citizen inquiries admitted that his studies held "little promise of adding proportionately to our knowledge."[95] The bad publicity that the department received was likely the most convenient excuse to act on a feeling already floating around the department. Although Paul Hellyer indicated that Smith still had a good reputation within the DOT in the late 1960s, he was probably remembering the department's opinion of the work Smith had done that was unrelated to UFOs. Smith, despite his foray into this "unwanted" and "virtually disowned" work, still did his job well and colleagues respected his technical expertise.

There is also an element of boundary work in Smith's story. This chapter, and the next, both deal with the state's attempts to set clear boundaries around what it considered to be legitimate scientific work. Smith's work tended to blur the boundaries between acceptable and unacceptable knowledge, and the state had a problem with how the two became conflated in discussions about UFOs. What is most interesting here, however, is not the status of either truth claim but the fact of boundary formation itself – an act that becomes most visible during times of controversy, as in this case.[96] Bruno Latour has written that it is the making of the boundary between objects that should be interrogated, not necessarily the objects themselves, as a boundary is a historical construction.[97] Writing about the conflict between local and expert knowledge, Tina Loo similarly argues that "it might be more productive to consider such labels as the outcomes of conflict, not the causes of them."[98] In this sense, Smith's and the state's efforts were the cause, not the outcome, of the boundary between "legitimate" scientific work and "illegitimate" ufological work.

UFOs were clearly a phenomenon of some substance, if only because people believed they existed and expected the Canadian government to do something about them. The fact that the government could not explain their origin, purpose, or even method of propulsion was, on the one hand, an embarrassment that the civil servants involved simply wanted to ignore. On the other hand, it had never been deemed a matter to engage with in the first place, given that Smith's colleagues simply did not believe that UFOs actually existed. Smith explained to a citizen inquirer that "when certain government people came face to face with the reality of the space people, and realized that there wasn't anything they could do about it, they promptly closed their eyes and hoped that the whole business would fade out and go away!"[99] Smith's conviction that the Canadian government was too cowardly to look into the matter seriously only became stronger after Magnet ended in 1954. It seems that his employment as a senior engineer in the Broadcast and Measurements division at the DOT was never threatened by the legacy of Magnet. Indeed, by 1959 he had been promoted to Superintendent of Radio Regulations.[100] Considering the fear of many scientists for their reputations if found to be involved in the study of UFOs, Smith was probably fortunate.

But he never forgave his department, or the government in general, for shutting down what he thought was fundamental research that might have led to incalculable discoveries. Smith's bitterness is apparent in a 1959 letter to a citizen correspondent: "I am amused at your attempts to get a copy of my Project Magnet report [from the DOT]. You will recall that I remarked last March that I didn't think you had the chance of the proverbial snowball of prying it loose. No Minister in his right mind is going to release ANY report which in any way might prove embarrassing or give rise to questions which he or his colleagues might find difficult to answer."[101]

Project Magnet highlighted three ways in which state and citizen began to come into conflict: first, the problem of communication between government departments, which was minimal at best and led to duplication of efforts and confusion among citizen correspondents; second, the emergence of citizens unafraid to accuse the government of a cover-up or, eventually, to advance claims of a conspiracy theory; and third, the state's inability to respond to these claims satisfactorily and to take citizens' concerns seriously, based on its official position of disbelief in UFOs and its more general disbelief that citizens would be taken with such unorthodox ideas in the first place. These three seeds of conflict were planted with Project Magnet and, while they may not have been sufficiently obvious at first to take more comprehensive action, they would become so sooner rather than later.

The end of Project Magnet was not the end of Canada's investigation into UFOs. Even before Magnet was terminated, Project Second Storey was formed to look into the UFO phenomenon. The difference between the two projects is striking.

2

Project Second Storey, 1952–54

J. Allen Hynek, astronomer and ufologist, was a consultant with the US government's Project Blue Book during the 1950s. In later years, he became very critical of the project and how investigators fished for certain answers: "What investigations were carried out … and what questions were asked were almost always aimed at establishing a misperception, and the questions were so directed."[1] In his words, Blue Book operated using the theorem, "it can't be, therefore it isn't."[2] Following America's lead, the Canadian government took the same approach.

In 1952, the Defence Research Board, Canada's military science agency, established Project Second Storey (PSS), a committee tasked with investigating the UFO phenomenon. Whereas Project Magnet was the brainchild of one individual, Project Second Storey drew its members from the various arms of Canadian military intelligence. The committee held a total of six meetings until its termination in 1954. Just as the question of how the Canadian government first became involved with UFOs animated the previous chapter, the question of why the government formed a *second* project guides this one. What did the Defence Research Board expect Project Second Storey to accomplish that Wilbert Smith had not done with Project Magnet? What was the point, given that by this time the US had repeatedly debunked the subject? And why did it last only two years?

The establishment of Project Second Storey was the government's first major strike back against what they saw as the disaster of Project Magnet. Adding to this tension, citizens had begun to demonstrate anti-authority and anti-establishment views earlier than the 1960s, the decade normally associated with this kind of radicalism. Specifically, some citizens began accusing the government of a cover-up or of participating in a conspiracy. The history of UFOs in Canada demonstrates how some of these radical views came into being: chiefly through the distrust that citizens came to feel about their government, in concert with the government's conclusion that it needed to clear away superstition and ignorance – in this case, belief in UFOs – and educate citizens on the merits of scientifically grounded knowledge. If the experience of Project Magnet was a false start in the state's attempt to draw on the cultural authority of science, then Project Second Storey was its attempt to overcome this failure and assert its expertise by debunking UFOs.

HOT TOMALLEY

In early April 1950, the minister of national defence Brooke Claxton put an item on the agenda for the next meeting of the Joint Intelligence Committee (JIC). The JIC's members were the directors of intelligence services from each branch of the Canadian Armed Forces as well as representatives from the RCMP and the Department of External Affairs. The goal of the committee was to make it easier to collaborate and share information across agencies. Claxton wanted Omond Solandt, the chairman of the newly formed Defence Research Board, "to seek the cooperation of the [armed] Services in reporting on the occurrences or alleged occurrences of Flying Saucers passing over Canada."[3]

The 220th meeting of the JIC included Item VI – "Flying Saucers (Restricted)." The meeting minutes suggest that discussion of the matter was brief and action-oriented rather than philosophical. They noted that a number of reports had come in from across the country and that perhaps "the field intelligence officers of the three Services and the Royal Canadian Mounted Police might be instructed to investigate these incidents and report thereon to the Department of National Defence." The meeting ended with a suggestion that the Directorate of Air Intelligence (DAI) and the Directorate of Scientific Intelligence (DSI) develop a questionnaire to assist with these investigations, which they would circulate to the various departments.[4]

These recommendations do not at first seem significant, but they marked the beginning of a forty-five-year period during which UFO sighting reports were collected, as well as an attempt to make sense of the bureaucracy supporting investigation of the phenomenon and who exactly would be responsible for the baffling reports. Indeed, a sighting report submitted just one month earlier by two RCAF officers expressed confusion: "It is not known if official credence is given to the existence of 'flying saucers' at any level." The author of the report simply wished to pass on the information in case it was "of interest to higher authority," whatever that authority might be.[5]

Further to the abovementioned meeting of the JIC, the RCAF had already communicated with the US Air Force to obtain whatever information might be available on their end. Air Commodore H.H. Hendrick requested a copy of the US flying saucer study only to be told that the "final study was not reproduced for distribution but is available for examination" at USAF headquarters in Washington.[6] An RCAF official made the trip in May 1950 and his report became the subject of further correspondence.[7]

The US study had concluded that "any further publicity in regard to 'flying saucers' would tend to induce further sightings of an imaginative character." In other words, the US was concerned about "copycat" sightings, where an initial sighting report inspired further reports. This would become a recognizable phenomenon as the years passed – especially following notable media reports about a UFO sighting, or the release of a new film such as, years later, *Close Encounters of the Third Kind*. As a result, the USAF adopted a policy to "play down" the subject and deal with reports in a more ad hoc manner. "It seems to me," wrote DAI group captain W.W. Bean, "that a similar policy on our part would be wise and that it would be undesirable therefore for us to produce a special questionnaire or make any special arrangements for investigation since this would tend to give emphasis to the matter."[8] Bean's colleagues ignored his suggestion. The only progress that the DSI and DAI members made on the matter for the rest of the year and throughout 1951 was, in fact, the development of a preliminary questionnaire.

They designed the "interrogation" form to obtain information about the UFO witness, about their observation, and also about the interrogator, "including his opinion of the reliability of the observer."[9] From this point on, reliability became a constant concern throughout the vast majority of reports and was ascribed to UFO witnesses according to factors such as age, education, excitability, and sobriety. It is remarkable that this questionnaire – just a draft drawn up quickly and without any consultation with other departments – contained the essential questions that all later versions would contain. Not much would change over the course of the next several decades when it came to reporting mechanisms.

Included in correspondence about the initial questionnaire was the suggestion that, "should the Flying Saucer actually make a landing on Canadian territory, the nearest RCAF Command should be advised immediately by telegram or something of the sort."[10] This is as close as any document would get to preparing for actual contact, and the somewhat offhand tone of the statement belies just how unlikely officials deemed this eventuality. Other than several sighting reports forwarded to various departments during 1950 and 1951, there was no more correspondence on the matter until the formation of Project Second Storey.

By 1952, various Canadian government departments were receiving letters from citizens – variously concerned, ecstatic, confused – which detailed all manner of flying saucer sightings. One writer referred to it all as "some of the mysteries which are taking place in the heavens."[11] Solandt himself received several of these directly addressed to him. "It may be of interest to you," read one letter, "to know that what appeared to be a flying saucer was seen by me on April 7."[12] A 1953 letter asked about "the forces which caused and maintain moons [*sic*] orbit, the cause of 'flying saucers' and with reference to magnetic propulsion in man made craft."[13] A 1955 letter indicated that some members of the public saw Solandt as an expert in the matter. The writer was contacting a number of individuals "with similar technical knowledge in the hope [they could] interpret for the public some of these strange phenomena."[14]

Despite Solandt's best efforts, the UFO enigma clung to him. Historian Jason Ridler writes that by 1952, Solandt had become "the public face for the DRB and did his best to weather the distortions and accusations that cropped up about him, his organization, and its fields of research."[15] In his biography of Solandt, Ridler is not shy about discounting the UFO phenomenon, noting that "a full examination of this trivial but publicly popular part of the DRB's existence cannot be dealt with here." Ridler adds: "one can only imagine the pragmatic Solandt politely dealing with this bizarre episode before focusing his mind on the serious matters of modern warfare."[16] Solandt was indeed polite about the issue. He publicly maintained an open mind about UFOs, but was clearly never convinced by what he saw as a total lack of direct evidence of their existence: "I do not feel able to make any useful comment concerning these reports. I naturally follow such reports with great interest but still feel that the best I can do is to reserve judgement concerning the nature of the objects that are reported to have been seen."[17] Nevertheless, public interest forced him to take action: "For three years he … had quietly ignored the rising tide of interest in 'flying saucers' in Canada and the United States, but by 1952, so many reports had been made and so much interest had been generated that [he was] forced to respond."[18]

Certainly, Hollywood and other media outlets did not make Solandt's job any easier. By this time, American and Canadian audiences were consuming even more science fiction films about outer space and extraterrestrials. Among them were the aforementioned *The Thing from Another World* along with *When Worlds Collide*, *Red Planet Mars*, and *Superman and the Mole Men*, the first feature-length film adaptation of Clark Kent's story.[19] Becoming prominent in these films was the theme of advanced extraterrestrial races who had achieved utopia, their alien lives free from such concerns as world hunger and poverty and, especially significant, the threat of nuclear war.

Back in Ottawa, Solandt chaired a general "Meeting to Discuss 'Flying Saucers' Sighting" on 22 April 1952. Eleven people were present, including astronomer Peter Millman from the Dominion Observatory, Wilbert Smith from the Department of Transport, and the DRB's secretary, H.C. Oatway. Three more members were from the DRB, one from the JIC, one from the DAI, one from the Directorate of Navy Intelligence, and one from the Directorate of Military Operations and Plans. The goal of the meeting was "to determine if a more serious effort is justified and, if so, ways and means of implementing an organized effort." Solandt opened the meeting by remarking that the "frequency and persistence of the sightings would tend to discount the theory of 'hallucinations,'" but that "the gathering of reports was rather haphazard and the reaction of the [armed] Services was passive." The committee lamented that "precise and realistic details were lacking in all known reports" and agreed that it would be "desirable to obtain information from U.S. interviews obtained under proper interrogation procedure, but to avoid the U.S. analysis of these interviews which was often unacceptable to some members of this Committee." The minutes do not indicate exactly which members found the US conclusions unacceptable, but it is safe to say at the very least that Smith had voiced his discontent with them, given his ongoing correspondence on the matter. The minutes also indicate that Smith was given some time to outline the extraterrestrial hypothesis and other potential celestial origins for sightings. In contrast, Solandt provided the terrestrial origin theory, "namely a new type of aircraft (presumably Russian) … [which] had some discrepancies, [but] the aerodynamics were worth following as, even if of extra-terrestrial origin, the bodies would have to follow aerodynamic theory within the earth atmosphere."

The members concluded that the various services involved (such as Defence and the RCMP) should undertake a more active investigation into UFOs, but that the role of the DRB would be mainly advisory. The committee, following through on the earlier recommendation, agreed to prepare reporting instructions and a questionnaire to ensure more standardized and reliable observation and "interrogations" of witnesses. This appears to be, at least, the second version of a questionnaire. Smith noted that the ionosphere section of the DoT had also written up reporting instructions independently and distributed them to the stations, making for a third, separate questionnaire.

There is ample evidence throughout the archives that departments communicated with one another about UFOs very infrequently.[20] Officials created and submitted documents within their departments that never made it to other departments for analysis or investigation, and there was often confusion about who exactly had responsibility for the matter. Only days before the DRB meeting, the DoT controller of telecommunications G.C.W. Browne had forwarded a memo to the officers in charge of ionosphere stations throughout the country. "A study of some of the traces taken at our Ionosphere Stations," Browne wrote, "indicates that reflections have been obtained from conducting objects approximately overhead. From the character of the traces it is concluded that these may be associated with the so called Flying Saucer phenomena and all stations are requested to keep a sharp lookout for unidentified aerial objects. Any trace not conforming with the general established pattern should be regarded with suspicion and the sky promptly scrutinized for any visible object which might be responsible." The instructions indicated specific information that the stations were to carefully note, including any accompanying sounds, the shape, luminosity, and maximum dimensions of the object, and the time it took "to travel through a certain arc."[21]

Prior to the 22 April DRB general meeting, those within the government who confronted the UFO issue were slow to respond (if they responded at all), but the newly formed committee acted quickly. It met for the first time only two days later, on 24 April. The first conspicuous difference between the two meetings is that Peter Millman replaced Solandt as chairman. Given Ridler's assessment of Solandt's attitude toward UFOs, it would seem that Solandt was doing everything he could to distance himself from the subject and continue his work on matters of greater importance. Millman shared Solandt's skepticism regarding UFOs and this likely had a significant effect on the tone of the committee's meetings and the conclusion that it eventually reached. A total of eight members attended the 24 April meeting, compared to eleven at the previous one. The meeting was brief. Millman tabled three UFO books as "worthy [of] study," including one by Donald Keyhoe, before assigning to the committee's work a security classification of "confidential."[22]

Millman went so far as to suggest that the committee adopt a name for itself, but one "entirely without meaning" in order "to divorce this work from the questionable title of 'Flying Saucers.'" His suggestion of "Project Theta" was adopted, seemingly because no one could think of anything better. The remainder of the meeting concerned the questionnaire that the committee was to develop, and with that the first official meeting of Canada's UFO committee came to a close.[23] Several days later, Oatway distributed the date of the next meeting and revealed that the name "Theta" could not be used because of security regulations. He instead suggested "Hot Tomalley" but admitted that "other suggestions are in order."[24] Perhaps mirroring the situation in the US, the name suggests that the committee felt the whole subject was embarrassing, given the government's implicit position that UFOs were not actually real.

JUST AN ADVISORY COMMITTEE

Nevertheless, the committee forged on and held its second meeting on 19 May. "Dr. Millman cautioned the members with respect to dealing with the press and public ... Contacts with the press or public are <u>not</u> to be made." The last thing Solandt wanted was the newspapers getting wind of what the committee was up to, any more than they had already done concerning Wilbert Smith's work. In some cases, this media ban did indeed work, as one news article from May 1952 makes clear: "So we are not to know, after all, what our Government members think about [UFOs], or whether they regard them as any more fantastic than the gyrations of the Federal budget, which last year missed its mark in the fiscal stratosphere by hundreds of millions of dollars."[25] In any case, the Project Second Storey members agreed to change the committee's name from "Theta" to "Second Storey," without giving any indication of its meaning or origin.[26]

With housekeeping out of the way, the committee turned again to the issue of sighting reports and the theories behind them. Millman brought up the work of Donald Howard Menzel, an astronomer with the Harvard University Observatory. In an article published in *Look* magazine, Menzel concluded that the things people were seeing and reporting as UFOs were in fact real, just not extraterrestrial in origin. Rather, they were optical illusions of various kinds. Often witnesses were misidentifying natural phenomena, such as the planet Venus; if only more information was available, all UFO sightings would be identified as perfectly prosaic, natural events. Other critics had come to the same conclusion even earlier and, given Menzel's stature in the scientific community, this view gained even more traction. Menzel believed in this approach, despite having seen a UFO himself. "I do NOT believe that what I saw," he wrote, "or anything anyone has reported seeing, were missiles or messengers or vehicles from the moon or Mars or space. I do NOT believe they were missiles or messengers or vehicles from Russia or any other foreign country. Indeed, how simple science and life would be if every time we encountered some seemingly inexplicable fact, we could blame it on some outside force over which we have no control."[27]

Menzel's conclusions clearly swayed Millman. Given his later correspondence, it is likely that Millman did not allow for much debate in the meetings. For example, in a 1968 letter, Millman thanked an army captain for his cooperation in the investigation of an incident at a local farm. "It is very helpful," Millman confided, "to have someone run these things down to earth. I am afraid that the more I study this field, the more I realize how much hoaxing has occurred on the part of pranksters and publicity seekers."[28]

Millman's opinion of the UFO phenomenon continued to decline over the years, and his experience with Project Second Storey laid the foundation for this. The remainder of the 19 May meeting concerned information that the committee might be able to glean from their US counterparts, as well as the questionnaire in development. The committee agreed that the armed services involved would only "follow up particular sightings provided that personnel and time [were] available," and that they would approve the "interrogation form" at the next meeting. Finally, "an attempt would be made to have Lt. Ruppelt visit Canada and describe the USAF project to the Committee."[29] By this time, the US Air Force had initiated Project Blue Book, the successor to Projects Sign and Grudge, with Lieutenant Ruppelt at the head of the investigation. Blue Book was intended to collect and analyze sighting reports in much the same way that Project Second Storey was set up to do, and the 19 May meeting minutes suggest that the Canadian government, while developing its own reporting procedures, was also looking to the south for guidance and potential answers to the problem.

Canada has had a complicated relationship with America's postwar leadership. Several historians of Canada's military endeavours have argued that the state was very self-conscious of its status as a "junior partner" to the US and, as a result, tried very hard to chart its own course in domestic and international affairs. Many Canadian government officials, especially those within the Department of External Affairs, were fearful for Canadian sovereignty. After the Second World War, US influence over Canada's policy decisions became incredibly strong, and so creating a clearly Canadian path forward became a necessary task.

Andrew Richter, for instance, laments that when it came to nuclear weapons, conventional wisdom holds that Canada "lacked an independent capacity to articulate its interests" and thus simply deferred to US policy. Richter argues the opposite – that in fact Canada had its own unique and robust strategy, and took every opportunity to challenge US policy and implement its own.[30] Similarly, Andrew Godefroy laments that critics have viewed the Canadian Army as a force that, "aside from brief bouts of professionalism," was "confused and generally met with failure." In contrast, Godefroy argues that the Army, like Canada's nuclear weapons strategy, innovated and adapted in its own unique ways to serve its specific geopolitical interests.[31]

This was *not* the case with UFOs. There is no evidence to suggest that the Canadian government attempted or even wished at all to chart its own path when it came to UFO investigation. Other than a few isolated individuals like Wilbert Smith, government officials were happy to let the US take the lead. It is clear even from the earliest intragovernmental correspondence on the matter that UFOs were something confusing, with which the government wanted as little involvement as possible. In this singular case, the Americanization of Canadian military and political policy was actually desired – and quite explicitly, as the meeting minutes and the attitudes of Canadian officials like Peter Millman demonstrate.

Project Second Storey met for the third time on 31 July 1952, and quickly approved a draft interrogation form. Wilbert Smith then proposed several ideas, each of them shot down in turn: that the committee subscribe to a press clipping service to keep abreast of UFO sightings in case investigation was warranted;[32] that the committee attempt to obtain as many reports as possible of each sighting to aid in analysis; that the committee conduct an experiment to test the observational capacities of citizens (his balloon experiment, discussed in Chapter 1, he nevertheless conducted himself); and that the committee respond to a letter from "Civilian Saucer Investigations,"[33] a UFO club based in Los Angeles.[34]

Smith was unhappy with how things were going. Just one week later, he wrote to Donald Keyhoe: "I do not feel that the present effort of merely correlating and cataloguing sighting data is nearly sufficient. I maintain that it takes only one black sheep to prove that all sheep are not white, and one unexplained saucer sighting should be enough to warrant establishing a serious scientific study group."[35] Despite the involvement of established and well-respected scientists like Omond Solandt and Peter Millman, Smith felt that PSS was inadequate, if not an outright farce.

THE SIGHTING FORM

What exactly did the sighting form look like? What was the result of all the months of preparation and deliberation? Did the form take a unique approach, asking questions that cut straight to the core of the witness experience? By all accounts, it did no such thing; there appeared to be nothing remarkable or innovative about it. The form contained elements common to most any other official form, with sections for describing the observer,[36] the thing observed,[37] other witnesses, other "contributory evidence" such as photographs and, finally, details about the "interrogator."[38]

In addition to the form itself, more extensive "complementary" instructions, referred to in the third PSS meeting, were included in the form of three appendices. The extra material began with a general statement: "In collecting data on unknown flying objects, accuracy of observation and record is of prime importance. The observer should report carefully and precisely what he sees and hears with a minimum of private personal interpretation. Accurate numerical data to the best of the observer's ability are most desirable. Confirmation of the observation by others is also desirable, particularly if other observers are located some distance away so that they may have a slightly different view of the object." Thomas Porter has written that as scientific communities grew larger, new methods were needed to ensure that one could trust the results of experiments done elsewhere, out of sight and reach. The most effective way to do this was to trust in numbers rather than personal testimony.[39] In the case of Project Second Storey's UFO sighting form, there is an obvious emphasis on the desire for quantitative and objective data. In a practical sense, this often meant limiting or eliminating altogether any narrative or testimonial account of a sighting. As a 1953 correspondence between DoT employees made clear, it was always preferable to "prepare a formal sighting report rather than attempt to convey the information in narrative form."[40] Emphasis was also placed on physical evidence: "an effort should be made to uncover any evidence of a photographic, electronic, magnetic or radioactive nature which might have some association with the sighting. No unusual happenings at the time or place of sighting should be overlooked."

Beyond these instructions, one appendix dealt with the "weighting factors" that Smith developed for the PSS committee. It also began with a general statement: "In the analysis of sighting reports it is fairly obvious that different reports will have widely different values from the viewpoint of reliability, confirmation and lucidity. A formula has been devised giving approximately the same significance to each of these factors and derived from numerical values assigned to the answers given to the various questions on the Project Second Storey sighting report form." Smith introduced the formula as a way of scoring each sighting by "obtaining numerical values for each of the factors" presented.[41]

Finally, the complementary instructions contained an appendix with "Descriptions of Normal Phenomena which might cause reports of unidentified aerial objects," including such common things as balloons, aircraft, and meteors.[42] What is ironic about the inclusion of these is that the committee assumed observers *would* misidentify natural phenomena. The committee took special care to emphasize the need for unbiased reporting and interrogation, yet prefaced the entire operation with a convenient list of possible origins for the UFOs sighted. It is this kind of detail that critics, especially the citizen UFO investigators who would later come to antagonize the government so much, latched onto when claiming the government was not taking the issue seriously. Wilbert Smith himself said as much when he lamented the committee's limited mandate. It is hard to keep an open mind and conduct a serious scientific investigation, he said, when the options are so foreclosed from the start. This also demonstrates, as Zygmunt Bauman argues, the state's goal of educating the public by clearing away ignorance, or even the possibility of ignorance. By precluding the possibility of a misidentification, the state was putting UFOs to social and political work, by using the phenomenon to shape how citizens thought in order to lift them up and make them more rational.

The presence of these descriptions within the complementary instructions is clear, if subtly placed, evidence of PSS's position on UFOs and those who witnessed them. To the committee members, UFOs were nothing but misidentified phenomena about which we have either known for some time or have yet to discover or fully explore, but they were nevertheless *natural* and not supernatural or extraterrestrial phenomena. People were simply inexperienced at observing nature and comprehending what they saw, and so the sighting form and instructions were meant to clarify for investigators what was, to the scientifically inept public, an unclear and even miraculous experience. This was a commonsensical position to take given the public's limited scientific literacy.

An article published around the same time helps to demonstrate why the Canadian government saw things this way. An Alberta newspaper published a small piece about a researcher who claimed to have discovered a manuscript proving that monks at an English monastery in AD 1290 had been "terrorized" by a flying saucer.[43] The sheer ambiguity of such an article, and the lack of corroborating details, likely would have made government scientists roll their eyes and try to forget about the whole affair.

Of the approximately 4,500 sighting reports made between the late 1940s and 1995, only about a dozen were submitted using the PSS form – a minuscule fraction of the overall total. Of this dozen, all were made in the mid-1950s, immediately after the form was first developed and distributed to other government departments. Almost as soon as PSS made the form available, other departments either ignored it or translated it into a different format, one that suited its own needs.

The two most common types of alternative reports were the RCMP reports – especially beginning in the mid-1960s – and telex messages sent to the National Research Council.[44] Sometimes, if relevant, the forms would conclude with a statement about the reliability of the witness. Reliability was usually simply positive or negative: either the witness was highly reliable due to their training as a pilot or some other kind of assumedly objective observer, or the witness displayed low reliability, because according to the investigator they seemed to be intoxicated, were too young to make an objective observation, or were "excitable." This last factor, in particular, was often used to describe women, invariably housewives, who reported sightings. Reports often noted that their husbands had discredited their statements.

Citizen UFO investigators usually created their own versions of the form. They would track down witnesses and submit a report to the government for consideration. These citizen reports very closely mirrored the government reports and provided much of the same kind of information. Beyond such formal reports, witnesses sent numerous sightings to the government in the form of handwritten or typed letters, which usually offered narrative accounts of the experience rather than any objective accounting of details. For PSS, these narratives were fatally subjective: irrelevant, and harmful to a proper scientific analysis. They wanted reports to stick to the objective facts. Some citizens may have been upset that PSS and other government officials did not take seriously their narrative accounts, but in the government's defence, it was unclear exactly what value a story about a UFO observation could offer to an analysis, especially if the writer included this description at the expense of hard details.

In short, a number of different departments were obliged to report UFO sightings, but they did so in ways that were tailored to their specific needs, and this is reflected in the kind, and scope, of information collected on the forms. The PSS form was far too detailed for most investigators, and so some elements of it were used and others discarded.

To some citizens, there appeared to be a contradiction between how the committee articulated its mandate and the kind of information they designed the form to elicit. The form may have read as if the committee intended to make a rigorous, detailed study of a particular sighting, as though a scientific study into the UFO phenomenon was actually taking place; however, the PSS committee also made it clear that it existed only as an advisory body and was not in fact tasked to investigate anything. As such, some felt that the form and the mandate did not very closely match. However, this feeling only arose if one assumed that PSS operated under the assumption that UFOs were real. PSS did not, and when this fact is taken into account, the sighting form becomes a means by which to ascertain misidentifications of natural phenomena, not to undertake a study on the nature of UFOs. As such, the form represented very different things to different people depending on their perspectives and beliefs regarding UFOs, rather in the same way that all parties involved put UFOs to work in different ways according to their goals.

These differences in belief also explain why other government departments were confused about the responsibility for reporting and investigation. The very same Edward Ruppelt with whom the PSS committee was seeking to consult later wrote that the USAF tackled the UFO problem with "organized confusion."[45] The Canadian government seems to have done the same. On the one hand, this is understandable. Ruppelt also wrote that "the military wants answers, not mysteries."[46] The military is pragmatic and requires concrete threats to tackle. Yet, this organized confusion is also the reason why people like Wilbert Smith, and later a number of Canadian citizens, became frustrated with, and came to mistrust, the government's efforts. A local newspaper made it clear what some citizens thought about the government's response: "Since those who believe in flying saucers are in a minority in official circles, it is unlikely any official information will be made public unless and until science can produce proof."[47]

WINDING DOWN

In the vast majority of cases, once an investigator filed a UFO sighting report, the investigation ceased. This could have been because the interrogator felt they could obtain no further information; or perhaps the departments to which the report was submitted lacked the time or interest to investigate further. Another reason was because government officials, especially those on PSS, felt that once the form was filled out, all due diligence had been done. The committee assumed that the majority of reports would provide evidence of misidentified natural phenomena, or that if confusion existed it was only because of insufficient information. It was inconceivable to the committee, as indeed to anyone who accepted the logic used to create the form, that anything other than a natural, prosaic phenomenon had occurred, and so it was only natural, in turn, that the investigation would cease after the form was completed. The evidence would be thus recorded and made available to those qualified to carry out further study, but the committee understood that this invariably meant personnel from some other, unspecified department. In other words, the work was done, and if someone else wanted to take it up further, that was their business. In fact, PSS's mandate supported this attitude given that it articulated itself as an advisory committee. It fostered a desire for competent reporting but certainly not for analysis.

RCMP reporting procedures, which began in earnest in the early 1960s, mirrored this attitude. Thousands of pages of documentation of UFO sightings exist in RCMP files, but this is all there is. There was great consistency in how RCMP officers reported UFOs. They were diligent in recording all the pertinent details – observer's information, location and time of sighting, weather conditions, etc. – but only very rarely did their reports offer any further opinion on what exactly the observer had seen. Comment on the possible origin of sighted objects was always withheld in favour of meticulous documentation of the observer's report.

Historian Steve Hewitt notes that the RCMP was particularly skilled at producing mountains of paperwork, but inept at actual analysis of the material they accumulated. Hewitt describes the service as "drowning in a sea of reports, all with red margins."[48] In the early 1950s, the Canadian government was overwhelmed by the idea of UFO reports (even if the actual number of such reports was low) and the disproportionate amount of attention they seemed to demand. The government felt that this attention was unnecessary; but I argue that it was also simply unable to provide it given the constraints that the government placed around its own investigation, namely proceeding under the assumption that UFO reports were no more than misidentified natural phenomena.

The number and quality of sightings did not seem to convince government officials that UFOs deserved serious attention. Several colourful reports and inquiries were made in 1952. The RCAF received a letter on 16 September from a German man living in Mont-Joli, Quebec, who claimed to be an aeronautical engineer who had worked under Hitler during the Second World War building secret aircraft. The man cautioned the Canadian government not to take seriously the claims that UFOs were extraterrestrial, as he knew from personal experience that they constituted nothing less than "Hitler's secret weapon."[49]

Only days later, the DOT received a report describing a government official's attempt to interview Mr Gabriel Durocher, of Windsor, Ontario, about his observation of a UFO. However, the official was unsuccessful in tracking the witness down, and a local reporter with the *Windsor Daily Star* informed him that "Mr. Durocher is a psychopath and usually after heavy drinking steals a bicycle and then gets himself mixed up with the law. He has appeared in court a number of times on charges of theft but always seems to get off on suspended sentence."[50]

Just the month before, the lighthouse keeper at the station at Nootka, British Columbia, spotted something that he could not identify and reported it to his superior at the DOT, describing it thus: "It was a smooth job whatever it was!"[51] A letter of 6 December addressed to the DND began with the line: "This is not a crank letter and should have been written on my own stationary at the office yesterday but it slipped my mind at the time."[52]

Such oddities were no doubt part of the reason why the government tried so hard to keep reports from the media. In January 1953, officials from the DOT again attempted to reinforce the ban on media contact. Several reports came in from the Regina, Saskatchewan area containing testimony from concerned citizens that "would appear to indicate that some unknown objects are landing and taking off." Andrew Thomson, a DOT controller, advised government weather observers in the area to give special attention to the sightings for the next few weeks, but also warned them "that the matter is confidential and it is most desirable that the newspapers do not get hold of any information in regard to our interest in this matter."[53] H.V. Anderson, the director of marine services, stated that while the sighting forms he had sent out to weather observers to assist in their observations did not bear any classification, "they are to be considered as Confidential and, under no circumstances, should they be released to the Press."[54]

The PSS committee met again on 17 November 1952 and then on 9 March 1953. Both meetings were short and uneventful. The committee continued its work of refining the sighting form and debating how long it should take an investigator to complete (ten minutes maximum, it was decided).[55] Attendance at the meetings continued to decline, with only Millman, Smith, and H.C. Oatway regularly attending. Interest was obviously waning by this point.

The committee was also thinking about the need for centralization of UFO reports. They decided that the Directorate of Scientific Intelligence "would henceforth act as the central agency, and reports received through the various Services would be forwarded to DSI for filing." The decision to centralize the collection of UFO reports within the *scientific* intelligence branch further indicates that the committee did not believe UFOs were a security threat. It also foreshadowed the transfer of responsibility for all reports to the NRC – a shift that would take place in 1968, as discussed in Chapter 5. Even as early as March 1953, it was clear that officials within the government – military or otherwise – deemed it a chore and were seeking to hand it off.

This attitude was most clearly reflected in Millman's remarks at the meeting. After discussions with Solandt, Millman "pointed out that [the] evidence to date did not seem to warrant an all out investigation by the Canadian Services." Millman reiterated that he "considered [it] unnecessary" for the "Committee or any other section of D.N.D. to undertake a detailed analysis of the reports received," but that "other government organizations may persue [*sic*] these investigations more actively on their own initiative." UFOs were, in Oatway's words, a "Hot Tomalley." Should another organization be foolhardy enough to investigate, they were welcome to the reports. But Millman made it clear that PSS, officially, had no interest in contributing in any way beyond standardizing and coordinating reports.[56]

THE LAST MEETING

For the next year, UFO witnesses continued to report sightings. Investigators used the PSS form several times, but uptake was minimal. Nevertheless, while Millman and the PSS committee (Smith excluded) were not particularly interested in UFOs, other departments maintained an active interest in reporting sightings, if not fully investigating them. RCAF squadron leader G.C. Campbell stated that while his air command was "not prepared to undertake scientific analysis of unidentified flying object reports, it does have primary interest in current reports on this subject."[57] At the very least, other departments retained an active interest just in case a security issue might arise, and to remain reasonably informed of what was going on. This attitude would persist for at least two more decades, until the late 1960s, when major changes were made in regard to how the government received reports.

In the meantime, citizens began articulating more unorthodox views. For example, Leonard H. Stringfield, of Cincinnati, Ohio, wrote to the DRB:

> In common cause and in the spirit of International cooperation, this writer earnestly believes the world can no longer be restricted from certain overt truths regarding one of the greatest riddles of our time – UFO phenomena! I am aware that your Government has viewed this subject seriously and is presently working, under wraps of secrecy, toward its resolution … I am convinced "saucers" are controlled devices from some extraterrestrial Intelligence. Unfortunately, at the present time, our [US] Air Force, through a policy of contradiction, is embarrassed before the public. However, anyone who has weighed the massive evidence can find only one logical answer – the Interplanetary answer![58]

Stringfield addressed his letter to "Project Magnet," no doubt a result of the press that Smith's UFO observatory had garnered by late 1953. Of course, as noted earlier, all this attention that Smith was receiving was reflected in popular entertainment at the time. In their letters to Smith and others, citizens were taking stronger views on the possibility of alien invasion, a theme then manifesting in such Hollywood films as *War of the Worlds*, the story of Martian invaders whose weapons can vaporize human beings.[59]

It was not just Americans who were taking an interest in the Canadian UFO work. Elmore Philpott, the member of Parliament for Vancouver South, wrote to Wilbert Smith in November 1953 after reading about his work: "I don't know how much of your enterprise is confidential. But the purpose of this letter is to let you know that I am intensely interested in what you are trying to do. If the time ever comes when you have anything which you can report without violation of your instructions, I should greatly appreciate being informed."[60] It seems that even members of parliament were no more privy to the work of PSS and Project Magnet than the general public, but were in some cases equally interested.

As mentioned in the last chapter, once the public learned of Smith's UFO observatory, the DOT began receiving scores of letters. The period between November 1953 and February 1954 was a tense time for the DOT and DRB. Government information officers attempted to quell interest in the subject. Sufficient press had reached the departments by New Year that Millman called another PSS meeting. On 22 February 1954, six members met for the committee's sixth meeting, one of the most perfunctory yet. Millman raised three items of interest. He noted that no progress had been made since the last meeting a year earlier in bringing the USAF's Captain Ruppelt (since promoted from the rank of lieutenant) to Ottawa. Millman also mentioned "the latest book on the newstands [*sic*] entitled 'Flying Saucers have Landed,' by Leslie and Adamski,"[61] which to his mind appeared "to be of doubtful authenticity and must not be taken too seriously." Finally, before adjourning, he gave Smith some time to review three items: "(a) what the [DOT] is now doing with reference to analysis of reports and any conclusions arrived at … (b) methods used by the DOT sighting station … [and] (c) future plans."[62]

This was to be the committee's last meeting. The members were frustrated that they had not been able to bring Ruppelt to Ottawa, and there is no evidence to suggest he ever made such a trip. Although Millman felt that the committee would have benefitted from the advice and wisdom of the US investigation, it is clear that bilateral relations in this case were severely restricted. During this time, different departments made a number of unsuccessful attempts to obtain information, UFO-related or otherwise, from their US counterparts, confirming an uneven distribution of power within the relationship. And while Millman's opening remark might have indicated that the committee was still interested in UFOs, his disparagement of Leslie and Adamski's book suggested that this interest was narrowly confined to specific cases, such as tracking meteorites and fireballs. In other words, Millman was interested in UFO reports only insofar as they could provide detailed information about recognizable natural phenomena.

Nothing was included in the minutes that gives an indication of how the committee received Smith's report, but by this time it is safe to say that Millman wanted the details only for purposes of knowing how far Smith had gone in communicating his work and how much damage control the DOT and other departments would have to do. The fact that the PSS committee never met again indicates that Millman and other committee members felt, as they had previously admitted, that UFOs did not present a viable scientific object of study and were unworthy of serious consideration. There is also evidence to suggest that, as anticlimactic as this sixth and final meeting was, Millman had called it only grudgingly. Several months earlier, in November 1953, he had authored a summary report of PSS activities in the belief that the committee would not be required to meet again. This report encapsulated Millman's thoughts on the matters before the committee.

It began by emphasizing the committee's advisory role. "An attempt was made," Millman wrote, "to eliminate, as much as possible, the subjective element from the sightings. The majority of sightings reported to date have over-stressed irrelevant personal opinions rather than the straight-forward objective facts." He concluded: "The committee as a whole has felt that, owing to the impossibility of checking independently the details of the majority of the sightings, most of the observational material does not lend itself to a scientific method of investigation."[63] In speaking for the committee, Millman excluded Smith's opinions. He made it clear to anyone coming to the subject after the fact that they were wasting their time.

Earlier that year, the Central Intelligence Agency had convened the Robertson Panel, a meeting of American scientists to discuss UFOs. Although this panel did not release its report publicly, the Canadian and American governments were clearly on the same page. The panel concluded that UFOs did not represent a security threat but did provide the circumstances for an outbreak of public hysteria. As Hynek lamented, "the Robertson panel did get someplace: they made the subject of UFOs scientifically unrespectable, and for nearly 20 years not enough attention was paid to the subject to acquire the kind of data needed even to decide the nature of the UFO phenomenon. Air force public relations in this area was egregious, and the public was left with its own decisions to make: was the air force attitude a result of 'cover-up' or of foul-up and confusion?"[64] PSS did not specifically mention the problem of mass panic, but did share the same general view of UFOs as the Robertson Panel. With Millman's final report in place and the sixth and last meeting adjourned, Project Second Storey was quietly terminated, establishing the conditions for the very kind of public suspicion and confusion that Hynek described.

The one task that occupied the majority of the Project Second Storey committee's time was the sighting form. Yet some doubted whether such a form was necessary at all. In 1952, after only the second PSS meeting, the DoT's controller of telecommunications G.C.W. Browne wrote to a colleague: "I would advise that we have not considered it necessary to supply all offices with the sighting report forms, since there appears to be little justification for the wide distribution of these forms in order to meet the requirements of the relatively few actual sightings." Even after PSS worked on developing a sighting form, others were not convinced it was needed. "As a matter of fact," Browne continued, "it is the information pertinent to the sighting which we require, rather than the completion of the form itself and if the same information is forthcoming in the form of a letter or memorandum we consider it of equal value to a completed sighting report."[65]

Millman felt that the standardized sighting form was necessary in order to obtain just the "straight-forward objective facts," as narrative accounts sent by handwritten letter, for instance, tended to include "over-stressed irrelevant personal opinions." Millman was not alone in this. As J. Allen Hynek wrote: "The problem [with the phenomenon] is compounded by the fact that most UFO reports are frustrating in the extreme. They contain so few facts!"[66] Browne was of the opinion that it did not really matter at all what the physical format of the report was, so long as it contained the facts. Perhaps he felt that it was not too much trouble to take the time to "separate the grain from the chaff," as one observer would later put it.[67] This difference of opinion, however, is superficial. In the same letter, Browne thanked the correspondent for the information provided, as it was "precisely the type of information which we require in our investigations" – that is, the information was ultimately deemed sufficiently straightforward and "objective." Whatever the rationale for using a form or a narrative account, the government required unbiased reporting of what was observed, not subjective interpretations of the event. Interpretation was a job for the experts, and those experts invariably decided that UFO sightings were nothing more than misidentified natural phenomena.

Project Second Storey's conclusions accelerated the cycle of mistrust between government and citizen that Smith had previously become embroiled in during his time with Project Magnet. To the government, the aim of Project Second Storey was commonsensical. UFOs were clearly nothing other than misidentifications of natural phenomena, and some basic investigation proved this.

For Project Second Storey, UFOs were a waste of time because it was evident that they did not exist. To scientists like Millman, it was ludicrous to think that anyone would take the subject seriously. The only viable reason to continue collecting reports was to keep up to date on the latest developments, just in case something significant did occur. The assumption was, however, that anything of significance would not involve actual UFOs but rather something of a physical, likely meteorological nature – in other words, something that legitimate scientists could recognize and actually study. For the Canadian government, officially at least, prudence was the motivation for its involvement with UFOs from the early to mid-1950s. Others within the government, such as Smith, thought otherwise. It would become clear that many outspoken citizens did not share the government's conclusions. As the next chapter will show, these citizen investigators were not shy about making their opinions known.

3

Very Persistent Men, 1954–67

By the mid-1950s, a small group of disconnected Canadian citizens really wanted to know what the government was doing about UFOs. They began writing letters in earnest, posing all manner of questions about the alien crafts' origins and purposes. The government was not happy about this. In its estimation, Project Second Storey had proven that UFOs were not amenable to scientific inquiry; as such, government officials felt the matter required no further attention.

This chapter is about the increasing interaction between government and citizen after the two investigative projects – Projects Magnet and Second Storey – were terminated. These various points of contact are highlighted to show moments when each side attempted to put UFOs to work in the service of different ends. What this is really about is *letters* to the government. These citizen letters demanding answers to the UFO mystery reveal what Canadians expected from their government and their frustration at the responses they received. In short, these Canadian citizens wrote to the government for answers but instead felt betrayed.

This sense of betrayal and frustration was the result of several converging factors: first, the apparent lack of fit between Project Second Storey's mandate as an advisory rather than an investigative committee, and the nature of the sighting form that the committee developed. The dissonance between the committee's mandate and its sighting form caused confusion and frustration among citizens who felt the government was giving them the "go-around" and responding to their letters with "doubletalk."

However, this conflict was also the result of a second factor: a passive lack of communication between government departments. It was almost inevitable that citizens would receive different and sometimes contradictory answers about UFOs when communicating with multiple departments, each with its own approach to the phenomenon.

The third factor was the rise of conspiracy theory. Lest it seem that citizens were the only ones wronged in this situation, conspiracy theory began to infuse their letters in the late 1950s, further antagonizing the government and the rational skepticism it was trying to advocate. UFOs and conspiracy theory go hand in hand. Canadian citizens did not develop conspiracy theories about UFOs in isolation, nor were they the products of "delusional minds." Rather, citizens believed such ideas due to a combination of "normal psychological processes"[1] and as part of a broader critique of the establishment in the postwar years.

COMMUNICATION TROUBLES

In February 1955, Tom Eastham, a reporter for the newspaper *Chicago American*, wrote to DRB chairman Omond Solandt. "My investigations have convinced me," said Eastham, "that many people are seeing strange things that have not been satisfactorily explained." Eastham had been following the phenomenon for some time, clipping out newspaper articles about UFOs, and was trying to find technically qualified people "to interpret for the public some of these strange phenomena." Eastham asked: "What do you think saucers are? Are they fact or fantasy and what makes you think so?"[2] Solandt replied briefly, several days later: "I do not feel able to make any useful comment concerning these reports. I naturally follow such reports with great interest but still feel that the best I can do is to reserve judgment concerning the nature of the objects that are reported to have been seen."[3]

Solandt's reply would not prove to be an unusual one. The majority of government replies to curious citizens were noncommittal, and Solandt's tone is indicative of an attitude toward UFOs that the government had been cultivating for several years. Solandt himself, during the initial Joint Intelligence Committee meeting that called for the formation of Project Second Storey, had been polite but dismissive when it came to the subject. Officially, UFOs were bunk, and the many citizens writing in were either mistaken or delusional. This official conclusion would help fuel the rise of conspiracy theories among citizens interested in UFOs. It would also paint a picture of believers as pathological types prone to irrationality rather than people tapping into broader cultural trends or demonstrating normal psychological tendencies present throughout society.

The next year, Solandt went even further in his attempt to discredit the phenomenon. In February 1956, another American, Daniel Kamman, wrote to the DRB asking for information about Project Magnet and "a building 12 ft. square," which he believed acted as a flying saucer observatory, and if the Canadian government had ever released an official statement about UFOs.[4] Solandt's reply was again brief, indicating that Kamman's inquiry had been forwarded to Wilbert Smith. Solandt also provided Smith's personal address for further correspondence and concluded that "the Canadian government had not 'gone on record,' at any time, 'with any opinion as to the existence of flying saucers, or to the contrary.'"[5] This was true to the extent that the government had never made any public statement in this regard, although it is clear that PSS did uphold an official stance of disbelief. Certainly, some citizens had already experienced this, and others reported on it in local media. One author described the situation in Ottawa, specifically, as shrouded by a "veil of secrecy."[6]

The government's disinclination to make its stance known is not surprising, given how policy and political decisions more broadly were handled. Robert Bothwell has written that *caution* was at the base of Canada's politics, especially in foreign affairs, during and even before the postwar years. During the tenure of Prime Minister Mackenzie King, a desire to appeal as broadly as possible and to avoid "radical, violent change" was what animated policy. Good government, to King, was about "order and orderly procedures"[7] – things in their place and no fuss about it. This was especially evident when it came to relations with the UK and the US. Whereas English-Canadian loyalties clearly aligned with England before the Second World War, after the war they shifted significantly toward the United States. As a "middle power," Canada had to balance these loyalties, and so the ability to waffle and refuse to take sides became an effective skill.

Jack Granatstein argues that "the Ottawa men" – "an extraordinary group of civil servants who collectively had great influence and power in Ottawa from the Depression through to the late

1950s"[8] – were responsible for Canada's "one distinctive position" on foreign policy: "functionalism." The functional principle argued that a country's unique talents or abilities would decide what power it enjoyed on the international stage.[9] This was a very Canadian, middle-of-the-road approach to balancing power, neither pushing too forcefully nor acquiescing entirely, and it matched King's approach well.

When it came to UFOs, however, Canada denied any functional expertise, instead taking King's position of caution. This broader stance – essentially a reluctance to take a stance – could seem like disinterest. The DRB and DOT had adopted this disinterest by the mid-1950s, causing confusion among some rank-and-file personnel inside those departments. For instance, the DOT received a 1957 telegram reporting a sighting of three slow-moving UFOs over Etobicoke. A handwritten note at the bottom read: "I thought we had cancelled these reports."[10] Later that year, RCAF squadron leader J.C. Lovelace responded to correspondents from Ontario to tell them that he had forwarded their sighting report to Wilbert Smith, "the Canadian Chairman of the Committee on unidentified Flying Objects." Further, Lovelace wrote that the committee was international in its membership and studied all "reliable" reports in Canada and the US.[11] At first, these details seem inaccurate given that Projects Magnet and Second Storey had been terminated by that point. Lovelace may have been referring to the fact that Smith was the primary Canadian contact with the National Investigations Committee on Aerial Phenomena (NICAP), a US-based citizen organization headed by the writer Donald Keyhoe. After Projects Magnet and Second Storey were terminated, it became common for those who knew Smith to automatically forward all UFO-related correspondence and material to his desk, avowing ignorance of the topic. They were likely thankful for such an easy way out of the situation. Another memo similarly stated: "The RCAF does not have the investigative capability to deal with these phenomena. The Department of Transport however, has a Mr. W.B. Smith, who is ex-officio Canadian Chairman."[12]

The practice of automatically forwarding UFO correspondence to Smith continued into the 1960s, until his death. Afterward, it became common for DOT and other departments simply to plead ignorance of Project Magnet. Between Smith's death, in 1962, and 1965, more than a dozen government replies to citizens contained some combination of the following claims: that Smith carried out the work of Project Magnet on his own spare time, that it was never an official project, that a different department had the relevant files, or that the department in question had no knowledge of it.[13] In some cases, officials tasked with responding to UFO inquiries likely really did have no knowledge of the Canadian government's involvement given that the investigations were modest and classified. In other cases, the officials likely did have some knowledge of what work had been done to date but did not wish to engage in further correspondence. Whatever the case, once the two projects were terminated in 1954, a point of central communication no longer existed. This left each individual department to field inquiries as its officials saw fit.

It is not hard to imagine the intensity of interest in UFOs in the late 1950s, especially once the Russian satellite Sputnik 1 was launched in October 1957. Zuoyue Wang writes that US president Dwight D. Eisenhower understood Sputnik not as a military threat but as a political and scientific crisis. The real threat was one of diplomacy and propaganda, of America's public image when it came to scientific superiority.[14] This led to the creation of the President's Science Advisory Committee and, ultimately, the establishment of NASA in 1958.

The Canadian government was also concerned about Sputnik's potential political and scientific consequences, although it did not form any special committees or organizations. The Department of Transport, however, immediately began an initiative to monitor Sputnik's orbit, as well as that of a second Soviet satellite launched in November.[15] And, as in the case of UFOs, even while tracking this indubitably real object across the sky, communication issues were paramount. As DoT technician L.G. Cope wrote, the only "critical observation I have of this whole exercise is the pointed lack of communication facilities between Headquarters and our Monitoring Stations." The delays in relaying messages from the various ionosphere stations across the country to headquarters in Ottawa were, in his words, "annoying."[16]

MR JOHN PUBLIC

By 1956, the production of popular flying saucer and extraterrestrial invasion films continued unabated. That year saw the release of, among others, *Earth vs. the Flying Saucers*, *Forbidden Planet*, and *Invasion of the Body Snatchers*.[17] The public was clearly eating up whatever content could be found on the topic. For their part, of course, citizen UFO investigators were similarly annoyed at the poor communication, or the complete lack of it, which they had received from the government. Several lengthy exchanges between government and citizens occurred in the years after Sputnik. Major Donald Keyhoe, now the director of NICAP, had continued to publish books on the alleged flying saucer conspiracy, and in August 1958 he wrote to the DRB. He asked if any sighting reports might be made available to the public and "whether RCAF pilots are instructed not to discuss or make public UFO sightings, as is the case in the United States." Keyhoe also made sure to mention the names of several of NICAP's illustrious board members – former military and intelligence personnel, "and other distinguished citizens of the fields of religion, education, newscasting, etc." – and asked what his organization might do for the Canadian government in these matters, making the letter as much a gracious offer of expert assistance as a simple inquiry for information.[18]

The DRB did not respond until October. According to DRB public relations officer C.A. Pope, since 1947 various government departments had collected sighting reports "on a voluntary basis," but these had become sufficiently numerous by 1952 to justify the creation of an advisory committee. "In 1954," Pope continued, "the Committee felt that most of the observational material did not lend itself to a scientific method of investigation," and so the committee was disbanded. Pope concluded by stating that the DRB had no knowledge of any instructions issued to RCAF pilots. He referred Keyhoe back to Wilbert Smith, reminding the major that Smith was a member of Keyhoe's own organization and "would be the logical person to contact for information."[19] It is unclear exactly why Keyhoe felt the need to contact the DRB when he had full access to Smith, unless he was simply hoping to catch some government official unawares, or to solicit an "official" statement.

That same month, Keyhoe wrote back requesting the release of sighting reports collected since the termination of Project Second Storey in 1954. The copy of his letter in the archives has three handwritten notes at page bottom. The first, from Pope to PSS secretary Oatway, asked if they could in fact release the reports. The second note, addressed to DSI, read: "Release of information is your responsibility. If releasable, suggest you ensure that there is no implication of official endorsement." Finally, the third note was addressed back to Pope: "We spoke. Can we politely disengage ourselves from Keyhoe[?]"[20]

In his final reply, Pope again suggested to Keyhoe that he contact Smith for such information given that, in Pope's words, the "majority of the sighting reports received by the advisory committee are passed eventually to Mr. Smith whom I am sure would be glad to help you." Pope also noted that the DND "is somewhat reluctant to make [the reports] directly available for examination because they include assessments of the individuals who originally report the sightings."[21] That is, sighting reports contained personal contact details and the investigator's thoughts on the witness's reliability and reputation. Personal privacy was always a concern, right up until 1995 when the NRC finally stopped collecting reports; the only redactions made on any of the available UFO documents were of witness's names and addresses.

Whether or not Keyhoe obtained what he was looking for, he did not write to the DRB again. There was never any shortage of similar letters from citizens, though. In fact, a May 1959 RCAF memo lamented how that particular branch was "plagued from time to time by the submission of UFO Reports and by civilian letters following sensational newspaper accounts of unexplained lights in the sky."[22] The memo's wording indicates that the memo's author, an RCAF officer, believed citizens were refusing to listen to common sense. At the very least, the officer's comments speak to the "copycat" phenomenon of UFO sightings, which typically spike after a notable media report or the release of a film or a book. For instance, the previous year saw the release of *The Blob* and *It! The Terror from Beyond Space*, both of which feature murderous alien life forms finding their way to Earth.[23] And, beginning in the year 1959, those with a television set were able to tune into *The Twilight Zone*, the classic Rod Serling series that explored all manner of surreal and anomalous experiences.[24]

Later that year, Saskatoon resident D.M. Spicer wrote to the DOT: "It seems peculiar to me that with all these reports, both yourself and the armed forces have remained silent." Spicer wrote that a recent Vancouver sighting had "brought a 'No Comment' statement from your department in that area" and that it seemed "that you people are in a good position to either prove or disprove these sightings."[25] After receiving a reply with contact information for another

DOT official who apparently was in a better position to comment on UFOs, Spicer sent the same letter a second time. This second letter prompted an internal DOT memo titled "Another Letter from D.M. Spicer." The memo's author, Officer in Charge S.L. Young, wrote that he had no comments to make and had cautioned his staff "accordingly." The local Control Tower also declined to accept the letter and so Young sent it on to the regional director for air services in Winnipeg.[26]

Late in December, C.R. Brereton, the regional superintendent for air traffic control in Winnipeg, did reply to Spicer, informing him that "anything out of the ordinary which might be noted by our Controllers would be reported through this Office to Ottawa and under no circumstances would it be made public by the operators themselves or this Office."[27] This answer did not sit well with Spicer. He replied just two days later: "I am wondering in particular if you think that the public needs this protection or is it for the convenience of your own office?" Spicer reminded the DOT that he was simply interested in "clarification from authoritative sources" about what people might be seeing. "Failure to give such a service," he railed, "appears to infer that Mr John Public suffers hallucinations or spots before his eyes."[28] Of course, unofficially, that is exactly what scientists in Ottawa thought.

Spicer's letter prompted another internal memo, this time from the office in Winnipeg up the chain of command to the director general for air services in Ottawa. The memo noted that previous letters to Spicer had "attempted to discourage further enquiry" and that the UFOs to which Spicer was referring were "invariably" "high flying SAC [United States Strategic Air Command] aircraft shimmering in the bright sunlight." The office, naturally, could not divulge this information and thus was asking for guidance from headquarters.[29] However, this is the only time the government provided this specific explanation. No other letter ever mentioned Strategic Air Command as a potential origin for sightings. In February 1960, the director of civil aviation, R.W. Goodwin, provided his thoughts:

> Mr. D.M. Spicer, obviously, is a very persistent man. Your problem seems to be how to tell Mr. Spicer that he cannot obtain from this Department the information he wants. Perhaps the easiest solution would be to tell him that such suspected "Unidentified Flying Objects" as have been reported to and

> identified by ATC [Air Traffic Control], have actually been military aircraft, without revealing that they are foreign military aircraft.[30]

The available correspondence ends there, but presumably Spicer received a general response and was satisfied (or frustrated) enough that he did not write back.

Spicer's letters demonstrate at least some citizens' rapidly growing distrust of the government's statements and intentions. As other citizens shortly would as well, Spicer raised the prospect that the Canadian government might be intentionally covering up information. The documents show that what many would come to call a conspiracy was most likely the result of poor communication and convoluted bureaucracy, as well as the government's concern about public embarrassment given the nature of the subject. This conclusion does not detract, however, from what citizens were feeling in the moment; the aim here is not to single out a type of individual prone to believing in conspiracy theory but rather to explain why they might have held such beliefs in the late 1950s and 1960s.

The scholarly literature on conspiracy theory is still developing, but one of the most compelling sources is Joseph Uscinski and Joseph Parent's book *American Conspiracy Theories*. The two political scientists argue that people who believe in conspiracy theories are what they call "losers," which they intend entirely as a descriptive rather than a pejorative term. They are "losers" in the sense that they lack power, political or otherwise. Conspiracy theorists are usually on the margins of authority, and use conspiracy theory as a way of understanding the world and their place in it. Conspiracy theories, they argue, "are weapons of the weak and on balance an adaptive behaviour."[31]

While this political explanation is compelling, in this chapter I also want to foreground the importance of a combined historical and psychological approach. Uscinski and Parent focus heavily on the role of ideology and previous political affiliation as a means of determining predisposition toward certain conspiracy theory beliefs. I want to place conspiracy theory about the Canadian government's involvement in the UFO phenomenon within a more general framework of changing ideas about deference to authority during the postwar period.

Canadians were becoming less deferential toward the government as early as the 1950s. Citizens' letters about UFOs demonstrate how anti-establishment and anti-expertise views were becoming more common in the wake of the Second World War. Conspiracy theory is not necessarily the product of individual minds geared toward certain beliefs based on idiosyncratic pathologies or predispositions, but rather – at least in part – the product of wider cultural changes. Conspiracy theory about UFOs in Canada comes from the same place as changing ideas about the government's technoscientific and political expertise. Combined with Uscinski and Parent's ideas, for instance, this analysis puts letters from citizens like Spicer – and others described below – in the context of "the 'thinning out' of social discourse," what historian Christopher Dummitt characterizes as the key change underway in a wider cultural and political transformation that is present most obviously in the rebelliousness of the 1960s, but "was presaged by similar developments in the 1950s."[32] Similarly, in the context of the experience of modernity more generally, Marshall Berman describes this as "a radical flattening of perspective and shrinkage of imaginative range."[33]

This is not to say, though, that psychology plays no role in this phenomenon. Jan-Willem van Prooijen writes that conspiracy theory is not a pathological behaviour, not something that should be studied in clinical psychology, but rather falls within the domain of social psychology, the study of ordinary citizens, what they think, and why. That is, conspiracy theory is "rooted in similar, recognizable, and predictable psychological processes."[34] The need to construct conspiracy theories around momentous events or phenomena comes out of a combination of behaviours and features which psychologists have studied for decades. This includes the need for "sense-making" in times of crisis, when fear and uncertainty are common. In such situations, it is common for people to place blame on powerful institutions, especially if they did not trust these institutions to begin with.[35] The early Cold War was just such a situation, when politics and the changes taking place generally in society created a situation of uncertainty. Added to this is the observation that people seem to be hard-wired to find patterns everywhere they look, even where connections between people and events do not actually exist. In times of crisis, especially, people want to attribute agency to events beyond their control, to help make sense of them.[36]

There is also another, more prosaic reason why citizens were demonstrating a growing distrust of the government at this time: simply, that the government was providing ambiguous answers to the

UFO question. In one of the earliest UFO books, American journalist Frank Scully wrote that once the government's official investigations were closed, citizens had only one place to go for answers: their local newspapers.[37] Like others, Scully claimed that the government was covering up the phenomenon and that the only trustworthy sources were muckraking journalists like himself.

Local newspaper reports are mentioned throughout this book to demonstrate the attitude they took toward the UFO question, and how citizens might have absorbed these views in lieu of the government's official response. Unfortunately for the government, what Scully and his colleagues claimed was partly true: answers were not generally very forthcoming, and articles and books by people like Scully and Donald Keyhoe quickly filled the gap, convincing citizens of a cover-up. These factors help to explain why some Canadian citizens started to accuse the government of a cover-up, of being deceitful, but also that this behaviour – while not explicitly widespread – was not necessarily pathological but rooted in the political and social climate at the time, and further motivated by common psychological tendencies.

An example of citizens' views comes again from local newspapers. In August 1965, a reporter in British Columbia wrote about a personal UFO sighting and the fact that so many others had also seen something in the sky at the same time. Yet, he also lamented the government's reaction (or lack thereof): "If I am seeing things which the authorities claim do not exist, I have plenty of company."[38] This kind of commentary, and the fact that local newspapers had been reporting continuously on UFO sightings all around the country since the late 1940s (even if scientists in Ottawa took little notice), shows that citizens on the ground, at least, maintained an interest in, and open-mindedness about, the phenomenon.

WIDE OPEN FOR INSPECTION

In the same month that R.W. Goodwin called Spicer a "very persistent man," the RCAF was similarly bombarded. "What has Canada concluded about the UFOs?" asked Vancouver resident Ken Kaasen. "Are the UFOs a genuine threat to Canada? Do RCAF jets ever 'chase' UFOs? If you have the answers to these questions, can you tell them to me? The U.S. and Canada give the public nothing but doubletalk when it comes to the subject of Unidentified Flying Objects. I find the only way to get the facts is to write to someone who has them."[39] Flight Lieutenant J.S.D. Francis replied two weeks later, simply to say that the RCAF had no official responsibility for UFO reporting and thus had no answers.[40] Kaasen was not to be mollified so easily. He wrote to the Edmonton RCAF base, identifying himself this time as a member of NICAP, the citizen UFO investigative group based in Washington, DC. He posed a total of ten questions concerning sightings in Alberta, and specifically over Edmonton, as to whether any landings had been made in the province and whether or not the base adhered to JANAP 146 (D).

Joint Army-Navy-Air Force Publication (JANAP) 146 (D), implemented in 1953, was an order clarifying the reporting procedure for things in the sky that might be of "vital intelligence." As such, the order made it a crime for military personnel in the US to report a UFO sighting to the public, punishable under the Espionage Act. This military order did in fact extend to Canada, although likely without the same level of punishment. Air Force Regulation (AFR) 200-2, another US order implemented in 1954, complemented JANAP 146 (D) and required that all UFO sightings submitted to the Air Force had to be classified and made unavailable to the public, unless the case was officially solved (i.e., positively identified as a natural phenomenon or otherwise).[41]

It is likely that Kaasen found this information by reading Donald Keyhoe's UFO books. Keyhoe had written about these specific orders in, for instance, *The Flying Saucer Conspiracy*, showing the impact that such popular writers had on citizens and their views.[42] Kaasen's letters also demonstrate an assumption held by a number of UFO enthusiasts at this time: that surely Canada and the US must follow the same military policies given their unique partnership, reflecting the increased Americanization of Canadian society and thought. At the end of his letter, Kaasen attempted to wrap the RCAF respondent in a bind: "If you cannot answer my questions, I will know that you either have not got this information, or that you are under order of JANAP 146 (d)."[43]

After sending at least two internal memos that attempted to account for the UFO reporting structure within the DND and assess who had responsibility for replying to such inquiries,[44] RCAF group captain L.C. Dilworth finally responded to Kaasen. Dilworth confirmed that the RCAF had in fact implemented JANAP 146 (D) but that he was not at liberty to answer any of the other questions

Kaasen posed.[45] The next month, Kaasen wrote instead to DRB: "It is a fact that Canada and the United States are not in complete control of their skies ... As bad as it sounds, North America, and many other countries, are wide open for inspection by these unknown flying objects. Can you honestly deny that?" Kaasen was convinced that US congressional hearings would imminently "reveal hidden USAF information on UFOs" and that this disclosure would force the RCAF to do the same. Kaasen concluded his letter with a prayer: "I only hope the UFOs prove to be harmless."[46]

C.A. Pope replied the following month, hoping to curb any further correspondence. He admitted that the DRB had participated in Canadian investigations, but claimed (inaccurately) that it was not in charge of them. "You may be interested to learn," Pope concluded, "that the vast majority of reported sightings have been explained by known phenomena. The remainder have not supplied evidence that any threat to our country exists."[47] Kaasen wrote back two days later, countering Pope: "You may be interested to know that [NICAP] of Washington D.C. now has proof that UFOs (at times called flying saucers) are intelligently guided by an unknown race of beings, possibly from another planet, or more than one planet."[48] He did not indicate how NICAP had determined this or exactly what proof they possessed.

Kaasen did not write again until two months later. In a letter addressed to "UFO Investigations, RCAF," he again summarized his knowledge of the secret Air Force regulations and questioned why UFO reports must be kept secret at all. "While it is Air Force policy," he said, "to explain every UFO sighting away, I know how serious the UFO problem is ... If flying saucers do not exist, why does the Air Force spend time and money investigating something that does not exist?" To Kaasen, the only reasonable conclusion a member of the public could draw was that the RCAF, which was clearly withholding information from the press and public, must have themselves concluded that "UFOs are under intelligent control."[49]

It seems that no one at RCAF responded to Kaasen, perhaps realizing that they could not disentangle themselves from the correspondence any other way. Kaasen did not give up. The following year, he wrote to Douglas Harkness, the minister of national defence. Kaasen explained to Harkness that NICAP was a "fact-finding organization" that investigated UFOs and attempted to "offset official secrecy." Chapter 5 will explore this dimension of independent UFO investigations in more detail, arguing that the battle against secrecy was a logical conclusion of the citizen investigations, which began in response to perceived government inaction and soon took on the appearance of conspiracy theory. In other words, citizens began explicitly using UFOs to achieve political ends, such as demanding greater government transparency.

The remainder of Kaasen's letter was a lengthy condemnation of the government's secrecy. "If UFOs are nothing more than natural phenomena and mistaken identity, why not open all the files on UFOs and let the press investigate all reports for itself? This will not be done." Kaasen also wrote that making all information about UFOs public would help resist the Soviet Union. He argued that the Soviets crafted propaganda to convince the North American public that their governments were indeed hiding information and thus could not be trusted.[50] Whether or not Kaasen believed in such a threat is unclear; nevertheless, rising tensions with the Soviets were clearly playing into fears about UFOs.

Several days later, Harkness sent a brief reply in which he attempted to reassure Kaasen that in the event of a potential threat to Canada, no information would be kept from the public and that, indeed, the government had never in the past withheld such information.[51] Perhaps Harkness was naive, thinking his letter would sway Kaasen. Robert MacDougall has written that people who believe in theories that others label as pseudoscience often maintain beliefs that perform a kind of social or psychological work for them in maintaining their self-image.[52] Such people, conspiracy theorists or otherwise, think of themselves as iconoclasts "who cannot be fooled by authority figures." MacDougall, speaking of contemporary concerns, concludes that "you can't fight flat earthers or anti-vaxxers or any other brand of pseudoscience with arguments from authority. If you want to combat false belief, you have to ask, 'What work is this belief doing for the person who holds it?' Then you start from there."[53]

Iconoclasm is evident in the writings of UFO believers. According to citizen UFO investigators Bryant and Helen Reeve, for example, they were not "fooled by the glib and pat explanations with which orthodox scientists and entrenched officialdom have essayed to explain away and 'whitewash' the entire saucer phenomenon."[54] They further argued: "There is no ignorance so dense as 'educated' or 'scientific' ignorance – the kind that can always prove to its own satisfaction that nothing can possibly 'be' outside of its own limited concepts. Scientific finality is the death of scientific progress. The answers we are looking for are not to be found in the realms of eminent, respectable, conventional teachings – even though they bear the label of 'science' and the seal of time."[55]

This kind of language had become common by the mid-1960s. Wilbert Smith had used similar language ten years earlier, when describing opposition to his own ideas, showing an increasing distrust of established authority and a progression of ideas involving government secrecy and the role of scientific knowledge in society.

As such, further appeals from authority figures within the Canadian government rarely appeased UFO enthusiasts, who distrusted the state to begin with. To Ken Kaasen, Douglas Harkness's reply was nothing short of a challenge. "Statements from the RCAF concerning UFOs," Kaasen replied to Harkness, "completely contradict your stand on UFOs." Kaasen referenced a RCAF letter from the previous year in which an officer explicitly stated that information *would* indeed be withheld from the public, and again explained his understanding of the secret Air Force regulations and lamented the Canadian public's lack of awareness of the secrecy.[56] Kaasen's letter prompted an internal memo debating how to proceed. "As Mr. Kaasen apparently wants to believe that we are hiding something," wrote Wing Commander W.H. Muncy, "it will be difficult to convince him otherwise, but in view of the apparent contradictions in our statements, it would seem desirable to attempt to do so."[57]

Based on this memo, Harkness responded again, caught up in the correspondence. He told Kaasen that the contradictions arose from differing definitions of "UFOs." If the term meant objects piloted by extraterrestrials, then the information would not be withheld from the public. However, if the term meant foreign aircraft, then "prudence and the requirements of military security" demanded that the information remain classified.[58] Again, this exchange speaks to how the efforts of the government and citizens like Kaasen grew from completely different roots, based on whether or not one already believed in the reality of UFOs. Harkness and other government officials simply could not fathom why someone would write letters like Kaasen's given that UFOs, to their minds, clearly did not exist.

The final documents in this exchange reveal confusion within the RCAF about the secret regulations that Kaasen repeatedly mentioned. Wing Commander Muncy wrote an internal memo asking whether or not Canada did in fact follow the same air force regulations as the

US, as this was apparently not common knowledge even within the service. In some cases, it seems, it took an intrepid UFO investigator to force military personnel to obtain knowledge about their own operations. This inquiry prompted what appeared to be Harkness's last letter to Kaasen, accessible only as a draft, from April 1962. Harkness clarified that AFR 200-2 did not apply to Canadian personnel; and that, in the US, it only applied to base commanders, as final investigations and conclusions were the domain of "higher headquarters." Harkness finished his letter by stating that he saw no useful reason why UFO reports should be released anyway given that no investigations to date had revealed any security threat.[59] In other words, what Kaasen and others interpreted as official secrecy, Harkness simply saw as expediency. Why release the information if those in the know saw in it no "useful purpose" and no reason why it should require assistance from the public? Whether or not this satisfied Kaasen, it does not appear that he wrote back, and his two-year correspondence regarding secret air force orders came to an end.

It is not hard to understand why Kaasen was so upset. It was clear that the RCAF *was* withholding information, given the government's contradictory answers. Of course, the government disagreed with the conclusions that Kaasen drew, but this difference in views illustrates the nature of this aspect of conspiracy theory. Kaasen's belief in UFOs was not necessarily the product of what the government had previously called a "pathological" or "delusional" mind, but it was rooted in common psychological behaviour. The government, for its part, subscribed to historian Richard Hofstadter's seminal characterization of the "paranoid style" of American politics, arguing that "the paranoid" feels dispossessed, as though his very way of life is under attack by "the existence of a vast, insidious, preternaturally effective international conspiratorial network designed to perpetuate acts of the most fiendish character."[60] This is a clinical psychological approach to diagnosing the problem, which scholars have argued impedes rather than supports research.[61] Rather, in combination with the common features of social psychology that van Prooijen articulates, Kaasen was responding to the government's own statements and tapping into a broader change in what citizens expected from their government and how they engaged with it. In other words, Kaasen was using UFOs as a way to engage with the state, which might otherwise have been difficult or impossible.

COMMON COURTESY BECOMES THE GO-AROUND

Around the same time that Ken Kaasen began demanding answers, the government established a new reporting procedure. Starting in April 1960, a new plan for "the reporting of vital intelligence sightings during peacetime" would come into effect. The purpose of the plan, known as CIRVIS-MERINT, was to extend the continental early warning defence system by providing instruction on how to report all air and water sightings of potentially hostile craft.[62] Witnesses were to report their sightings by radio to the nearest ground station. A poster was designed that gave examples of what might constitute a potentially hostile sighting. Ufologists have made much ado about this poster because of one particular detail: it contained a drawing of a UFO.[63] The poster depicted other, more conventional objects such as submarines, warships, aircraft, and missiles, but it also included a drawing of a rocket ship and a flying saucer whizzing through the sky. The caption underneath confirmed this: witnesses were to report any "Unidentified Flying Objects or unidentified objects in the water" using the CIRVIS method.[64] The bottom of the poster indicated that the DND authorized it for display in post offices, which meant they intended it for public as well as military use.

Whatever the intended use, the posters caused confusion. Various DOT and DND offices received dozens of copies, often without a covering letter explaining their purpose. A memo from the Winnipeg Regional Office is representative of one reaction: "A package of 33 posters entitled 'CIRVIS-MERINT Reporting Procedure' has been received by mail with no covering instructions ... It would be appreciated if Headquarters would advise the intended distribution of these posters."[65] A number of handwritten notes on the memo further illustrate the confusion. One official wrote that their department had only sent five copies; they had no idea where the others came from. Another note indicated that they had sent out forty copies, while another simply passed the memo onward, stating: "Appear to be yours – please action."

An incident of two years earlier demonstrates the limits that departments placed on their own operations, interest, and abilities when it came to UFO investigation. At about 6:00 p.m. on 22 June 1960, a camper at Clan Lake, Northwest Territories, heard a strange noise from the sky, "like a big plane in the distance." The camper looked up

EARLY WARNING IN DEFENCE OF THE NORTH AMERICAN CONTINENT

CIRVIS-MERINT REPORTING PROCEDURE

1. MESSAGE IDENTIFICATION

(a) Reports made from airborne and land-based sources will be identified by CIRVIS (pronounced SUR-VEES) as the first word of the text.

(b) Reports made by waterborne sources will be identified by MERINT (pronounced MUR-ENT) as the first word of the text.

2. WHAT TO REPORT

Report immediately all airborne and waterborne objects which appear to be HOSTILE, are UNIDENTIFIED or are acting suspiciously.

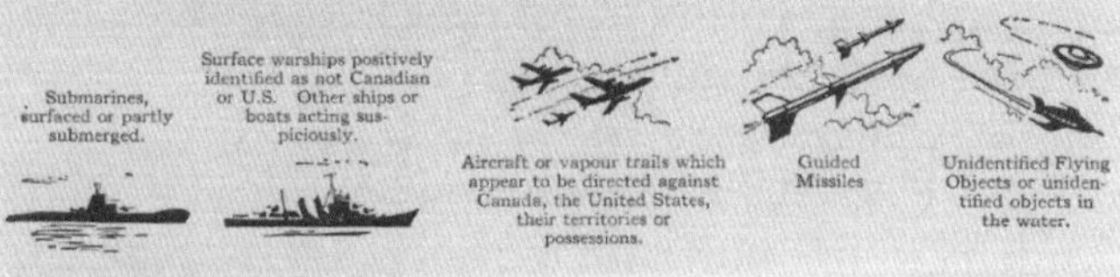

3. SEND TO ANY

Canadian Military Establishment,
RCMP Post,
Department of Transport or Fisheries Representative,
Hudson's Bay Company Northern Radio-Equipped Store, or
The nearest open Canadian Telegraph Office. (By telephone if necessary.)

Use the quickest possible means to make your report.

4. SEND THIS KIND OF MESSAGE

(a) Begin your message with the word "CIRVIS" or "MERINT" as applicable.
(b) Give the identification of the observer, aircraft or vessel making the report.
(c) Describe briefly the objects sighted.
(d) Indicate where and when the objects were sighted.
(e) If objects are airborne, estimate altitude as "low", "medium", "high".
(f) Give direction of travel of sighted objects.
(g) Estimate and give speed of sighted objects.
(h) Give other significant information.

5. SEND IMMEDIATELY

DO NOT DELAY YOUR REPORT DUE TO INCOMPLETE INFORMATION.

NOTE

There are no charges to the originator in the handling of CIRVIS or MERINT messages.

Authorized by Department of National Defence
Authorized for display in Post Offices by the Postmaster General

Figure 3.1 | CERVIS-MERINT reporting procedure poster featuring an illustration of a flying saucer. The print at the bottom of the poster indicates it was intended for distribution to the general public in post offices, implying that the government was soliciting reports from the public.

but could not locate the origin of the sound, which grew in intensity until suddenly he heard something strike the water. "I turned around," the camper's statement to the RCMP read, and "saw a splash and what appeared to be some object with arms or spokes rotating in the water." The object gradually slowed and sunk below the water's surface. The camper and his partner paddled out to the spot in a canoe and found that the tall grasses growing above the water from the mud below were burnt all around the impact site. Feeling with their paddles, they could discern "a channel [in the mud underwater] which corresponded to the cut path of grass." The RCMP report noted that the camper "is well known in this country having lived in and around Yellowknife for many years. He has a good knowledge of bush life as he is a prospector and woodcutter by trade. He is considered very reliable."[66]

The report was evidently detailed and seemed reliable enough that it called for an actual investigation. An aerial patrol went to view the site from above and determined that something likely had hit the lake, although nothing could be found.[67] The next month, a RCMP inspector recommended using a skin diver to search the area underwater[68] and also mused "that possibly the object which fell into Clan Lake may be a nose cone of a rocket or some other scientific object," and would thus call for some "extra endeavour."[69] He notified the DND at this point, but they demurred: "It is our view that R.C.A.F. are much better equipped to handle matters such as this than we are and it is obvious that if there is anything in this story which seems to be quite reliable and objective, it is certainly more of R.C.A.F. interest than ours. With personnel and equipment at their disposal, it does not seem that we should be spending any time or effort on this matter until we are provided with the ability to do the job."[70]

Later that month, the RCMP commissioner received a report stating that a patrol had checked out the site with a Geiger counter and probed the mud underwater with a rod, all with negative results.[71] A month later, a DND memo to the RCMP stated that as far as they were concerned, the object was likely a meteorite that had disintegrated as it fell. "On the strength of investigations to date," the report read, "we doubt that the object has significance as far as National Defence is concerned."[72] In May 1961, the RCMP followed up. They were unsuccessful in finding a qualified person to conduct a magnetometer reading of the site, but Ian Halliday, an NRC scientist, concurred with the theory that the object was likely a meteor.[73] It seems that the investigation ended at this point.

The incident is illuminating in two ways. First, it shows the limits of any department's ability and interest to investigate. The DND no longer cared once they decided that the object was probably a meteorite and not a piece of space technology. Another example also illustrates this point. In August 1965, an object fell to the ground in Foster, Quebec. The DND was quick to investigate but soon stopped. "Because the object is man-made and its markings are in English, it is no longer of direct interest."[74] In other words, the objects in these two cases no longer constituted a potential security threat – the first because it was deemed a natural phenomenon and the second because it was not a foreign-made (i.e., Soviet) object. The incidents were outside the operations of the department, something that the DND would later claim about UFOs more generally to justify ridding themselves of the responsibility. The RCMP apparently only had limited resources and took the investigation as far as these allowed.

Second, the Clan Lake incident shows the power of potential physical evidence of UFOs. Investigations of this sort, in which helicopters and multiple teams were sent out to investigate alleged sightings, were only ordered in cases where physical evidence might have been accessible. This aspect of the phenomenon will be explored in more detail in Chapter 4.

Despite the relative clarity behind the rationale for the previous two investigations, one of the main issues plaguing the military and civilians alike was the continued confusion surrounding how (or if) the government was supposed to investigate UFOs. An earlier RCAF memo from June 1959 makes this clear. Flight Lieutenant J.S.R. Francis noted that the public relations officer had been "hard-pressed to supply satisfactory answers" to inquiries from press and public about recent sightings, and that it was "unreasonable" to continue "without official recognition and some policy direction."

Francis had attempted, in vain, to dig up some form of official statement: "There seems to be no recorded instance of the Canadian Government having any interest whatsoever in 'flying saucers.' No RCAF organization has ever been charged with the responsibility for handling UFO reports either to investigate or simply to acknowledge receipt of letters from observers." He noted that Squadron Leader Lovelace had, since the previous year, attempted to reply to inquiries "on the basis of common courtesy – feeling that persons who took the time to write the Department about what appeared to them an important defence matter, deserve an official reply – as at that time all such reports seemed to get the 'go-around.'"[75] Francis and Lovelace were obviously among the more sympathetic military personnel, whether or not they shared Wilbert Smith's or Ken Kaasen's views about the origins of the objects.

Unfortunately, despite Lovelace's best intentions, it seems that citizens regularly received the "go-around." For example, in April 1966, a citizen sent a three-page handwritten letter to the Prime Minister's Office: "Sir, you must excuse me if I doubt very much whether the general public will ever get an honest and truthful report from the government on such matters." Nonetheless, the writer continued: "We do look forward to the day when the authorities will have the courage to release the truth, but with all due respect to you and your office, I doubt it."[76]

Another citizen, Wilfrid Daniels, from Stafford, England, wrote to the DOT in frustration. He had received two replies regarding inquiries about Wilbert Smith's research that directly contradicted each other, prompting him to ask if someone could "please make up their mind and give me a factual, unambiguous reply to the question … One way or another, I am determined to elicit the truth of this; I have been, with reluctance on my part and considerable distaste, drawn into what seems to me to be an incredible web of evasion, prevarication, circumlocution and downright 'double-talk.'"[77]

Later that year, J.J.A. Hennessey, another Englishman, wrote to the chief of the Air Staff with the same intention. He pointed out a contradiction in letters he had received regarding whether or not Project Magnet was an official government initiative, and asked for a clear answer. All throughout his letter, he politely expressed his regrets and apologies for troubling the government with such an inquiry.[78]

Examples such as these make it easy to see how some citizens concluded that the government was covering up information. Especially when it came to Wilbert Smith – at this point, more than a year after his death – and after the DOT's attempts to distance itself from his work, it must have been difficult to confirm any details. However, it is important to keep in mind the scope of such beliefs. A 1966 Gallup poll asked Americans if they had ever seen a UFO. Five per cent responded positively.[79] Gallup had yet to ask Canadians the same question, but it is likely that even fewer Canadians had seen one given the difference in such data from later polls.[80]

Again, there was very little national press attention on the issue. In May 1966, *Maclean's* published an article titled "Look, Ma! It's Flying Saucer Time Again," lampooning the "20th-century community sport of UFO-hunting [which] abides by no fixed rules."[81] The article mentioned some recent sightings, including one by Canadian heavyweight boxer George Chuvalo, who claimed to see a UFO shortly after his heavyweight title loss to Muhammad Ali on 29 March. Despite the overall tone of the article, it nevertheless also stated that scientists were taking the issue more seriously than ever before.

The seriousness with which many Canadians understood UFOs is better reflected in another national story, published in *Weekend* magazine, spanning five pages and reporting on all manner of recent sightings and government statements. More a survey of events than a focused report, the article was clearly more sympathetic than *Maclean's* to those who claimed to see a UFO. The article's length is an indication of the interest that readers took in the subject and, while the author was skeptical of certain aspects of the phenomenon – such as abductees – he nevertheless treated every aspect of the subject with an open mind and concluded that no one really seemed to have the answers.[82]

Beyond newspaper accounts, there were plenty of other media to turn to for answers or speculation. Earlier, in 1963, for instance, the television show *The Outer Limits* had premiered. Inspired by *The Twilight Zone*, it pushed even further into science fiction territory.[83] Then, in 1966, another watershed moment for those captivated by the space age: the premiere of *Star Trek*, which would go on to create a franchise comprising multiple films, television series, books, and merchandise.[84]

There was only ever a handful of Canadians actively interrogating the government for information, but through their bombastic letters they made their presence well known. It is possible that they even inflated the government's concerns as to how widespread these conspiratorial ideas were. Nonetheless, by the mid-1960s, changes in how citizens related to their government were clearly reflected in these activists' letters. Some citizens doubted that they would ever receive a truthful reply. Whatever responses citizens did receive seemed only to obfuscate the issue, drawing them further into the belief that the government was covering up information, that perhaps there was some kind of conspiracy.

These letters show that this distrust was mutually reinforced, with its origin in the various points of contact since the 1950s which seemed only to antagonize and confirm each side's lack of confidence in the other. It was not the case that all citizens writing about UFOs began in the assumption that the government was covering up. Rather, many citizens were open-minded and initially respected the need for secrecy, only to become frustrated and disillusioned with the process after months, sometimes years, of the government "go-around."

The Canadian government was not unaware of this situation. In January 1966, John R. Kohr, a community relations officer at the NRC, wrote to the DRB's public relations officer Charles Pope. Kohr enclosed an article from a Montreal newspaper that apparently quoted "Dr." Wilbert Smith speaking about his attempt to analyze a piece of metal that had fallen from the sky. "In view of the fact," Kohr wrote, "that Wilbur [*sic*] Smith died several years ago, I assume that the article is based on some warmed-up and badly garbled incident."[85] However, the degree to which information about UFOs was "garbled" was due mostly to inept and disinterested communications between departments rather than a conscious conspiracy. In other words, it was a cock-up rather than a cover-up.

It was inevitable that if a citizen dug deeply and wrote to enough departments, they would receive contradictory statements. When it came to UFOs, departments rarely communicated with one another and the answers they gave to citizens, in the absence of any coordinated procedures or guidelines, were done using personal discretion. It was also the case, simply, that those within the government or military who received letters usually had no information themselves; but this lack of, or gap in, understanding would have been unacceptable to admit to the public. The government did not intend, maliciously, to mislead the public. There were moments, moreover, when secrecy was necessary – legitimate cases of protecting information relevant to national security.

Nevertheless, the government's responses contributed to a growing distrust swirling within the wider milieu. It is tempting to say that there had always been those citizens who would insist on the more fantastic explanation. This is inadequate, though, because it again privileges the idea that conspiracy theory is solely the product of warped minds rather than broader social change. Especially by the mid-1960s, citizens writing about UFOs were tapping into the counterculture of the era. UFOs may have been an especially unorthodox topic, but they still fit within the search for personal, rather than expert, truth.[86] To this end, van Prooijen argues that conspiracy belief is rooted in an intuitive rather than an analytical mode of thinking, whereby people rely on gut feeling to come to conclusions.[87]

In July 1966, the same letter writer who, earlier in April, had looked forward to the day when the government would have the courage to release the truth, now sent a twelve-page letter to the DND outlining his views on extraterrestrial visitation. The writer defined the public as "a strange body" that holds contradictory viewpoints and suffers "from a psychological condition termed 'Fear.'" This strange body was divided into "The Non-Believers" and "The Believers," the latter broken down further into "A Soft Core" and "A Hard Core." The "Soft Core" held relatively agnostic views about UFOs, while the "Hard Core" believed that flying saucers were under intelligent extraterrestrial control.

This writer was convinced that aliens had made face-to-face contact with humans, especially those in government and in the military. "Our Prime Minister Pearson," this author wrote, "would probably be among one of those who have been so contacted." The rest of the letter contained numerous and confident statements about how, for instance, the aliens spoke all earthly languages, the US government was in possession of "bulging" files of information on UFOs, and it was the duty of all human beings to follow the wishes of the extraterrestrials in "revamping" the world's monetary system, its research initiatives, and its military and police powers in order to create a more equitable, safer world. In closing, the writer was careful to state that they were "NOT [a] member of any 'Ban-the Bomb-Movement,' Communist or Communist inclined-party or organization." The goal of his work was more universal than this. In matters of knowledge about things unknown, which could affect the welfare of all humankind, "the real problem is what quality proof does the modern, ignorant man require, and when he gets it, is he willing to accept it?"[88]

The rest of this "Hard Core" citizen's lengthy letter is meandering and tangential, but his questions were central ones: what is the threshold for belief in UFOs as extraterrestrial craft? What evidence is required to exceed that threshold? Despite the significance of these questions, the DND's response was to dismiss and debunk. In his reply, Commodore F.B. Caldwell referred to the "Hard Core" citizen's description of several sightings in the Montreal area, remarking that the latter's comments "respecting these sightings reflect a slight prejudice against explainable events and in favour of the unknown."

Caldwell went on to debunk each observation as nothing more than a misidentified sighting of a satellite or jet aircraft.[89] Again, the government's attitude was that such people were all idiosyncratic cases. UFO enthusiasts, they thought, were predisposed to believing in odd things, and nothing could be done about the situation except to debunk it or ignore it – to ignore the "cranks." This was, for the government officials, a common-sense view that accorded with their understanding of the world. It did not acknowledge interest in UFOs as part of a broader change happening in Canada, but rather considered the belief akin to a superstition which the state was responsible for clearing up in an attempt to educate the public.

As in other cases, rather than shutting down the correspondence, Caldwell's letter only invited further debate. The "Hard Core" citizen responded the following month with a mélange of information invoking, for instance, the questions surrounding JANAP 146 (D) and AFR 200-2 and rebutting Caldwell's claims about satellites and jet aircraft. "As time goes on," he concluded, "and as the sightings continue, the efforts of people all over the world to get at the truth and have it brought before the public will be found to have been useful."[90]

It seems that something in this "Hard Core" citizen's letters prompted yet another internal review of the procedure for dealing with such matters. A DND memo noted that, "periodically," the department received a sighting report that might make headlines if reported to the press. "To date, no system has been established for the follow-up of such reports before the embarrassing questions are asked."[91] As in the case of the DOT's reaction to Wilbert Smith's work, what the UFO problem often came down to in operational terms was bad publicity.

Caldwell again replied to the "Hard Core" citizen: "You continue to suggest that information is being withheld from the general public by the Department of National Defence. I can assure you that such is not the case ... As our responsibility to the Canadian people is to provide for their security, we are only concerned with the possibility of unidentified flying objects being a threat to Canada. All evidence points to the fact that there is no threat from them." Caldwell again attempted to dissuade further correspondence: "We are not prepared to prolong the discussion on this matter, as it is really only a matter of judgment."[92] On the very same day, Caldwell replied to yet another, similar inquiry. One paragraph in particular is significant in terms of its candidness about the DND's position:

> We do not criticise you for your beliefs and in fact are glad to see that individuals are prepared to devote their time and energy to searching for the possibility of a new truth in a mass of reports which are often coloured by emotional distortion and a near-religious certainty of the existence of an extraterrestrial presence. Within the Department of National Defence we are expected to be pragmatists and this makes us appear disinterested in views such as yours.[93]

The political theorist Frederic Jameson described conspiracy theory as the "poor man's cognitive mapping." Jameson meant that people use conspiracy theory as a way of making sense of the world by connecting what might otherwise be unrelated dots.[94] Jonathan Kay calls this process "historical hopscotch," whereby conspiracy theorists connect events and people across time and space as a way of unifying their ideas.[95] Probably Commodore Caldwell would have agreed with this assessment given his views on how emotionally loaded the UFO subject was. Again, however, this characterization belittles individuals. It is easy to label conspiracy theorists as cranks, but their ideas are the result of common and predictable psychological processes, further motivated by the broader cultural changes that began in the 1950s, which mutually reinforced tension and distrust between citizens and the government.

Belief in UFOs is also not an isolated phenomenon. A number of commentators have proposed a continuity between this specific postwar belief and beliefs in, for instance, fairy folklore and medieval apparitions; or they have examined similar phenomena from a historical rather than a purely psychological perspective. Carlo Ginzburg, for instance, in analyzing sixteenth- and seventeenth-century witchcraft in Italy, argues that the phenomenon "can not be explained on pathological grounds." Rather, because belief in witchcraft was so widespread, "the boundaries between a healthy and diseased state become vague"; instead, the beliefs had "a precise cultural basis."[96]

Two other commentators have written specifically about UFOs in this respect. Computer scientist and venture capitalist Jacques Vallée understands postwar UFO belief as one aspect "in a much wider tapestry blending the mysteries of antiquity with the wonders of the Space Age."[97] To Vallée, people throughout history have always seen objects in the sky "under forms best adapted to the believer's country, race, and social regime."[98] To this end, he traces a history of folklore to show continuity with previous tales of visitation by otherworldly beings, arguing that modern flying saucers are not so different from religious visions but simply reflect postwar technoscientific concerns and aspirations.

Similarly, the psychoanalyst Carl Jung characterized the UFO phenomenon as a "living myth" – a modern myth in the making: "We have here a golden opportunity of seeing how a legend is formed, and how in a difficult and dark time for humanity a miraculous tale grows up of an attempted intervention by extra-terrestrial 'heavenly' powers – and this at the very time when human fantasy is seriously considering the possibility of space travel and of visiting or even invading other planets."[99] By drawing on examples of dream analysis and objects in paintings from medieval to modern times, Jung argued that the prospect of heavenly intervention was simply a matter of course in previous eras, and that people are no longer "rooted enough in the tradition of earlier centuries" to make sense of this.[100] In other words, people have been seeing "UFOs" for centuries, simply in different guises and filtered through the lens of the day. What all of this says about UFOs in Canada during the 1950s and 1960s is that the phenomenon was potentially more widespread than the concern over literal flying saucers in the sky, and speaks to much broader psychological and cultural trends.

CITIZENS ORGANIZE EARLY UFO CLUBS

One person who was prepared to devote their time and energy to the search for a new truth, as Commodore F.B. Caldwell wrote, was Wilbert Smith. The termination of Project Magnet forced Smith to conduct his work independently. He soon realized that even if the government had no interest in UFOs, there were plenty of other citizens who were open-minded about the possibility of extraterrestrial existence. Smith began meeting and speaking with like-minded people outside of work and, in March 1957, formally established the Ottawa Flying Saucer Club. The OFSC met each month in Smith's basement at his house in City View, a suburb of Ottawa.

Anywhere from a dozen to forty people attended. Club members would regularly travel to these meetings, some from as far away as New York City and even, occasionally, from places farther afield such as Finland. According to Smith's son Jim, the mood of the meetings was always excited and positive.[101] By 1960, the club's presence was substantial enough that Smith began publishing a regular newsletter called *Topside* – in reference to the "Boys from Topside," namely the extraterrestrials he claimed were perched above the Earth in the topside ionosphere. *Topside* contained reviews of recent sightings, the odd piece of poetry, and longer essays that Smith or other club members wrote on such topics as the theory of gravitation, Soviet science, and the relationship between religion and science.

It is clear from the newsletter that the club's mission was to disseminate the kind of information and reasoning about UFOs that the club thought the government was unprepared or unwilling to undertake. "I maintain," Smith wrote, "that it takes only one black sheep to prove that all sheep are not white, and one unexplained saucer sighting should be enough to warrant establishing a serious scientific study group."[102] Of course, Smith had hoped that his own Project Magnet, as well as Project Second Storey, would be the solution, only to be disappointed. Now, instead, he used the OFSC to pursue this goal.

Government scientists, in Smith's view, were too close-minded for this kind of work and so the task fell instead to citizen organizations like the OFSC. This development was not unique to Canada. A Gallup poll for 1974 concluded that 11 per cent of Americans were UFO witnesses who, together with the many other people interested in the subject, were unable to obtain clear answers from the government about their experiences. As such, "grassroots organizations" like the OFSC, in the case of Canada, became the only available sources of information, thereby creating a shared experience across the border which, again, speaks to the increasing Americanization of Canadian life.[103] As another article from a local newspaper stated, even a member of Parliament asking about UFOs in the House of Commons could elicit no clear response from the government. Edward Schreyer, MP for Springfield, Manitoba, and the future premier of that province and governor general of Canada, asked the minister of transport "whether he had received any formal report containing the rather strange information that approximately 20 sightings have been made in a period of six weeks or less of unidentified flying objects in a relatively limited area of eastern Manitoba, including sightings by RCMP."[104] In the end: "No solution has been offered."[105]

A similar situation prevailed in the US. For example, in their book *Flying Saucer Pilgrimage*, two UFO researchers, Bryant and Helen Reeve, described meeting in their basement recreation room with other like-minded enthusiasts as well as tape recording lectures by prominent ufologists they had brought to their city. They then copied and distributed these taped lectures to spread the word, another grassroots method by which these citizens organized.[106] In other words, some citizens felt compelled to form their own groups to investigate the problem because of the government's failure to provide unambiguous answers. To the government, however, such people were unwilling to accept expert opinion.

In another sense, it is perhaps unsurprising that these enthusiasts turned away from authority and toward one another. Writing specifically about the US, Robert D. Putnam argues that during "the first two-thirds of the twentieth century a powerful tide bore Americans into ever deeper engagement in the life of their communities."[107] After the Second World War, civic engagement was at a high point, especially as the baby boomers began to come of age. Whereas Putnam tracks a decline in civic engagement in the last third of the twentieth century, during the 1950s and '60s, "community groups across America had seemed to stand on the threshold of a new era of expanded involvement."[108] It seems safe to say that this trend extended to suburban Canada and influenced, at least in part, the formation of UFO study groups at this specific time.

If not the first, the OFSC seems to have been one of the earliest, and certainly the most organized and productive, clubs in Canada. The Vancouver Area Flying Saucer Club was also founded in the 1950s, although very little documentation remains of its activities. At least as early as 1956, members began meeting to discuss the topic and quickly set out to recruit "younger folk, say from 9 or 10 years, to 15 years," given that adults were "not the only ones who ask questions about U.F.O.'s!" as the VAFSC's "Chairman" Margaret Fewster wrote in the club's February 1957 newsletter. The club had been successful, noted Fewster, at starting up a junior branch that rotated the bi-monthly Sunday afternoon meetings among the members' houses ("rumpus rooms are ideal"). "The younger people," Fewster wrote, "ask extremely intelligent, and often strangely penetrating questions, and they deserve an opportunity to receive answers of the same caliber."[109]

One such youngster was Ramon McGuire, who later went on to become the vocalist for the Canadian rock band Trooper. McGuire described attending VAFSC meetings sometime in the mid-1960s, as its youngest member: "My Mom and Dad took turns driving me to meetings in Kits[ilano], and I was warmly welcomed by an eccentric group of truth-seekers who thought I was just the cutest thing – until the night I stood up and mockingly questioned a presentation about two Australian boys and their suspicious close encounter of the third kind." According to McGuire, that was his very last meeting with the VAFSC club – apparently his questions were *too* penetrating.[110]

Beyond recruiting youth, the VAFSC, like other groups, collected sighting reports, mused over cosmic questions like the unification of space and time, and brought guest speakers to Vancouver. On 7 May 1964, for instance, the club hosted George Van Tassel, an aircraft mechanic and contactee who ran a private airport in California that also played host to an annual UFO convention.[111] A number of other organizations with similar goals and activities were established in the 1960s, whether independently or as a branch of an American club. Several examples of these will be explored in further detail in Chapter 5.

Of course, not all citizens were, at least at first, convinced by what they saw in the sky. What the experience of seeing a UFO comes down to, in part, is the question of doubt and knowledge production. It is clear that the government response was doubt, but this was also, at first, the default response for many citizens. For instance, a citizen from Rodney, Ontario, wrote to the DND in August 1958 about a brilliant white light that he had seen rise up steadily from the horizon. He prefaced his report with the phrase "at the risk of seeming a little 'off,'" before stating that he had "always taken the reports of flying objects with 'a grain of salt' but this one [had him] wondering."[112] A telex report from July 1965 described a witness to another sighting, this time in Vancouver, as "an intelligent business man" and noted that "he did not believe in UFOs until this morning."[113] Similarly, in a detailed statement about a June 1989 sighting in Meldrum Creek, British Columbia, a witness stated that she saw a UFO "beaming" with orange and yellow lights, with "what appeared to be windows on the bottom half" of the object. "I could not believe what I saw," the witness wrote. "I thought that this only happened in magazines that you read."[114] As the "Hard Core believers" often said, it usually took a personal experience to convince someone of the reality of UFOs.

An RCMP memo illustrates this in a case involving one of its own officers. In January 1967, one Constable Ford saw a UFO in the area of Inuvik, Northwest Territories. Upon investigation, Ford's superior, Inspector K.D. Smith, concluded that he had "no doubt" that Ford had seen what he described in his report. However, Ford's fellow constables St-Jean and Kaminski "showed little confidence" in his story. Inspector Smith was not happy about the latter's reactions. Apparently, St-Jean and Kaminski made little effort to confirm Ford's sighting and limited "their observations to looking out a window in the general direction he indicated." Ford's two colleagues simply attributed his sighting to a star. "These three members are all single and live in barracks," Inspector Smith wrote in his report, "and I suspect that both Csts ST-JEAN and KAMINSKI believed that he was trying to play a joke on them. I have told [St-Jean and Kaminski] that I expect them to be more receptive to observations of their fellow members, and I am satisfied that their apparent indifference in this instance was an isolated case that occurred only because of the subject under discussion."[115]

As internal memos illustrate, the DND still took a dim view of the subject. CBC Winnipeg, intent on doing a program on UFO sightings, contacted the DND in February 1965 asking for background information on the department's procedures when dealing with reports. Colonel L.A. Bourgeois, the department's information services director, instructed his colleagues: "This HQ does not wish to become involved with such a program. It is policy to stay clear of this subject whenever possible … Please tactfully say 'NO' to CBC."[116]

What these examples show is that citizens had begun to doubt not only the government's intentions but also the authority of the scientific establishment. Some citizens doubted that scientists could actually make authoritative statements about the natural world, or that at least there were hard limits on how broadly their statements applied. For example, the tone of an article from the *Peninsula Times*, a newspaper serving British Columbia's Sunshine Coast region, makes it clear what some citizens thought of the scientific community. The article recounts the sinking of a tugboat off the Sechelt coast and speculates that this may have been linked to various sightings of UFOs in the area at the time, despite the fact that the

Department of Transport was skeptical of the connection. "As the situation now stands," the author wrote, "official denials of undersea unidentified objects will remain as constant as official denials of atmospheric UFO activity. Unless a bathysphere has a head-on collision with one of these secretive submarines, we shall be asked to believe that commercial fishermen, coastal and freshwater area residents, and power station employees are seeing nothing but 'seaweed gas.'"[117] The author was clearly skeptical of the government's position and authority, as the comment about undersea head-on collision indicates. The "seaweed gas" comment also makes this clear – an allusion to a gaffe made by J. Allen Hynek just two years before. Hynek had been investigating a UFO sighting over swampland in Michigan and concluded that what witnesses had seen was nothing more than "swamp gas," a naturally occurring phenomenon. For his comment, Hynek was roundly lampooned in UFO circles.[118]

One of the main drivers of some citizens' lack of confidence in scientists were the early writings of journalists and UFO enthusiasts, who aimed to seed doubt about the abilities of scientists. There are several examples that demonstrate this. Donald Keyhoe was one of the first to make such a claim. In writing about Albert Einstein's theory of gravity, Keyhoe quoted a colleague of his, who manufactured aircraft and electronic equipment, as saying that flying saucers were real and operated by manipulating gravity. Keyhoe's colleague described gravity control as the "missing link" in Einstein's theory, concluding that one of the most successful scientific theories of all time was only partially correct.[119] Keyhoe also wrote into his books scattered references to how slow the public and the scientific community were to accept new ideas. The UFO evidence, he predicted, would eventually prove the existence of extraterrestrials, if only scientists would be more open-minded. Similarly, Edward Ruppelt, the head of Project Blue Book, claimed that scientists had previously been slow to recognize new discoveries, such as meteorites, and that UFOs were clearly, to him, another such case.[120]

There were even more vocal opponents of the scientific community writing and influencing citizens at the time. Desmond Leslie and George Adamski's bestselling book *The Flying Saucers Have Landed* was explicit in its condemnation of scientists: "No, it is all too easy to trot out a few facts wrapped up in a bit of highly scientific sounding mumbo-jumbo, to convince a great many simple, unquestioning souls to who the very word 'scientific' is sufficient label to raise the whole matter to the realms of Hallowed Dogma where further dispute is out of the question."[121] To Leslie and Adamski, "a certain doubt lingers in the mind," despite scientific statements to the contrary.[122]

What is more, it was not just popular writers planting this doubt but actual scientists too, on occasion. The prominent astronomer J. Allen Hynek wrote: "The fact of the matter is that many of my colleagues who have undraped their dignity long enough to take a hard look at the reports have joined the growing ranks of the puzzled scientists."[123] It is understandable that some UFO enthusiasts, denied access to official information on the topic, might turn to, and be persuaded by, these more accessible texts. As will become clearer in Chapter 5, an even smaller number of these UFO enthusiasts went even further than simply reading these books and attempted to act on the information. Bryant and Helen Reeve embarked on a cross-country journey to discover the truth about UFOs. There was no clear precedent for UFO research, they wrote, and so anyone doing it was a pioneer, setting "upon a lonely and uncharted path."[124]

Indeed, it is exactly to this kind of person that Leslie and Adamski dedicated their book: "It is to this sort of fool; to the lonely heretic who likes to walk down strange untrodden paths; to him who believes that all things are possible, particularly those things held by other men to be impossible; to him who leaves no stone unturned, and to him who gives a second chance to 'the stone rejected by the builders,' that this book is dedicated."[125] This type of writing was persuasive to those confused by responses they received from the government, and to those, such as D.M. Spicer and Ken Kaasen, who may already have believed the government was deceiving them. Such writings arguably convinced some of an alternative truth, and convinced others to act on it – to become one of these fearless pioneers seeking out the truth, such as the citizens profiled in this chapter and in Chapter 5.

In other words, this chapter attempts to make sense of the efforts of these citizens writing to the government and demanding answers. There were multiple motivations for believing in UFOs: some sought a religious or spiritual truth, others yearned for an advanced civilization to save humans from their own (atomic) destruction, and others were concerned about government secrecy. Whatever the motivation, and whatever kind of work UFOs did for citizens, popular books like those described above helped to seed doubt about the abilities of scientists, and science itself, as a means of understanding the natural world, which in turn helped to foment conspiracy theory.[126] What is clear is that the two sides – government and citizen – failed to understand what each side expected of the other.

The previous two chapters were about discrete government projects aimed at investigating UFOs. In contrast, this chapter presented the first real efforts that a handful of citizens made to interrogate the government for its knowledge about UFOs. The government had received letters of this sort from the earliest days, but such correspondence accelerated following the termination of Projects Magnet and Second Storey. The government took the position that UFOs were nothing other than misidentified natural phenomena. Many citizens disagreed, some of them vehemently.

Citizens like D.M. Spicer and Ken Kaasen made their views known by writing one letter after another. Others formed UFO clubs at a time when this grassroots movement had only just begun, in direct response to perceived government inaction. UFO enthusiasts tapped into broader countercultural movements taking place simultaneously. As Lara Campbell and Dominique Clément write, Canada was "a hotbed of activism": students, women's rights groups, gay rights organizations, environmental, Indigenous, and Black activists all fought for greater recognition and rights, "while advocates for children's rights, prisoners' rights, animal rights, peace, poverty, and official languages organized in unprecedented numbers."[127] One of the main ideas all these various movements had in common was a sense of the postwar period, and especially "the sixties," as an idea, or moment, of questioning established and hierarchical authority.

Conspiracy theory about UFOs in Canada was, in part, a manifestation of the growing distrust that citizens felt for their government in the postwar years. It was not necessarily a purely psychological phenomenon that "paranoid" individuals experienced on their own, although psychology clearly did play a role. There are established psychological processes, such as pattern recognition and the need to attribute agency to events and causes – especially to institutions believed to be untrustworthy – that influence the generation and spread of conspiracy theory.

On a much broader level, however, these ideas were the result of historical changes taking place that affected political deference and trust in established authority. Some citizens felt that the government was not living up to its obligations to provide for them, whether through national defence or scientific knowledge, and they were not shy in making this opinion known. This conflict was also the result of the state coming up against these changing views even as they attempted to educate the masses. The Canadian state attempted to put UFOs to work, socially and politically, as a means of pointing out the irrational nature of the everyday citizen, to educate them and thereby lift them up and out of the morass of superstition. By making pronouncements about the unreality of UFOs through the voices of its officials, the state sought to shore up its authority and clear away uncertainty. Unfortunately for the state, times were changing and the people they were attempting to educate considered themselves, as Robert MacDougall writes, to be iconoclasts who would not be fooled by the establishment. What resulted was two sides butting heads, neither willing to relent.

4

Three Cases of High Strangeness, 1967

The year 1967 was filled with what the astronomer and ufologist J. Allen Hynek called "high strangeness."[1] The year was Canada's centennial, celebrated by events and activities across the country, most notably Expo 67 in Montreal, which attracted millions of visitors. Journalist Tom Hawthorn argues that the Canada of today "owes more to the decisions made in the wake of 1967 than to the negotiations conducted in 1867."[2] The greatest achievement of the year, he writes, was "a seductive awakening of the spirit."[3] At least one place explicitly connected this awakened spirit to the UFO phenomenon: the Canadian government declared the small city of St Paul, Alberta, the "Centennial Capital" after it built a UFO landing pad. The former defence minister, Paul Hellyer, opened the pad with a speech about the wonder of space travel and the promise of a technological future.[4]

In addition to national pride, however, a number of stranger phenomena occurred, and not just in Canada. John Keel's book *The Mothman Prophecies* described a series of bizarre encounters involving UFOs and a moth-like creature in the area of Point Pleasant, West Virginia, that culminated in a fatal bridge collapse that December.[5] The infamous Patterson-Gimlin film was shot in October, depicting one of the most controversial images of an alleged Sasquatch.[6] In Canada, witnesses reported a record number of UFO sightings in 1967, jumping to 169 from just fifty-five the previous year. The numbers continued to climb in the late 1960s and into the 1970s, but it was 1967 that clearly marked a shift in UFO activity in Canada.

Indeed, in November 1967, *Maclean's* ran another article on UFOs, one that contrasted dramatically with their article the previous year. In 1966, the writer was clearly skeptical, but the 1967 article, which ran to nearly five pages, was full of detailed sighting information and extensive quotes from both government scientists and citizen investigators.[7] Clearly, something had changed to pique new interest in the topic, however one might account for this.

The year also marked a hinge point in the Canadian government's response to UFOs. Official interest in the subject culminated in this year but then dropped off almost immediately afterward. As Chapter 5 will show in detail, the DND, clearly deeming the researches performed to date to be sufficient and further efforts unnecessary, took steps to rid itself of responsibility for UFO investigation. However, the events of that year did not make this easy for the department.

This chapter explores three UFO cases in 1967 that produced *physical* evidence: Stefan Michalak's encounter at Falcon Lake, Manitoba; the Duhamel, Alberta crop circles; and the Shag Harbour, Nova Scotia crash. Scientists in Ottawa felt they could not ignore the evidence they found at these sites. Hynek characterized UFO encounters that left physical traces as Close Encounters of the Second Kind. As he wrote: "The significance of such physical interactions is obvious; they offer opportunity for physical measurement and the promise of 'hard data.'"[8] When, how, and why did government investigators find these cases sufficiently compelling to take seriously? The year 1967 was the moment at which the reality of UFOs coalesced most convincingly.

The three cases of physical evidence are discussed directly in departmental briefings, indicating that the government was well aware that physical evidence commanded special attention. In November 1967, the minister of national defence Leo Cadieux wrote the following to the minister of industry C.M. Drury: "Most frequently reported, are sightings of aerial phenomena which, in general, cannot be fruitfully investigated after the event. Occasionally, however, there are associated physical phenomena on the ground that require scientific investigation."[9]

Those involved with these UFO investigations were aware of the differing values placed on different types of evidence, and agreed that anything physical warranted more serious attention. Again, as Hynek wrote, "Close Encounters of the Second Kind bear a special importance, for when it is reported that a UFO has left tangible evidence of its presence, here is clearly the area in which to begin digging for 'scientific paydirt.'"[10] This chapter will explore what this digging actually comprised and why, in the end, even the physical evidence failed to yield paydirt.

THE MICHALAK CASE

The Falcon Lake incident is easily the most extensively documented Canadian UFO case. Scattered across several files are approximately 250 pages of material documenting the investigation. The incident is one of the most frequently cited Canadian cases,[11] and was even recently the subject of an entire book.[12] So why the intense interest in this specific case? Why did the Canadian government invest so much more time and energy into this case than any other?

Compared to the vast majority of other UFO sighting reports, which only offer descriptions of ambiguous lights in the sky, the Falcon Lake incident came with a cornucopia of physical evidence. The government was able to get its hands on *something*. The fact of physical material that could be collected and tested, in addition to a witness statement and a drawing, lent the alleged UFOs a greater reality than any other case had done.

The story began on 19 May 1967. Stefan Michalak, fifty-one years old at the time, was a mechanic and amateur gold prospector who lived in Winnipeg, Manitoba. He decided to prospect in Whiteshell Provincial Park and so took a Greyhound bus to the site, about 150 kilometres east of Winnipeg, close to the Ontario border. He checked into a motel for the night and, in the early morning of 20 May, gathered his gear and headed into the forest. He spent the morning surveying near Falcon Lake and then set up a small camp for lunch. What had started out as a routine trip soon took a bizarre turn that plagued Michalak for years.

After lunch, Michalak went back to a vein of quartz he had found that morning. The sounds of geese flying overhead soon distracted him. Michalak looked up and saw two cigar-shaped UFOs. They were in plain sight, in the middle of the day, and less than two hundred feet away. Michalak wrote that they descended steadily and at the exact same rate. One stopped in mid-air, while the other continued to descend and landed about 160 feet away atop a flat rock. The first UFO hovered above Michalak for several minutes before ascending and disappearing into the sky. The UFO on the ground began to change colour, "turning from red to grey-red to light grey and then to the colour of hot stainless steel, with a golden glow around it."[13] Michalak noticed an opening at the top of the craft that emitted a brilliant purple light as well as waves of warm air. The stench of sulphur emanated from within.

The craft remained motionless long enough for Michalak to sketch it on his note pad, producing the drawing shown in figure 4.1. He had brought no camera as there was no need for one on a prospecting trip. Michalak thought it must be some kind of advanced, likely American technology, but could see no identifying marks. He eventually approached and heard two human-like voices coming from inside the craft. After attempting to hail the occupants in several different languages to no avail, Michalak approached and stuck his head into an opening in the side. He reported seeing "a maze of lights" within, all flashing randomly.

Michalak stepped back and touched the UFO with his gloved hand, scorching the fingertips. Then the UFO moved. As it began to ascend, a wave of hot air blasted out of what appeared to be a ventilation screen. The heat struck Michalak in the chest, burning his shirt and skin, and then disappeared into the sky, leaving Michalak confused and injured.

If this encounter was not strange enough, the investigation was even odder. Michalak collected his gear and noticed that the needle on his compass was spinning wildly. He moved to inspect the landing site but was overcome with nausea and a severe headache. He began vomiting and, once he was able, staggered through the woods to the highway, heaving the whole way. By this point, it was about 3:00 p.m. The burn on his chest had resolved into a pattern of red marks much like the holes in a grate. By a stroke of luck, Michalak was able to flag down an RCMP cruiser driving down Highway 1.

At this point, accounts of the incident begin to conflict. Michalak maintained that he tried to explain his story to the RCMP officer, Constable Solotki. Michalak warned Solotki to stay away from him in case he was irradiated, but also asked Solotki for medical assistance. Solotki apparently did not believe Michalak and left him on the road. Michalak was forced to walk back to his motel, check out, and take the bus back to Winnipeg that same night.

Solotki's version frames Michalak differently. In an RCMP report dated 26 May, Corporal Davis – an investigator on the case – summarized what Solotki had witnessed. Michalak told Solotki that his shirt had been burned and so he had put it in his briefcase. However, Michalak refused to show it because "he didn't want any publicity." Michalak later said he refused to show it because he was afraid that the shirt would emit radiation. Solotki assumed that Michalak had been drinking and was hungover, as "his eyes were red and he acted in a very irrational manner." Every time Solotki approached him, Michalak would back away. Michalak also refused to show the constable the landing site, again because he wanted to avoid publicity. He did show Solotki the marks on his chest, which, the constable reported, "looked like marks that were caused by rubbing ash onto the skin." As Michalak was so uncooperative, Solotki was forced to leave him on the road.[14]

Once back in Winnipeg with his wife and three children, Michalak continued to feel the effects of his encounter. He had lost weight, could not rid his mouth of the taste of sulphur, saw pink dots in his field of vision, and would vomit anytime he tried to eat or drink. Despite his statements to Solotki that he wished to avoid publicity, one of the first things he did upon arriving back home was to call the local press. One of Michalak's sons, Stan, later recalled that his father felt a moral duty to report his experience, lest the public be left unaware of a potential danger.[15] A reporter showed up that same evening, 21 May, and began what Michalak himself characterized as the "beginning of [a] long series of questions and harassment by the press, radio, television, the air force and various authorities."

Michalak was right. Interest in his case continued for a number of months, as RCMP and RCAF officers conducted interviews, followed up on soil sample tests, and hunted for the elusive landing site near Falcon Lake. At subsequent meetings with RCMP officers, representatives from citizen UFO organizations accompanied Michalak. For instance, on 23 May, just two days after Michalak's return to Winnipeg, when RCMP constables Zacharias and Davis visited him at his home, one J.B. Thompson of the Aerial Phenomena Research Organization (APRO) was also present. Michalak himself had gotten in touch with APRO. At this meeting, Michalak reported that he had been treated at the hospital and again by his family doctor for the burns on his chest, which resembled severe sunburns. He said he did not want to reveal the location of the landing site because he had "a good nickel strike in the area and [did] not want it to be common knowledge just where he [had] been prospecting."[16]

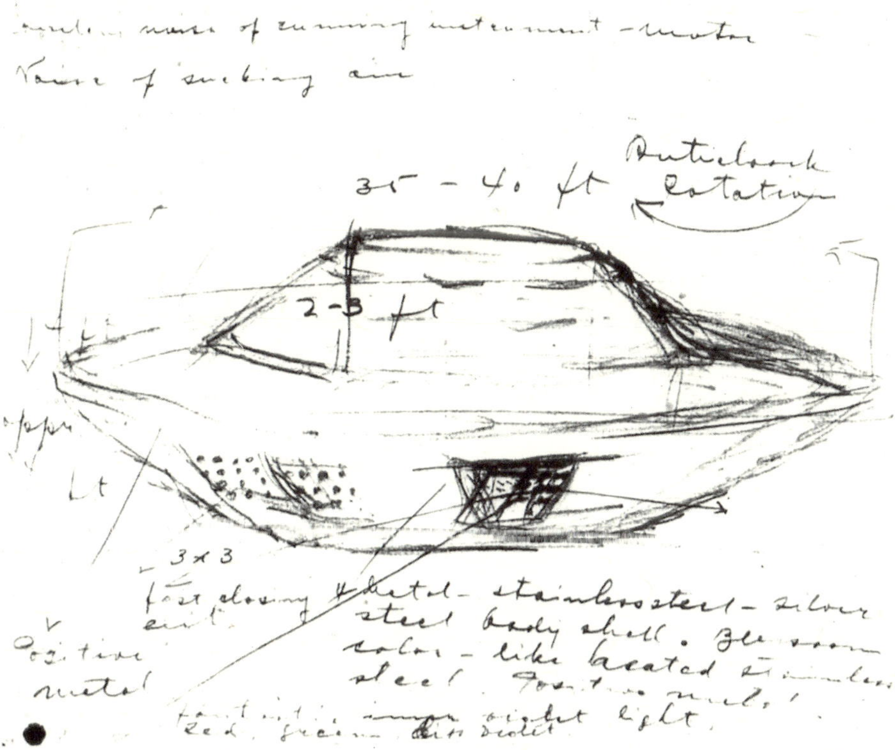

Figure 4.1 | This sketch of a UFO, which Stephan Michalak made for investigators, shows an exhaust panel that appears to match the burn pattern on Michalak's chest. Michalak admitted, however, that the value of a drawing of this sort in conveying useful information was limited; a Canadian geologist working with the federal government later ridiculed the drawing.

RCMP officers followed up with Michalak on a number of occasions afterward, recording interviews with him and trying to convince him to take officers to the landing site. Michalak said he would not go back out until he was physically well enough and had assurances that the site would not be publicized. In the meantime, Michalak's shirt was tested for radioactivity and the results came back negative. The RCMP officers attempted to acquire Michalak's burned glove for testing, but were told that Thompson from APRO had taken it without the RCMP's knowledge. As Michalak was too ill to go, RCMP officers headed out to the Falcon Lake area themselves in an unsuccessful attempt to find the site. To them, Michalak's story did not seem totally consistent. For instance, on their search, the RCMP found several landmarks near Falcon Lake which Michalak had described, but the actual landing site remained elusive. They also interviewed the bartender at Michalak's motel near the site, who was convinced he had served Michalak several beers the evening of 19 May. Michalak maintained he had drunk only coffee.

Adding to the case's strangeness, Michalak eventually returned to the area alone and found the site. This was after several unsuccessful trips that Michalak took, with investigators in tow. Squadron Leader Bissky, the RCAF investigator, noted several times that Michalak seemed to be stonewalling him and withholding information about his experience – perhaps, Bissky suggested, for private gain. In any case, the landing site was much smaller than Michalak had led the authorities to believe, but it did contain the flat rock on which the UFO had come to rest, as well as some of the prospecting gear he had left behind. The flat rock was completely free of grass or moss, as if it had been burned away.

The area was tested for radioactivity, and this time higher-than-normal levels were detected. S.E. Hunt, from the Department of Health and Welfare, concluded that the radioactive material detected was radium-226, an element commonly found in radioactive waste, but the level was not high enough to be a public hazard. Hunt also noted the confusing nature of the case, given the variety of actors involved and their general unwillingness to cooperate.[17] He was also appalled that Michalak, once he had located the landing site, had taken his soil and rock samples and contaminated them by placing them all in the same bag with his prospecting gear and storing it in his basement. In short, to an outsider, Michalak appeared at times inebriated, confused, and disingenuous; he maintained, however, that he had experienced a traumatic event that scarred him for the rest of his life, and that he had only the public's best interests in mind.

In the end, the investigators could make no more headway. They could only interview Michalak so many times before they stopped receiving new information. Michalak's burns eventually healed, although they would apparently flare up intermittently in the months and years to come. Radioactivity at the site was detected, but remained within relatively normal ranges. The case had received a considerable amount of press attention, which attracted dubious characters like Thompson from APRO. And despite the ample documentation of the events of 20 May onward, there were no more witnesses to the actual events and Michalak's account lacked the kind of objectivity and consistency that was needed to make a more rigorous assessment. Ultimately, however, the investigators "were unable to provide evidence which would dispute Mr. Michalak's story."[18] The case remains unsolved.

Nevertheless, it is clear that what prompted such interest in this story was the amount of physical material on offer. Regardless of the truth of Michalak's account, there were pieces of evidence that defied explanation. Michalak had severe burns on his chest in the pattern of a ventilation grate, matching the drawing he made. The burns never blistered, but they were certainly not minor. His general behaviour after the event, including the vomiting and pain, were consistent with radiation poisoning. His clothing displayed burns of a similar force. The flat rock at the landing site was conspicuously absent of vegetation and the radiation levels there were unaccountable. These were simply elements of the story that could not be ignored, whatever their origin.

SEVEN DAY WONDER

It was not until the late 1970s and early 1980s that crop circles entered the popular imagination.[19] When they first began appearing in farmers' fields, ufologists immediately linked them to the UFO phenomenon. Many witnesses assumed that only saucer-like craft could have made the unique shapes of these circles. Only a flying saucer could descend, leave a perfect impression upon the ground, and then lift off again without leaving any other trace. As interest grew and more crop circles appeared – mostly in the UK – the designs they traced in fields grew more complex. Viewed from the air, many crop circles looked like works of art. Perfectly geometrical and displaying a variety of unique designs, many witnesses saw in them an otherworldly mystique.

It did not matter that a number of people eventually admitted that crop circles were hoaxes.[20] Almost as well known as the impressions themselves is the image of several mischievous men toiling through the night, pressing down cornstalks using nothing more than simple wooden boards looped through with rope.[21] As David Clarke writes, ufologists "depended upon UFOs retaining an aura of mystery." When it came to crop circles, "few ufologists wanted a resolution. The integrity of the enigma had to be defended at all costs."[22] Interest in crop circles never entirely abated. For example, the 2014 documentary film *A Field Full of Secrets* attempted to revive interest in crop circles, arguing that they are more than just interesting shapes on the ground and are, in fact, two-dimensional designs for "free energy" spacecraft – that is, craft that operate using free, renewable sources of energy and produce no emissions, such as the gravitationally driven type of spacecraft that Wilbert Smith had sought to research.[23]

While crop circles were predominantly a British obsession, a number of them did appear in farmers' fields in North America. Even before ufologists gave them the moniker "crop circles," Canada was host to one of the earliest appearances. The 1967 case of the "reputed UFO landing marks" at Duhamel, Alberta, remains a mystery. While the Canadian government clearly maintained an official stance toward UFOs of indifference, if not outright disbelief, any physical traces discovered were cause for concern and investigation. Like the case of Michalak, the Duhamel crop circles represent a time and place when UFOs *came into being* in a way not previously experienced. No other case of physical depressions on the ground warranted an investigation like Duhamel. Although the effort put toward the mystery's resolution was relatively minimal – documentation of the incident amounts to only about twenty-five pages – it is nevertheless a fact that the Department of National Defence did assume the marks represented some kind of physical reality that could be investigated.

The mystery allegedly began several weeks before the crop circles themselves were discovered. A number of citizens in the hamlet of Duhamel, near the small city of Camrose, Alberta, had reported instances of UFO sightings to friends, family, and the local newspaper. In the words of G.H.S. Jones, the investigating Defence Research Board scientist, two schoolgirls reported seeing "a UFO, largish, creamish, standardish, at a range of not more than two or three hundred yards, bobbing up and down near the ground 'as if to attract attention.'" Jones was not impressed with the sighting, and noted that "this description could be taken from any of many previously published reports." As is often the case, one sighting begets another, especially when media coverage is involved, and so, in this respect, Duhamel was ripe for a more spectacular occurrence.

There was a heavy rain the night before the crop circles appeared on Edgar Schielke's land. Schielke, a local farmer, had not been out to his fields in weeks. He stated that he only went out if his cows did not come home for the night.[24] On the morning of 5 August, he trudged across the soft ground to his pasture to locate his cattle and "immediately noticed a circular mark some thirty feet in diameter on a region of relatively high ground." He thought little of the mark and more on getting his cows back home. Word of the crop circle might never have leaked out if Schielke had not "casually" mentioned it to his neighbour, who immediately assumed it was from a flying saucer. The neighbour then informed a local schoolteacher and amateur ufologist, Ray Sanders, who – in Jones's words – "became the <u>obvious</u> prime-mover in the growth of the story and its distribution to the Press, a UFO society in Edmonton, and in due course to the CBC."[25]

Schielke maintained from the beginning that he did not believe in UFOs but also that none of his farming equipment could have made the marks. Rather, he assumed they were the result of "some strange lightning phenomenon." The farmer gave Sanders permission to visit the site and conduct an investigation. For several days after Schielke first noticed the mark, nobody thought to contact authorities. Instead, Sanders and several others repeatedly visited the site, leaving tire tracks throughout the field. They found three additional circles, of similar size and quality, and also took soil samples, which they forwarded to the Edmonton UFO society. Ken Patridge, a reporter with the *Camrose Canadian*, visited the site on 8 August. A story, with accompanying photographs, was published the next day.[26]

At this point, Patridge directly contacted Canadian Forces Headquarters. On 9 August, priority telexes went out ordering an investigation and indicating the following: "Four rings in ground as though round large object settled into ground. Depressions heavier to one side. Ring diameter of 34 ft to 36 ft[.] No scorch. Clearly marked teeth or claw like marks around edge."[27] Two days later, on 11 August, a government team arrived at the site.

The investigating scientist, G.H.S. Jones, worked with the nearby Defence Research Establishment Suffield, a military research facility and DRB branch. Jones introduced his report on the Duhamel investigation by lamenting the sorry state of the process used to clear his travel logistics to and from the site. Jones noted that "the use of a staff car [to drive to the site] would have meant that the inspection became a weekend affair." This was clearly an unacceptable prospect, as Jones anticipated the job could be done in a single day – that is, it did not require wasting any more time. He then attempted to arrange passage on an RCAF aircraft, which was coincidentally flying into the area, only to encounter a two-hour delay to arrange the necessary clearance, which "involved numerous expensive phone calls."

Jones eventually made it to the site and met up with the reporter, Patridge, as well as Captain Walker, a helicopter pilot with the Royal Canadian Army Service Corps. Jones was tasked with conducting a scientific inspection of the site, Patridge with taking more photographs, and Walker with carrying out interviews with all the relevant witnesses. As Jones wrote: "By the time the inspection team visited the site, it had been, literally, a seven day wonder." Tire tracks from "droves of people" covered the pasture (but not the marks themselves). Schielke, oddly, seemed unconcerned about the damage to his pasture and "maintained an attitude of nonchalance towards the whole business." Despite the damage by the visitors and the heavy rainfall several days earlier, the marks were still clearly visible. Jones, however, did admit his disappointment upon first seeing the circles, again lamenting that he "had been brought so far to look at so little."

Nevertheless, the crop circles left him puzzled. Jones's five-page report gives a detailed explanation of what he encountered and his attempts to account for the circles. In total, Jones and Walker identified six circular marks, ranging in diameter from thirty-one to thirty-six feet. According to a map of the site that Walker drew as part of his own report, the marks were randomly arranged within the single field, isolated from one another. All of the circles were "incomplete" on one side and contained within them tread or lug marks. Jones thought they looked as if a rolling tire had made them, although not a single tire track led to or from the circles. He further observed that the "droves" of visitors' tire tracks criss-crossing the field offered a reliable comparison; the crop circle marks were obviously made by something heavier than a normal car or truck. He was also skeptical of anyone's ability to carry and roll a tire with the weight required to make such "sharply impressed" marks.

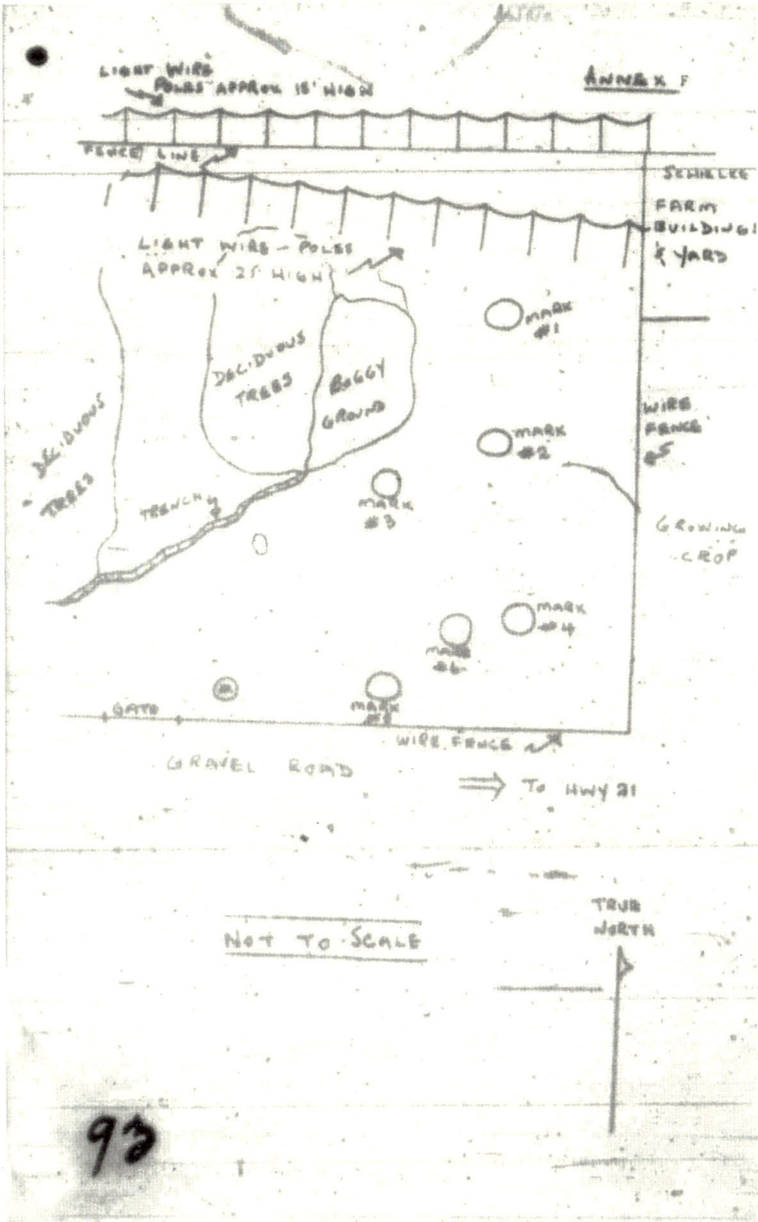

Figure 4.2 | Drawing by helicopter pilot Captain Walker, Royal Canadian Army Service Corps, of six crop circles found in a farmer's field near Camrose, Alberta.

Jones considered the possibility that the circles were a hoax, although he concluded that he was "unable to find anything which would lend strength to this supposition."[28] Lastly, he considered "the UFO possibility." After some quick calculations of potential load versus area, he concluded that the necessary load to make such marks would be 135 tons, "in [the] right ball park for a large aircraft, or presumably, small space craft." In the end, Jones was equivocal: he could neither confirm nor deny the possibility of a hoax, and the previous evidence of strange phenomena in the area could have been "a lead-in" to the hoax. A rolling wheel could have produced the marks, although it was unclear how this would have been accomplished; and the marks were "sufficiently unique" in his experience to "state categorically" that he would likely discount the possibility of a hoax were he to encounter such marks again.[29]

Walker's report was similarly detailed and also withheld firm judgment. He gave a general description of the site and specifics for each of the marks found. The cattle seemed unaffected: "There is no evidence, physical or verbal, of any change in their habits." He found no evidence of "deliberate interference" or "chemical involvement." He also noted that Jones had tested the area with a Geiger counter, which returned normal background radiation readings.

On 15 August, Walker returned to the site to collect soil samples. A Department of National Defence summary of the incident dated 25 August indicated that the soil sample was ordered as a direct result of the ambiguity encountered during the Michalak case. Tests of the soil taken from the Falcon Lake site had shown higher-than-normal radioactivity levels, and so "it was deemed advisable" to test the Duhamel site as well. The defence department sent the Duhamel soil to the University of Alberta to test "for foreign matter." The DND summary notes that nobody reported any further UFO activity after Schielke discovered the marks, and that "it has not been possible to arrive at a conclusion" regarding the incident. Rather, it was advisable to wait until the soil sample tests came back from the laboratory.[30]

Unfortunately, and perhaps predictably, the tests were inconclusive. A 17 October memo indicated that gamma-ray spectral analysis of the soil samples revealed entirely normal levels of radioactivity.[31] In the new year and in response to a ministerial inquiry, a DND staff member, Commodore F.B. Caldwell, blandly summarized the incident by stating that "DND is unable to arrive at a solution as to what caused the impression on the property of Mr Ed Schielke of Duhamel, Alberta."[32] No official filed a further report on the matter and those involved with the incident moved on.

DARK OBJECT

Flying saucer crashes hold a special wonder for ufologists. Sightings of mysterious lights in the sky are relatively commonplace; the archives are full of them. An actual crash, however, is rare, with only a handful around the world reported. Perhaps the most infamous is the alleged 1947 Roswell crash, which, in combination with pilot Kenneth Arnold's sighting, kickstarted the modern era of UFOs. Ufologists and conspiracy theorists have built and maintained an extensive mythology around the Roswell crash. Arguably the basis, or at least one of the founding pillars, of the American UFO phenomenon, it continues to fuel speculation and commercial interests.

Canada has its own UFO crash mythology, although it developed much later and is, in many ways, a much more believable one. Whereas the evidence for the Roswell crash is largely speculative and has become so convoluted it is difficult to trust, the evidence for "Canada's Roswell," as some ufologists have called the 1967 UFO incident at Shag Harbour, Nova Scotia, has retained an uncommon consistency. As with the Michalak and Duhamel cases, the Shag Harbour crash yielded an amount of physical evidence convincing enough to warrant a serious DND investigation. It is likely that if the crash had comprised only eyewitness testimony, and not the possibility of finding an actual craft, then the Canadian government would have handled the case like any other – that is, interviewed the witnesses and shelved the report.

Shag Harbour is a small fishing village on the South Shore of Nova Scotia, right at the southwest corner of the province. The place is so small that it is served exclusively by the RCMP, which has a detachment in the nearby town of Barrington, about fifteen kilometres away. On 4 October 1967, close to midnight, the detachment received several calls – one right after the other within a span of fifteen minutes – about an airplane that had crashed into the harbour. Corporal Wercicky was the officer in the station at the time and, after taking the calls, drove down to the harbour with a second officer. A third officer met them there. Thus, there were three RCMP officers as well as half a dozen citizen witnesses to the event.

ICA128PEA133 OEB076 COA038 UU

DE RCEOC 29 05/1320Z

P 051320Z OCT 67

FM RCC HALIFAX

PRIORITY

OCT 5 14 19 '67

O.P.I.

TO CANFORCEHED

BT

UNCLAS RCC076

FOR CFOC. UFO REPORT

A 050210Z OCT 67

B NIGHT CLEAR , NO MOON

C CPL WERCICKY RCMP BARRINGTON PASSAGE

D OUTSIDE LOWER WOODS HARBOUR, N S

E 6 OTHER WITNESSES - NAMES KNOW TO RCMP CPL

F DARK OBJECT - IN EXCESS OF 60 FT - 4 WHITE LIGHTS HORIZONTALLY 15 FT SPACING - MOVEMENT EASTERLY LOW ALTITUDE ON DOWN TO WATER SURFACE

G UNKNOWN BUT IN EXCESS OF FIVE MINUTES

H UFO DESCENDED RAPIDLY TO WATER WITH HIGH WHISTLING SOUND. BRIGHT FLASH ON HITTING WATER. SINGLE LIGHT FLOATING ON SURFACE REMAINED FOR LONG TIME SAND BEFORE RCMP COULD GET BOAT TO IT. AREA SEARCHED EXTENSIVELY BY CCG LIFEBOAT 101 AND

PAGE 2 RCEOC 29 UNCLAS

MANY SMALL BOATS - NIL RESULTS. POSITION OF LAST SIGHTING 4330.5N 6545W. ALL OTHER POSSIBLE LEADS (A/C , FLARES, ETC.) CHECKED - NIL RESULTS. FOLLOW UP: AT 051215Z COAST GUARD CUTTER 101 PROCEEDING TO AREA WITH RCMP ON BOARD TO RESEARCH AREA BASED ON A/REF DATUM POINT.

BT

Figure 4.3 | Telex report detailing the Shag Harbour incident, in which the UFO is described as a "dark object." The report, typical to its kind, contained only the most basic information about the sighting.

The citizens had first noticed the UFO as nothing more than an object with lights that moved silently and slowly across the night sky. Witnesses later described it as an object "in excess of 60 feet in diameter [that] carried four white lights spaced horizontally at a distance of 15 feet." Suddenly, as a DND report put it, the object descended rapidly to the water with a high whistling sound and made a bright flash upon impact. The object floated on the water, a single light still visible. At this point, the RCMP officers arrived and stood on the shore with the other witnesses watching the curious object. It was obvious to them that this was no ordinary aircraft. Subsequent inquiries about "all other possible leads" – such as "aircraft, flares, floats, or any other known objects" – had come back negative, and investigators determined that no commercial or military aircraft were operating in the area.[33]

After watching the object for several minutes, the RCMP officers commandeered a fishing boat and piloted into the harbour. They thought it possible that survivors of the craft might be in need of rescue. Although this detail is not contained in the official documentation, subsequent accounts have noted that as the boat approached the craft, it "entered a swath of glittering yellow foam estimated to be eighty feet wide by a half mile long and three to four inches thick."[34] Before the boat could reach the exact site, the remaining light on the UFO went dark and the object quickly sank under the water.

The following day, 5 October, the RCMP detachment reported the incident to DND. A helicopter airlifted a three-man diving team to the site the same day, along with 400 pounds of equipment, to search the water for the craft or any other physical traces.[35] A local boat was hired to assist with the operation, and DND requested regular updates from the team. Unfortunately, the search did not go well. A DND memo from Ottawa indicates that "two days of underwater search by divers of probability area under good conditions has produced nil results." The divers were unable to locate any trace of the craft and the memo concluded that if no results were obtained by end of day on 8 October, the search would be terminated.[36]

At the same time, DND was receiving letters regarding the incident. One citizen from Quebec requested that the department "give [him] all available information about it," while another from Calgary expressed his concern and ventured that he was "sensible enough to realize that what was seen there was some kind of 'flying machine/vehicle,' and it was either man made or of alien construction."[37] The RCMP officers involved had given the story to the press, which followed developments closely. The Halifax *Chronicle Herald* reported that officials in Ottawa were very interested in the search results. One article quoted a Squadron Leader Bain, apparently a spokesman for "a special and little known Royal Canadian Air Force department" that investigated UFOs, as saying that the Shag Harbour crash was one of the few reports where they might find "something concrete."[38] There is no evidence for a special RCAF department of this kind, but it was certainly the case that DND thought something more tangible might come of this particular investigation, especially given that three of the witnesses were RCMP officers and thus considered more reliable than the other witnesses.

Alas, only disappointment followed. On 9 October, DND terminated the search.[39] The divers found no trace of the craft, and went home. In response to one citizen's inquiry, the operations director for the DND's Maritime Command, W.W. Turner, wrote: "A search of the area failed to produce any material evidence which would assist in explaining or establishing the identity of the object. An underwater search conducted by divers from the Department of National Defence also failed to locate any tangible evidence which could be used to arrive at an explainable conclusion."[40]

As with the previous two cases, the Shag Harbour incident officially remains unsolved; but this has not stopped amateur ufologists from investigating the case themselves to unearth new details. Chris Styles, a Nova Scotia-based ufologist, has published two books on the incident. Styles claims that there is in fact evidence for a second crash site, further along the shore, which DND investigated in secret. He argues that it is possible that the craft travelled underwater to this second spot and that DND was aware of this movement. In any case, nothing was recovered from this site either.[41]

Despite this speculation, accounts of the Shag Harbour incident retain an uncommon consistency. The story has remained essentially the same since 1967, with very little embellishment. This is likely due, mostly, to the fact that there is very clear documentation in the archives regarding who witnessed the event and what appeared to occur. The event has also remained mostly a local phenomenon. While others outside of Nova Scotia are aware of the Shag Harbour incident, it has not been publicized to the same extent as, for instance, the Roswell crash.

Nevertheless, like the Duhamel case, there is actually very little documentation about the Shag Harbour crash. Curiously, despite the fact that three of the witnesses – and in the DND's mind, the most reliable ones – were RCMP officers, no RCMP files regarding the Shag Harbour crash have survived in the archives. All available documentation, which amounts to about twenty-five pages, comes from either DND or National Research Council files. This is especially odd given that RCMP personnel are habitually detail-oriented and their files on UFO sightings are some of the most detailed and complete of any department. There is no satisfactory way to account for this omission.

Despite its official stance of indifference, the Canadian government was obviously paying attention to UFO sightings within its borders. This was especially so in the case of any sighting that involved a physical encounter. The Michalak incident was the most heavily investigated of all UFO sightings in the history of Canadian interest in the phenomenon due to its relative abundance of tangible evidence. It even informed future investigations: soil sample tests were ordered for the Duhamel crop circle case in large part because of the radioactivity that analysts found at the Falcon Lake site. However, despite the physical evidence on offer at Falcon Lake, Duhamel, and Shag Harbour, investigators remained unconvinced of the reality of UFOs.

J. Allen Hynek called cases like these Close Encounters of the Second Kind and argued that only such cases had the power to disrupt mainstream understandings of the topic. Physical evidence left behind commanded attention in a way that nothing else seemed able to do. Scientists measure things. Their quantitative measurements are the means by which they claim to produce, and not merely communicate, knowledge. Trust in numbers, as science historian Theodore Porter put it, is a thoroughly modern means of understanding the natural world; as such, the state's investigations into these cases, where physical evidence was available, fit neatly into the image of itself that it was attempting to construct. For this reason, these three cases were able, if only briefly, to overcome the threshold of legitimate evidence. This moment in 1967, when the physical evidence left behind in these cases made UFOs coalesce into reality the most concretely, represents the culmination of Canadian UFO investigation. In other words, investigators looking into these cases believed, more than they had ever done, that there might actually be something to the phenomenon.

This change of attitude was short-lived. In the end, the government declared each case a mystery, and they remain unsolved. Despite the relative abundance of evidence, there still was not enough to move forward in any systematic way. Nonetheless, the cases presented what seemed to be isolated instances that investigators could not explain away as a generalized type, and that fit the pattern of anomalies that fell outside acceptable scientific boundaries. Again, it is not hard to see why – namely the appearance that there may have been evidence that leant itself to scientific study, such as radiation readings and bodily harm. When evidence did present itself, however, it was impossible to do much more with it. The investigations simply hit a wall that they could not scale.

As a result, the Canadian government would take steps to remove itself from the UFO phenomenon altogether, given that years of investigation had apparently yielded nothing useful. The next chapter describes the process by which the government closed out its investigation, as well as how citizen UFO investigators took up the task instead, in opposition to and in conflict with the government, concluding the narrative of how each side perpetuated this dynamic of mutual mistrust.

5

The End, 1967–95

On 20 June 1968, D. Davies, an administrator at the Department of Indian Affairs and Northern Development, wrote to the National Research Council to report a UFO sighting above Frobisher Bay: "The object appeared to be a star moving very slowly across the sky in a west to east direction. The local camera enthusiasts were out in full force." Davies consulted with the local Department of Transport office, which informed him that the object was likely a weather balloon flying at high altitude. Davies concluded his letter by reassuring the NRC: "There have been no reports of landing by little green men or other weird non-world creatures. Furthermore, there have been no reports that all our women are pregnant."[1] Davies was clearly no believer in the UFO phenomenon. He also assumed the letter's recipient shared his views and would appreciate the joke. Letters like this one clearly demonstrate the government's derisive stance toward UFOs.

What was less clear by the late 1960s was what certain members of the public thought. Chapter 3 explored some citizens' early attempts at eliciting information from the government. They were largely unsuccessful, leading some UFO enthusiasts to accuse the government of a cover-up. Conspiracy theories about UFOs emerged in the context of changing attitudes toward expertise and deference. This chapter will continue the narrative after 1967, again arguing for a mainly historical approach to conspiracy theory. Citizens continued to write to the government about UFOs, seemingly trusting the official responses they received less and less.

However, a transformation began to take place in the late 1960s and into the 1970s. Whereas previous correspondents like D.M.

Spicer and Ken Kaasen were primarily concerned with information about UFOs, some of the Canadians introduced in this chapter became just as concerned about government secrecy more broadly. It seems that at least some of the earlier efforts at achieving UFO disclosure found their logical conclusion in attempts during the 1970s to advocate for more effective access to information policies. The efforts of UFO enthusiasts in Canada during the period between 1967 and 1980 are best placed within the broader history of changing ideas about government secrecy and information, a history that culminated with the introduction of access to information and privacy (ATIP) legislation in the early 1980s.

Citizens were as responsible as the government for the confusion about UFOs. The available documents show that the government was not covering up any information regarding UFOs. They show instead that there was significant confusion about responsibility for the investigation, arising mostly from a lack of communication and political will to pursue the matter. However, some citizens' responses to this situation were not justified, and served only to further inflame the tension between them and the government.

More specifically, the particular manner in which some citizens approached the government about UFOs was antagonistic. Some were brazen in their demands, rude and unforgiving, and sometimes made personal attacks against government officials. They tried many ways of making themselves seem more credible, such as affiliating with UFO research organizations, but the government saw these as mere pretenses. This kind of approach did not endear these citizens to the government, which generalized this behaviour across the broader field of UFO activism, framing everyone in it as simply more examples of ignorance and superstition that impeded the state's task of educating the public and maintaining its modern image.

TRANSFER OF RESPONSIBILITY

Early in the 1950s, the Department of National Defence concluded that UFOs did not present a security risk. The only thing left to do, in the department's mind, was to leave the investigation to scientists, who might be able to make something of it. When it became obvious that even Canada's foremost astronomers, such as Peter Millman, were similarly uninterested in the topic, the DND pushed even harder to dissociate itself from the phenomenon.

"DND should NOT be put in the position of appearing to be responsible for this subject," read a 1967 memo, "thus linking these phenomena, in the public mind, with some sort of threat to the national security."[2] Attempts to ignore and brush aside citizen investigators culminated in late 1967. By June of that year, word began to circulate that the DND might be transferring responsibility for collecting UFO sighting reports and that the National Research Council would be the obvious choice to take it over.

John H. Hodgson, director of the Observatories Branch within the Department of Energy, Mines and Resources, wrote to DRB chairman R.J. Uffen to report that the Dominion Observatory has "in their files a number of reports about UFO's" and to ask "if any agency in Canada is interested in maintaining a file on these reports." A response noted that Hodgson was told to hold off on transferring any files until discussions between the NRC and DND could determine the responsible agency.[3]

The next month, RCAF air commodore R.M. Aldwinckle asked an unidentified recipient to "assume responsibility for determining the Department's [DND] position with respect to UFO's and communicating this to [NRC scientist] Dr. Rettie." Aldwinckle also noted his personal interest in the subject and that he would "appreciate being kept in the picture."[4] Even at this time, it was unclear who had responsibility for the subject. It was a necessary task in and of itself to identify someone simply to look into the matter, let alone decide who would eventually take on the project.

Later that month, H. Sheffer, scientific advisor to the vice chief of the defence staff, wrote that the DND had positively identified the NRC as the ideal candidate for UFO responsibility: "I agree that it would be a good idea to transfer responsibility for investigation of UFOs to the National Research Council if they are willing to undertake this responsibility. One of the reasons given by DOps [the DND's Directorate of Operations] for wishing to relinquish responsibility is lack of sufficient staff and necessary scientific assistance. NRC might well have the same objections. It is, after all, not an attractive field for investigation and there are very few scientists who will eagerly undertake the required studies." Sheffer asked if he should "explore informally NRC interest" or whether a formal ministerial inquiry would be more appropriate.[5] At this point, these discussions were taking place solely within the confines of DND.

Sheffer went ahead and informally inquired about NRC interest. W.G. Schneider, at the NRC, replied to Sheffer: "On the question of UFO's, we had a preliminary discussion here on this matter and it was decided we would not proceed further unless we had a request from your Minister addressed to ours." In other words, Schneider and others at the NRC decided to force the DND's hand. Schneider confirmed this by adding that, "after having gone through the exercise of fitting ourselves to our projected budget, which is rather sad, we are at the moment very chary about taking on anything that might involve any expenditures of funds."[6]

In September, RCAF wing commander D.F. Robertson drafted a letter to C.M. Drury, the minister of industry and defence production. Robertson indicated that Canadian Forces Headquarters (CFHQ) had carried out a study and determined that despite Schneider's misgivings, the NRC was the most appropriate agency to investigate the phenomenon due to the availability of its "scientific research facilities and trained personnel." Robertson outlined the procedure that CFHQ undertook upon receiving a UFO report. Each case would be classified into one of two categories: if the report contained information "which would suggest the type of phenomena associated with fireballs and meteorites," they were classified as Category One. If the report did "not conform to the physical patterns usually associated with fireballs or meteoritic activity," they became Category Two. Category One reports were automatically forwarded to NRC and, in fact, had been for some time before the discussions about transferring responsibility were initiated. Category Two reports would necessitate one of two responses: they were "either placed on file and annotated that no further action [was] required, or action [was] initiated to conduct a formal investigation of the report by a military officer." These investigations were rare, and the letter admitted that those done to date had "failed to disclose any evidence which would suggest that UFOs pose a threat to national security."

In an attempt to further justify the transfer of responsibility, Robertson added that rather than constituting a security threat, "a number of investigations suggest the possibility of UFOs exhibiting some unique scientific information or advanced technology which could possibly contribute to scientific or technical research." It also noted the recent formation of the Condon Committee at the

University of Colorado, which was tasked with solving the UFO enigma once and for all. Robertson used this example to demonstrate the need for a civilian scientific organization to look into the matter, rather than a military one.[7]

In October, the recommendation to transfer responsibility became a formal ministerial inquiry. The defence minister, Leo Cadieux, signed the letter that Robertson had drafted and sent it to Drury. Two weeks later, Drury replied. The NRC, according to Drury, acknowledged that immediately after the Second World War, there had been sufficient cause to justify a UFO investigation. This centred on two aspects: the "possibility of unexpected military innovations in or above the atmosphere" and "the sensitivity of the civil population to the remarkable scientific progress in upper atmosphere and space research."

However, Drury continued, "after some 15 years of publicity and of conditioning to the acceptance of natural explanations for unusual sightings," such an investigation was no longer warranted. Further, if any investigation was to take place, "it is one that should preferably arise by the natural extension of scientific work in progress rather than by the intrusion of UFO phenomena seeking explanation." In other words, UFOs were a bother to scientists, who were preoccupied with more rational pursuits.

Drury offered a revision of Cadieux's proposal to transfer wholesale responsibility to the NRC. Since he thought UFOs were an "intrusion" into normal science, Drury instead proposed "a substantial reduction in the government effort, in fact to something rather akin to a judicious sampling procedure."[8] Drury saw this not just as a means of transferring responsibility to another agency but an opportunity to reduce involvement to the most minimal level possible.

Cadieux agreed with Drury's assessment. The next month, he replied "that it is unnecessary and wasteful of effort to investigate all reported UFO sightings," although he admitted that investigation would be required in cases where physical evidence was available – such as those detailed in the foregoing chapter. Cadieux suggested that DND transfer to the NRC the responsibility for UFO reports but also, more specifically, the authority to determine when and where scientific investigation was warranted. This latter decision had a significant impact on how the government received UFO reports from that point forward.

By the end of 1967, the NRC had become responsible, willingly or otherwise, for UFO reports and inquiries. The DND wrote that the

NRC "has recently assumed responsibility for the scientific investigations of UFO's where such appear warranted" and that while no individual scientist had yet been identified as the lead investigator, all inquiries could be forwarded in the meantime to NRC scientist R.S. Rettie.[9] The DND wasted no time in spreading the word about the transfer and passing the buck on citizen inquiries.

LISTLESS APPROACH

Not all within the government were happy with this decision. The NRC, of course, had already expressed their reluctance to become more involved with the UFO "intrusion." Others at CFHQ were similarly dissatisfied. DND official E.W. Greenwood wrote that the NRC's intention was to undertake only a passive role. The organization would not actively investigate any cases and would not solicit information from observers. "All this adds up," Greenwood wrote, "to a quite listless approach; the NRC staff members concerned appear to be personally convinced that UFO sightings do not merit serious attention."[10]

Brigadier N.H. Ross, of the DND, also expressed his concern over the NRC's commitment: "This Division supports the views that should a scientific governmental agency accept the responsibility for investigating UFOs, the agency concerned must be prepared to undertake a serious and objective investigation." Of course, one could say that Ross was not overly concerned with UFOs per se but rather indignant that a publicly funded institution such as the NRC would shirk its responsibilities, whatever they were.

However, Ross also suggested that the NRC "be discreetly advised that the DND has a genuine interest in UFOs and it is intended to maintain a close association with any studies undertaken in this field."[11] It seems reasonable to conclude, however, that while Ross may have taken a personal interest in the subject, the department as a whole had not. Many in the government thought that a serious study of UFOs perhaps should be conducted but that another department – not their own – should be responsible. Since every department shared this view, it is clear why nobody undertook such a project.

To the UFO enthusiast, though, lacking the benefit of an inside view, it was very unclear why the government did not engage in the task. While a handful of military and government employees may have been dissatisfied with the result, the number of disgruntled and offended citizens was surely higher. Word of the decision to transfer responsibility to the NRC did not take long to travel among UFO enthusiasts. One such enthusiast was Allan K. Vezina, a chairman of the Canadian Aerial Phenomena Investigations Committee (CAPIC) based in Scarborough, Ontario. In early January 1968, Vezina wrote to Leo Cadieux to congratulate the minister – not on the successful transfer of responsibility but on winning CAPIC's "Booby of the Year Award." Given this chapter's argument that the way in which citizens presented themselves did nothing to help their credibility, it is worth quoting Vezina's letter at length:

> I simply cannot understand why you turned the UFO investigations project over to the Space Research branch of the National Research Council and expect to achieve something. Yes, it lifts responsibility from your shoulders, but why them? Why not some private agency which showed some semblance of open mindedness toward the subject?
>
> Dr. R.S. Rettie, the head of the space research branch stated: "The whole business is awfully like the belief in witches and hobgoblins." Now, that's just what scientific research needs; the head of a supposedly scientific project being so close-minded that he likens the item he is investigating to witches and hobgoblins. I am absolutely certain you will receive the answer you want from him about UFO's. But, will it be the right answer? I rather doubt it! Dr. Rettie does not have to investigate UFO's; to him, the answer is obvious – the whole thing is a myth. You really outdid yourself this time. Imagine, the government wasting money on an investigation where it already knows the answer.
>
> The Defense Department has stated that the UFO presents no threat to national security. So, what took you so long? The United States Defense Department issued that statement some twenty years ago!

Vezina reminded Cadieux of just how many readers his next editorial on the subject would draw, and that they all "expected a white-wash of this subject" anyway. "Again," Vezina wrote, "congratulations on winning our 1968 award so early in the year."[12] Vezina's letter was a passionate indictment of the Canadian government's efforts, or seeming lack thereof, to seriously investigate the issue. His observations followed from much of what Wilbert Smith argued a decade earlier, when Smith wrote about "official reticence" and the government's fear over what they might find.

Vezina's suggestion of a "private agency" to fill this gap was something he had previously called for. Seven months earlier, Vezina had written to Paul Hellyer, then minister of national defence, outlining CAPIC's mandate and history. CAPIC was a Canadian offshoot of an American citizen UFO investigation group. At its peak, it had about a thousand members ranging in age from "eleven years to sixty-five years," including "scientists, engineers, technicians, lawyers, radio announcers, and many other interested citizens." In his letter to Hellyer, Vezina proposed that CAPIC take over the duty of receiving and investigating UFO reports. To do so, Vezina wrote, it would be necessary to have the cooperation of the armed forces so as to facilitate the travel of a CAPIC investigator wherever they were needed in the country. Vezina also proposed "a small subsidy" in the form of "a permanent staff of, let's say, two persons – one of CAPIC's Directors and a secretary," along with "an office with office equipment such as typewriters, filing cabinets, etc.," and "an offset printing press so that we may publish our findings."

Vezina thought the total cost might come to about $20,000, which he acknowledged was "a great deal of money" but certainly "a great deal less than if the government set up a Royal Commission." Finally, Vezina felt the need to "emphasize this one point; we are not a so called 'crack-pot' organization."[13] Of course, the necessity of making such a statement rarely bolstered anyone's credibility.

Hellyer did not respond. Rather, the very same Leo Cadieux, at the time the associate minister of national defence, replied on Hellyer's behalf with a standard response thanking Vezina for his letter and assuring him it would be discussed "with the appropriate officials."[14] Cadieux wanted the correspondence to end. Vezina, however, was dogged. Only two days later, Vezina wrote back to Cadieux reiterating the sensibility of providing CAPIC with a grant to take the investigation off the government's hands. Vezina also appended a detailed budget, which included lines for office space rental costs, salaries for the director and secretary, stationary, equipment, and printing costs, generous expense accounts for "Auto travel, Air travel, lunches, etc." and "Miscellaneous Items and Expenses Incurred," as well as an "Apartment in Ottawa for Director." Whereas Vezina had quoted $20,000 in his letter to Hellyer, the budget proposed to Cadieux ran to $37,290.[15]

C.A.P.I.C.

canadian aerial phenomena investigations committee

p.o. box 98, postal stn. A, scarboro, ontario, canada

SUBSIDY BUDGET ESTIMATE

1. Rent of Office in Ottawa	12 mo. @ $250.00/mo.	$3,000.00/year
2. Salary for Director	12 mo. @ $100.00/week	$5,200.00/year
3. Salary for Secretary	12 mo. @ $ 80.00/week	$4,100.00/year
4. Publication	6 issues @ $900.00/issue	$4,500.00/year
5. Stationery, press releases, , and other printing costs -	or an offset press to do it ourselves	$4,000.00/year
6. Typewriters	2 @ $400.00 each	$ 800.00
7. Telephone	12 mo. @ $35.00/mo.	$ 420.00/year
8. Telex communication system - Toronto, Ottawa, Vancouver -	12 mo. @ $50.00 each per mo.	$1,800.00/year
9. Supplies used for Telex	12mo. @ $50.00 each per month	$1,800.00/year
10. Photostatic copier	1 @ $250.00	$ 250.00
11. Adding Machine	1 @ $300.00	$ 300.00
12. Office Equipment	- filing cabinets, desks, chairs, etc.	$4,000.00
13. Hydro Bill	12 mo. @ $50.00/mo.	$ 600.00/year
14. Expense account	- Auto travel, Air travel, lunches, etc.	$4,000.00/year
15. Apartment in Ottawa for Director	12 mo. @ $135.00/mo	$1,520.00/year
16. Miscellaneous Items and Expenses Incurred		$5,000.00/year
	TOTAL BUDGET	$37,290.00

Of this budget, $9,350.00 (if we are supplied with an offset machine) will be removed from the second year's expenses as they are equipment we will be using year after year.

Naturally, these estimates are for new equipment, but we will be able to do the job quite well with used equipment if necessary.

CHAIRMAN: A.K. VEZINA

SENIOR DIRECTOR: L. BLUESTEIN DIRECTOR: D. ELY 000138

Figure 5.1 | Budget for an independent, citizen UFO investigation, proposed by CAPIC chairman Allen K. Vezina to the minister of national defence.

Again, Cadieux replied with a standard response: "As previously advised, your representations are being investigated."[16] It would only be another two months before Cadieux succeeded Hellyer as defence minister and facilitated the transfer from the DND to the NRC, an act which, in Vezina's eyes, earned him CAPIC's Booby of the Year Award.

Vezina's letters, despite their antagonistic tone, reveal a feeling commonly held among citizens interested in the topic: that the government was not taking UFOs seriously and was shirking its duty to properly investigate all potential threats and follow up on scientific leads with an open mind. Unfortunately for CAPIC, the tone of Vezina's letters meant that Cadieux and the DND dismissed the organization as "crack-pots."

Vezina's tone was especially ill-advised considering that RCAF wing commander D.F. Robertson, who had drafted the original ministerial inquiry between Cadieux and Drury, had also written that since "the general public is becoming more interested in unusual aerial objects which can be neither identified nor explained … [m]any private citizens, many of whom are exceptionally well qualified, are either carrying out personal and independent research studies on UFOs, or have joined organisations established for this purpose."[17] Robertson had intended that any discussion of the Canadian UFO investigation after its transfer to the NRC should include mention of these "exceptionally well qualified" citizens, as they would undoubtedly have something to offer. After his exchange with CAPIC, however, it is doubtful that Cadieux would have placed Vezina in this category.

Another case from Alberta surely added to the government's doubt about the public's qualifications. The Canadian Forces base in Calgary forewarned CFHQ in Ottawa about William Albert Small, a man "actively engaged in the investigation of UFOs as a centennial project." Small was upset with the "passive" response he had received to his previous inquiries to the government and therefore intended to "visit Ottawa in the near future to contact senior governmental and defence officials." The memo was clear about how the government should approach him: "Mr Small is a crank and should be treated as such."[18] DND officials and NRC scientists thought very little of the public's qualifications on this matter, and so it is unlikely that those departments would have categorized any of them as "exceptionally well qualified."

Yet, citizens might make different judgments about expertise in this case. As explored in Chapter 3, many citizens turned to independently run UFO clubs, seeing these organizations' leaders and members as more trustworthy and knowledgeable. For another example, the *Newmarket Era* published a short piece around this time announcing that a Mrs Beverley Hall, who had reported several UFO sightings in the area, was to give a talk to a group of students in grades four through eight at a public school.[19] This aspect of how the UFO phenomenon was handled rarely makes it into official accounts: namely that over the years, some educators hosted guest talks on UFOs, usually by local residents who rarely had any formal training in this kind of work. Nevertheless, the fact of having seen a UFO and reported it made such witnesses, in some minds, experts on the matter, so much so that some public schools welcomed them.

Hollywood also continued to deliver during this time. The year 1968 saw the release of *Planet of the Apes*[20] along with Stanley Kubrick's *2001: A Space Odyssey* – two milestones in science fiction. Kubrick's film depicts an intelligent alien civilization that was responsible for initiating key evolutionary changes in the human race.[21] *2001* found the perfect companion in Erich von Däniken's best-selling book *Chariots of the Gods?* which claimed that many of the world's oldest structures and technologies could only have been possible through alien intervention during ancient times.[22] This theme would be followed up in later media, such as the more recent History Channel show *Ancient Aliens.* In other words, even if the Canadian government was mostly unwilling to engage with citizens about UFOs, and even less willing to give them classified information, then by this time, these same citizens had plenty of other places to turn to for speculation about the origins of what they were seeing in the skies. This kind of media filled in the gaps left by government correspondence.

DECLASSIFICATION

The National Research Council quickly settled into its passive role. In February 1968, Drury again wrote to Cadieux confirming that the NRC had "agreed to act as the repository of reports of unidentified flying objects ... [and that] investigations by NRC, if any, of these reports will depend on the degree of scientific interest in each case."[23] This wording left the NRC a great deal of leeway to decide on their level of interest in the topic. Peter Millman, for one, made his interest clear in a number of letters to colleagues and citizens. In March, he replied to A.F. McQuarrie, the officer in charge at the Gonzales Observatory in Victoria: "Apart from the fireball and meteor reports, we do not solicit unidentified object reports and we only investigate reports that seem to be of scientific interest."[24] The following month, Millman responded to Captain S.B. Goddard, of CFB Penhold, regarding an incident at a local farm: "It is very helpful to have someone run these things down to earth. I am afraid that the more I study this field, the more I realize how much hoaxing has occurred on the part of pranksters and publicity seekers."[25]

Nevertheless, Millman did take extra measures to make the collection of reports more efficient. He drew on one of the NRC's "associate committees," a program first established in 1917 and finally terminated in 1989. While in operation, associate committees served "as instruments to provide the opportunity to bring together experts for the study, coordination, and promotion of research on problems of national significance. When an associate committee studied a particular problem, it collected and collated pertinent information, delegated research problems, coordinated research, and suggested new avenues of research."[26] Millman outlined this program to the RCMP commissioner, writing that the NRC's associate committee on meteorites had been established "for some years" and that it would assist in collecting and cataloguing reports.

Members of this associate committee were scientists in a variety of fields scattered across Canada. There was usually representation from a university or observatory in each province, with the NRC in Ottawa serving as the link for Ontario and the northern territories. The committee members met in Ottawa regularly to discuss their latest findings. For instance, the twelfth meeting of the associate committee on meteorites took place on 5 April 1968 and included seventeen members representing various universities and observatories, the Royal Astronomical Society, the Geological Survey of Canada, the Royal Ontario Museum, the DRB, the DND, and the Department of Indian Affairs and Northern Development.[27] One member, University of Manitoba geologist Edward Leith, wrote to Millman a week after the meeting. Leith had encountered the latest article on the Michalak case and joked: "You can see that it must be an authentic 'saucer' because of the drawing made at the site!!!!"[28]

Other committee members likely shared Leith's and Millman's views of the subject.

Millman made it clear to the RCMP commissioner that his, and the committee's, real interest was in the scientific study of the nature of meteoritic objects, and their rapid recovery when found. UFO reports might be useful under this umbrella as a contribution to tracking meteorites and fireballs, but "all sighting reports that do not seem to refer to fireballs or meteors will be placed on the non-meteoritic sighting file which will be unclassified, as in general we do not deal with classified material in our research program."[29]

The creation of the non-meteoritic file marked a turning point in how the government responded to UFO reports and interacted with citizens looking for information. It was the first step in the process of declassification of Canada's UFO material, which Millman continued to spearhead. Greg Eghigian has written that the work of ufology has changed over the decades since the beginning of its modern period in 1947, and has come to include two distinct tasks. The first and better-known task, articulated in the early days, is about determining the nature of UFOs and whether or not they were extraterrestrial in origin. Part of this work has involved pressuring the government to reveal what it knows about the phenomenon, and ufologists have been successful at times at forcing the government to give up classified documents (an example of this follows below). According to Eghigian, "there has been a clear and consistent consensus among UFO investigators and enthusiasts that government authorities have to be pressured to disclose critical information they have kept from the public." This situation has engendered hostility and mistrust of government action, and contributed to the rise of citizen investigations. "Thus," Eghigian continues, "indignation over state secrecy has given birth to a second-order of work for UFO investigators, namely explaining and combating government crypticness [*sic*]."[30]

Ufologists also ran into these issues of secrecy and institutional inertia when attempting to access UFO documents. The standard practice since the beginning of Canada's involvement in the early 1950s was to place such documents under classification; and, despite the fact that the government decided soon afterward that UFOs were not a security risk, the documents remained classified. This was a frustrating situation for ufologists attempting to access information. Authors writing books about UFOs certainly helped to fuel these tensions. For example, Donald Keyhoe, perhaps the most noteworthy writer on the subject during the 1950s, began referring to "the secrecy group" as a way of describing what he concluded was a conspiracy within, and among, the world's governments.[31]

However, the documents at Library and Archives Canada tell a slightly different story, at least at a certain point. Millman was actually quite eager to declassify the UFO material. He thought of it as a burden that was best dumped in someone else's lap. Declassification was one way to stop the flood of citizen inquiries. If citizens could access the documents themselves, through an unclassified file of sighting reports, then there would be no further need for Millman and his colleagues to remain involved.

The DND was even more eager. In November 1967, Brigadier Ross wrote to the Directorate of Information Services noting the increasing number of "requests from private citizens, reporters and civilian organizations for the release of UFO material" and that the normal practice within the DND was to withhold material that contained confidential police reports and information from private sources. "However," Ross argued, "as a result of the nation-wide publicity being given to UFOs, it has become advisable to adjust this policy in order to avoid giving the impression that DND is 'hiding something' and attempting to suppress the release of UFO information to the general public."[32] This is the same Ross who earlier had lamented the NRC's lacklustre approach to the investigation, and who maintained, at least, a personal interest in the topic.

These early calls within the government for declassification pertained not merely to current sighting reports but also to older material, like the Project Second Storey documents. In March 1968, Millman wrote to the DRB requesting the declassification of the PSS material: "This Committee has been dormant for many years and I see no reason why the attached material could not be declassified and transferred to the NRC for their use as they see fit."[33]

The DRB obviously agreed with Millman's assessment, as they granted the declassification the following month.[34] In addition to the Project Second Storey material, Wilbert Smith's final report on Project Magnet was also declassified. Since the mid-1960s, several researchers, most notably Arthur Bray, had again started writing to various departments asking for information about Smith's work. Millman must have thought that including the Project Magnet material would also solve the problem of these specific inquiries. Millman's "Note on Project Magnet Report," dated 9 May 1968 and tacked to the report's cover, repeated a previous conclusion: "I have been informed by the Department of Transport that although Project Magnet was officially authorized by the Department, work on this Project was carried out almost entirely by Mr. W.B. Smith and was in the nature of a spare-time activity. The conclusions reached in this report are entirely those of Mr. Smith, and do not represent an official opinion of either the Department of Transport or of the Second Storey Committee."

What Millman and the citizen UFO investigators were battling was a tradition within the Canadian government of secrecy of information. Ann Rees describes secrecy as "an old and welcome friend" of the Canadian government.[35] Canada evolved as a country with a "'culture of secrecy' and citizen exclusion from government decision making."[36] Whereas the US introduced modern access to information legislation in 1966, Canada followed Britain's lead and maintained its right to withhold information from the public using the mandate of the Official Secrets Act. Americans hold "a powerful belief that citizen access to government information is a right." The Canadian government does not share this belief.[37] Canada adopted Britain's version of its secrecy legislation wholesale in the late nineteenth century and, notwithstanding minor modifications in the years since, it remained entirely intact until 1983, when Canada's own Access to Information Act (ATIA) was introduced.

This is a key difference between Canada and the US, precipitated by certain political events. The American law was the result of pressure by journalists fighting for better access to government information, especially in the wake of the assassination of President John F. Kennedy. The law was further "strengthened by several amendments during the 1970s in response to the loss of public trust over the unpopular war in Vietnam and President Richard Nixon's resignation over Watergate."[38] Americans had clear reasons to demand better access to government information. The Canadian government, however, was not as willing to oblige, and waited until 1983 to enact its own legislation. To the credit of Canadian citizen UFO investigators, it is not hard to imagine how frustrating this situation may have been, especially given that their American counterparts were able to file access-to-information requests as early as 1966. Many of the same pressures in the American context applied in Canada too, especially the decline of public trust in government. However, government secrecy was so entrenched in Canada that UFO investigators were stonewalled as a matter of course.

A FLAP OF CITIZEN INVESTIGATORS

If Millman and others at the NRC and DND thought declassifying the Project Second Storey and Project Magnet material would stop the citizen inquiries for good, they were sorely mistaken. In June 1968, Arthur Bray again wrote to the DND asking for information. His letter did not make it into the archives, but the department's director of operations, Colonel W.W. Turner, wrote a lengthy and revealing internal memo discussing the inquiry.

Bray had pointed out that his "close perusal" of the files transferred to the NRC revealed that no sighting reports prior to March 1965 were included. Rather, the only ones accessible were dated 1965–68. To account for this discrepancy, Turner explained that "prior to 1965 Air Defence Command (ADC) in cooperation with NORAD was the recognized defence agency primarily concerned with UFOs." As a result of their own "numerous" investigations, ADC had determined there was no security threat and thereupon transferred responsibility to CFHQ. Turner admitted that ADC "did not forward their UFO files to CFHQ and unofficial talks held with ADC suggest that the files were destroyed in accordance with normal disposal instructions." This means that a significant amount of UFO material in ADC's possession was destroyed as part of routine protocol. Clearly, the DND and other departments were simultaneously receiving UFO reports and debating what to do with them, but the timeline Turner suggests helps to explain why the archival material prior to 1965 is patchy.

Bray also lamented that the files which the NRC did receive were incomplete; he knew this because he had also examined RCMP files that listed sightings not referenced in the NRC material. Turner again had a ready explanation for this discrepancy: upon learning that the NRC was to take over responsibility for the UFO files, the RCMP decided to retain its own reports and correspondence rather than transfer them to the NRC. In the event that anyone from the NRC wished to see an RCMP report they were welcome to do so, but the files would remain with the originating department. This worked for all parties, as the "NRC advised that they did not think that the RCMP reports would be of any value, and if they felt that the reports were necessary they would negotiate directly with the RCMP." In other words, the NRC was not overly concerned that the files they received were incomplete, as they had no real intention of conducting investigations anyway.

This confirmed Bray's own observation that "very few sighting reports were actually investigated, and this is no doubt due to lack of funds and staff." Turner clarified this statement: it was true, in part, "however, our operational and scientific staff agree that it would be senseless to become engaged in a large scale, expensive investigation where no tangible evidence exists. The majority of UFO reports consists [*sic*] of information of objects moving quickly across the sky and disappearing [and so] it is suggested that to investigate such a report would be difficult if not impossible." Turner concluded his memo with instructions: "It is the opinion of this office that [Bray's letter is] designed for sensationalism purposes and suggests that DND are concealing or hiding something. It is recommended that ... Bray be advised of the information contained herein in order that any reference to DND reflects facts and not suppositions."[39]

Despite Millman's hopes for the value of an unclassified UFO file, researchers like Bray were clearly still disappointed with what they found. Nevertheless, the NRC and other departments forged ahead, trying their best to ignore the UFO issue altogether. During the remainder of 1968, witnesses continued to submit sighting reports. The RCMP maintained their vigilance in collecting reports, which invariably included a statement on the witness's reliability. As mentioned above, the majority of RCMP reports described observers as generally reliable. Reports of July sightings at Fort Resolution, Northwest Territories, in one case described the witness as a "steady, truthful individual and quite reliable"[40] and in another as "not the type to imagine or invent the sighting described."[41] A sighting report later that month from Amos, Quebec, attributed high reliability to the witness because of his "good knowledge of astronomy" and occupation as a notary with the county court.[42]

Amid the flood of sighting reports were inquiries for information. Colonel L.A. Bourgeois, the DND's director of information, received a letter requesting information about Wilbert Smith, his flying saucer observatory, and four of his colleagues who, so the writer had heard, had worked on Project Magnet. The writer, his name redacted, also asked for information about Omond Solandt, the DRB's previous chairman, and C.J. Mackenzie, the NRC's previous president, as well as records of UFO sightings from 1947 to the present.[43] This kind of citizen letter is typical in terms of the sheer number of requests it makes of the government official to whom it is addressed (if there is an addressee at all) but atypical in that the writer knew the specific names of a number of officials.

In addition to Vezina's organization CAPIC, other citizen investigators were coming on the scene. In October 1968, Donald Golding wrote to the DND's chief of defence staff on behalf of Canadian UFO Research (CUFOR), an organization based in Oshawa, Ontario. In the first half of the letter, Golding described seeing two bright objects in the sky that orbited one another. Thinking they might be US satellites, he contacted NASA, but an official there told him that such satellites would orbit beyond the limits of the naked eye. "The only thing I can suggest," Golding concluded, "is a couple of space stations maybe U.S.S.R. I must make clear that these two objects do not fit the right pattern to be U.F.O."

Having brought up the subject of UFOs, however, Golding felt the need to expound further: "I must say that in dealing with U.F.O. we must keep in mind, that we are dealing with matter and anti-matter objects." Golding then connected this realization with the government's decision the previous month to terminate its Intense Neutron Generator program, which conducted basic research in nuclear physics. "It is true that the generator is costly," Golding wrote, "how ever [*sic*] what we will learn from it in regards to anti-matter makes it worth while [*sic*] building. This country is making a very bad mistake by dropping the neutron generator project!"[44] For Golding, the government was failing its citizens not just when it came to UFOs but also in its commitments to basic science that might enrich the nation. And, of course, these two ideas were entwined.

Golding sent another document to the DND around the same time, likely attached to this letter. "Unidentified Flying Objects Report: 3 Year Study" was dated 1968 and consisted of five pages, the first of which was a title page. Perhaps the report contained more pages that did not make it into the archives. The one thing that is clear is that somebody at the NRC did read it, as they underlined all the spelling errors in the text. Again, it is unlikely that the presentation of this document added any credibility to the writer's cause. The second page contained a preface: "There are meney [*sic*] things about the universe unknown. Man is not the king of universe [*sic*] in which he lives. How can he even think such a silly idea as that [*sic*]. For we are but a small stone in a ocean of meney stars [*sic*]." The third page contained a suggested reading list of books on UFOs, while the fourth page was a partial photocopy of an unidentified summary of Project Blue Book. Above the photocopy, Golding expressed his astonishment that the USAF had spent $20 million on the program (it is unclear where he came by this number) and surmised that Blue Book was nothing more than a cover-up for the CIA. The last page contained Golding's conclusion:

> When our research started three years ago, we could not understand, how these unidentified objects could appear and disappear in mid air [*sic*]. How ever [*sic*] we now beleave [*sic*] to have to this problem, an answer which also explains ghost. In June 1962 Columbia and Brookhaven physicist [*sic*], completed an exeriment [*sic*] in the 33 billion volt atom smasher, that proved the neutrino particle is as closest to nothing as an [*sic*] thing can get. It has no charge but it does have a definte [*sic*] mass, and can pass though all forms of matter as if it didn't exist. now [*sic*] then if an anti matter electron can exist then so must the anti matter atom. Hence life may exist as we know it in anti matter form, hence some u.f.o. may be from the 4th diemention [*sic*]. What ever [*sic*] the case may be U.F.O. dose [*sic*] exist.[45]

In early 1969, another citizen investigation group entered the fray, albeit much more subtly. The Winnipeg-based Canadian Aerial Phenomena Research Organization (CAPRO) reported a 2 February 1969 sighting in Ste. Rose, Manitoba. CAPRO submitted the report on their own unique sighting form, which contained an internal file number and a host of meteorological information.[46] The report was very detailed and professionally composed, quite akin to Robertson's definition of "exceptionally well qualified" citizen investigators. Unfortunately for CAPRO, it was too little, too late. The NRC took no interest in the report other than to file it away with the others. Given Millman's entire disbelief in the matter of UFOs, it also likely did not help that Brian Cannon, a CAPRO member, wrote to him a month later admitting that the group had placed Stefan Michalak under hypnosis to glean information regarding the Falcon Lake incident. The results, Cannon wrote, "were about as expected. The story remained virtually the same with small differences although it is unfortunate that we waited this long to accomplish what may have been, a meaningful part of the investigation."[47]

In March, yet another citizen group made its presence known. Thomas James Cameron, handling public relations for the Montreal

UFO Study Group (MUFOSG), wrote directly to the top: Prime Minister Pierre Trudeau. MUFOSG had formed two years earlier and had more than two hundred paid members. The organization's aim was to investigate sightings and study reports to learn "the origin and/or construction of this phenomena; be it psychological or physical, natural or man-made, terrestrial or extra-terrestrial." The purposes of the letter, Cameron wrote, were information and cooperation. MUFOSG was "attempting to work along the lines of the now disbanded 'PROJECT MAGNET' – a former Canadian Government-sponsored investigating body, but on a much smaller scale, having neither the funds, nor the time (all persons involved, having outside full-time employment) to spare."[48]

Cameron and the others in the group were obviously unaware of how small an operation Magnet was to begin with given that it was essentially the work of Smith alone, using borrowed equipment. Cameron expressed the group's wish to meet in person with Trudeau, as well as with Leo Cadieux and Paul Hellyer, to discuss the matter. Six weeks later, Trudeau's appointments secretary, Mrs G.J. Cook, acknowledged the letter and informed MUFOSG that the prime minister's schedule was unfortunately "heavily committed" during the next several months and so a meeting would be impossible.[49]

The various citizen UFO groups continued to collect and report sightings, occasionally asking the DND or the NRC for further information. In April, CAPRO's Brian Cannon wrote to the commanding officer at CFB Esquimalt to ask whether the facility's radar had tracked an object in the skies over Victoria, British Columbia. Witnesses saw the object expel "some form of 'glowing' material that fell to the ground near a transformer."[50]

The same month, Arthur Bray again submitted his thoughts. He wrote to Bruce McIntosh, a scientist in the same division as Peter Millman at the NRC. Bray expressed his displeasure at certain remarks that McIntosh had made in the pages of the *Ottawa Citizen* regarding a 22 April 1969 UFO sighting near Ottawa that involved an object in the sky that looked like "a huge drinking cup turned upside-down."[51] McIntosh dismissed the sighting as a misidentified helicopter, despite the fact that the witness worked at the DND as a mechanic and had disagreed with McIntosh's assessment. Bray told McIntosh that "your conclusion would seem to be entirely unwarranted" and stands "on no apparent evidence to support it." Bray further lamented the "misinformation as well as lack of information" plaguing the public. "It is my belief," he wrote, "that government agencies and private researchers should work hand in hand in studying the UFO problem because often some information is available to one group which is not available to the other, and thus we stand a better chance of an eventual solution to the mystery."[52]

In May, CAPRO's director, Brian Cannon, again wrote to the DND to follow up on his previous letter. Having received no reply to his inquiry with CFB Esquimalt other than a form letter from a Captain Frewer, now he sought clarification on who exactly was now handling the UFO investigation: "We were under the impression that the matter had been turned over to Dr. Peter Millman and his staff at the National Research Council. However, I interpret Capt. Frewer's remarks as to indicate that the Defence Dept. is handling at least a portion of the cases."[53] Despite the best efforts of people like Arthur Bray and Brian Cannon, and their associated organizations, the "doubletalk" and "go-arounds" persisted.

MR X

In Gallup's first survey of the Canadian public regarding UFOs, in 1974, 67 per cent of people had heard of UFOs while 8 per cent thought they had seen one. When asked if they were real or just people's imagination, nearly 30 per cent had no answer, 15 per cent said they did not know, almost 20 per cent thought they were just imaginary, and 36 per cent thought they were real.[54] What this says is that more people believed that UFOs were real than that they were not. In addition, more than 1.8 million Canadians thought they had seen one, not an insignificant number. These numbers are much more conservative than those of the US Gallup poll in 1973 wherein 94 per cent of Americans had heard of UFOs, 11 per cent thought they had seen one, and 54 per cent thought they were real.[55] Of course, by this time, another momentous event had occurred: the moon landing, which no doubt helped to inflame the imaginations of UFO enthusiasts.

By 1978, the numbers had increased: 81 per cent of Canadians had heard of UFOs, 10 per cent thought they had seen one, and 46 per cent thought they were real.[56] The following year, Gallup asked Canadians to indicate their belief in UFOs: almost 61 per cent responded positively.[57] These rising numbers were reflected in local media. For instance, the *Winnipeg Tribune* ran a monthly writing contest, with the subject for March 1978 being UFOs. Contestants were given the beginning of a story about a man who saw a UFO while sitting at his desk job, and were required to finish the story. The winning entries would be published.[58] The timing of this article was likely inspired by the release the previous year of Steven Spielberg's *Close Encounters of the Third Kind*.[59] Added to this were other recent Hollywood releases: *Star Wars*, *The Andromeda Strain*, *Capricorn One*, *Alien*, various *Planet of the Apes* sequels, and *In Search of…*, a television series hosted by Leonard Nimoy, of *Star Trek* fame.[60] The 1970s were a veritable cornucopia of science fiction films with extraterrestrial characters and plots, no doubt contributing to this rising belief among Americans and Canadians. The government, certainly, was not prepared to divulge much information; as such, these numbers indicate that Canadians were finding information about UFOs from other sources: news reports, UFO clubs and citizen investigators, films, books, and TV shows.

However, despite these rising numbers indicating positive belief in UFOs, the phenomenon had a far less significant impact on the daily lives of most Canadians than upon those of the few enthusiasts mentioned here. UFOs held a very special allure for a small group of Canadian citizen investigators, such as the enigmatic "Mr X."

In May 1979, following an almost ten-year break in the kind of brazen citizen inquiries the government had been used to receiving, a new citizen investigator arrived on the scene. Based in Kingston, Ontario, Mr X wrote to the RCMP commissioner on letterhead describing him as the "Consulting Resologist of the Res Bureaux" and listing a Kingston post office box address. The "Res Bureaux" was his formal organization which, for a number of years in the late 1970s and into the 1980s, produced and posted to subscribers a printed bulletin containing the latest news regarding all manner of Fortean occurrences such as falls of frogs from the sky, giant worms on the ocean floor and, of course, UFO sightings.[61]

In his three-page letter, Mr X explained that he had researched the UFO phenomenon for five years and been unsuccessful at eliciting any straight answer on the subject from the Canadian government. He lamented the incompleteness of the NRC's UFO files and the DRB's decision to withhold documents pertaining to Project Second Storey. In his previous contacts with the RCMP, Mr X came to the conclusion that "the 'policy' of whether or not copies of UFO reports might be obtained is often determined not by any Force, Division, nor

Sub-Division commander but merely the Detachment commander or officer-in-charge." Furthermore, Mr X wrote,

> As I have been reading UFO reports made by or transmitted by members of the Royal Canadian Mounted Police for the last five years, I have gained considerable insight into the difficulties arising and confronting investigating members who are not experienced in UFO investigations. Many reports are of admirable quality and most professional, whereas others are regretfully lacking in the most basic of details and full of erroneous data. It is a pity so few members of the Force cannot distinguish between Venus, Jupiter, Saturn, and Mars nor the stars. They might thus be able to re-assure confused witnesses and readily determine the identity of the UFO in many instances. One cannot expect members of the Force to be knowledgable [*sic*] in astronomy considering their many tasks; but, as I suspect they might benefit by having access to information on celestial phenomena, which I am aware is not always forthcoming from astronomers at the National Research Council.

Mr X concluded his letter with a list of questions. He first asked if the RCMP would disclose how many, and what kinds, of reports they had gathered under Project Second Storey, and whether or not any policy governing such disclosure actually existed. He also asked if it would be possible "to distribute a supplementary questionaire [*sic*] to all detachments, which would provide more detailed data than currently asked for by the [NRC] Meteor Centre." He further asked if a civilian liaison might be identified "through which information of UFO reports received by the [RCMP] might be made available to serious investigators."[62]

Unlike several previous citizen investigators, and despite his lamentations about government secrecy and incomplete files, Mr X's letter demonstrated that he had managed to obtain very detailed information about the government's involvement with the UFO phenomenon. He knew about the involvement of the Department of Transport with Project Magnet, and of the DRB with Project Second Storey. He was also aware of the transfer of files to the NRC in 1967, and had personal experience with how departments might give citizens the runaround, inadvertently or purposefully, when inquiring about the subject. Neither the RCMP nor any department, for that matter, had a clear policy on how to investigate or communicate UFO sightings, leaving the matter to the lowly investigator to puzzle out, whether or not that person had any specialized training that could give them insight into what witnesses might have seen. In short, Mr X's letter was a concise diagnosis of some of the main administrative problems that the Canadian government had allowed to develop when it came to UFO reports.

Perhaps to be expected, however, the RCMP did not seriously engage with Mr X's questions. An internal memo dated two weeks later indicated that the police force was more concerned about his pseudonym: "Although not in agreement with corresponding with an anonymous person on matters such as this, it is felt if Mr. X is serious about conducting a bona-fide study then he should present himself at this Headquarters and outline what he wants exactly and establish his credentials."[63]

Two weeks later, Inspector D. Chiarot replied to Mr X, noting that his request would not be considered because the RCMP did not feel it could offer "too much additional information" beyond what the NRC had in its possession. "However," Chiarot continued, "for further consideration to be given to your request, you would be required to appear at this Headquarters to establish that this information will be utilized for a serious, bona-fide study as well as produce your credentials and establish your identity."[64] The wording of Chiarot's letter is unique. Nowhere else in the archival UFO materials does a government department or agency indicate that a citizen inquirer need to establish that they are conducting a "bona-fide" study. The usual response was a form letter thanking the writer for their interest and assuring them that the inquiry would be passed to the appropriate department. Perhaps Inspector Chiarot thought this unusual request would dissuade Mr X from further correspondence, in the assumption that the standard of a bona-fide study would be too high to meet. If this was the case, then Chiarot and the RCMP were unaware of the tenacity of UFO investigators, however misplaced it may have been.

Mr X responded to Chiarot a week later. His two-page letter acknowledged the question of his name: "As my inquiry into UFOs and my signature are not the Force's normal fare, I would not doubt that it may have elicited some strong scepticism and probably some chuckles." However, he continued: "I would point out that my true and legal name is 'X' and enjoy its recognition as such by Canada, the United Kingdom, and the United States of America. Its adoption was one of precedent for patent and copyright purposes; but, for more mundane matters, I still use my former Christian name as circumstances dictate." As such, Mr X wrote that he was including with his letter a copy of the court order changing his name; however, Library and Archives Canada (LAC) archivists removed this document from the archives at some point as it contained personal information. Obviously, Mr X was aware of how preposterous he appeared and that this would not help his appeal for information.

Despite the oddity of his persona, Mr X's letter again demonstrated a very clear grasp of the bureaucratic dynamics at work in the Canadian government. "Often it is a lack of clear communication," he wrote, "between government departments and a lack of departmental responsibility being designated to a single agency that has scattered UFO reports into the archives of several ministries. Yet, each UFO report is of importance, for the number of UFO reports is not as large as some enthusiasts would hold." Mr X noted that no agency or department had ever undertaken any effort beyond collecting reports, and that it was a shame that agencies like the RCMP have "received little support from other agencies in clearing the identity of UFOs or passing their investigation over to others with the knowledge and resources to deal with their analysis."[65]

Chiarot took more than three weeks to respond. His letter was short and to the point: "Before giving further consideration to your request for access to our files on U.F.O. sightings, additional information will be required." Chiarot asked for information on Mr X's date and place of birth, as well as his previous residences and documentation in the form of "something tangible to indicate you are a qualified researcher into this subject."[66] Chiarot did not make explicit what such tangible documentation might comprise. Given that the government had previously dismissed other qualified investigators – people trained in physics or engineering, for instance – it is unclear what would have sufficed. As mentioned above, it was an unusual step to ask for such documentation at all, given that no other correspondence mentioned such a requirement. Perhaps this burden of proof turned out to be too high, as Mr X does not appear to have replied. However, it may also be the case that a letter of reply was removed from the archives because of the personal information provided.

Whatever the case, Mr X continued the struggle. In December 1983, the RCMP's information commissioner sent him a letter together with photocopies of their UFO file – the very same file now publicly available at LAC. Mr X had asked for copies of the entire file and had sent a money order in the amount of $176.75 to cover the cost. He was closely following developments regarding how information was handled and was ready to act on them, as the Access to Information Act had been approved earlier that year. Mr X wasted no time in making use of the new service, and it seems appropriate that one of the earliest requests concerned UFO reports. In other words, Mr X finally achieved a victory. He obtained the RCMP files that earlier had been denied him. However, it is unlikely that Mr X found anything revelatory in the documents. What is more interesting was his feeling that *something* was hidden or covered up, and that he needed to expose it.

Mr X's efforts, and the fact that he obtained nothing more than routine, mundane documentation, speaks to a greater change in how the public came to think about government secrecy and the state. Mark Fenster notes that advocates of government disclosure began using the term *transparency*: "the metaphor presumes a problem and suggests its logical solution: The distant, invisible state must be revealed to the public."[67] He characterizes this logic as the "transparency fix," which presumes that the state is a large, faceless bureaucracy that operates at a remove from the public and routinely withholds information. This is the problem that must be fixed by opening it up to public scrutiny, a problem that the "visibility metaphor" presents as commonsensical. It is a powerful metaphor, Fenster argues, but is fundamentally flawed and therefore doomed to failure.

The main problem with the transparency fix is that even many diehard disclosure advocates admit that some secrecy is necessary to protect the nation-state. This is evident in various letters that Canadian UFO investigators sent to the government. Many UFO enthusiasts request information even as they acknowledge that disclosure might not be possible given the interests of national security. However, once this concession is made, transparency becomes only one value competing among many others for the attention of bureaucrats and politicians. Unfortunately for the public, furthermore, secrecy is easier to justify than transparency given the serious and varied threats that the state anticipates. In the case of Canada specifically, with its long culture of secrecy, classification of documents is far easier to effect than declassification. Fenster argues that transparency thus becomes a problem in and of itself, as it "becomes a term of concealment and opacity that promises more than it can deliver."[68] Transparency advocates can never muster as much political support as those advocating for national security. Even if disclosure advocates articulated the transparency fix in its strongest form – in terms of a completely open government that allows absolute access to all information – there remains sufficient doubt about the feasibility of such a plan that it becomes easy to dismiss. In other words, according to Fenster, those Canadians who requested UFO information from the government – and particularly given the way in which they did so, from the level of transparency they requested to how they presented themselves personally – were, in a way, also responsible for the responses they received.

THE NRC'S FINAL REPORT

A good sense of the NRC's position on UFOs by the late 1970s comes from an undated article titled "UFO's: What Are They?"[69] The author was A.G. McNamara, head of the NRC's Planetary Sciences Section and a close colleague of Peter Millman. The three-page report provided a select overview of the history of the UFO phenomenon as well as its terminology, and attempted to provide the most compelling scientific explanations for sightings known at the time. It is unclear for what purpose or audience McNamara wrote the article, but by this point it provided no novel information; rather, it rehearsed phrases well known to any serious ufologist. "There are some people," McNamara wrote, "often called 'believers,' who take the position that if [a UFO] is not identified [through investigation] then it must be of extra-terrestrial or supernatural origin … Actually, in the great majority of UFO reports there is no definite yes or no answer and there never can be, simply because the data recorded are either lacking entirely or insufficient to make an interpretation. The proper scientific attitude is to declare the observation to be indeterminate."

McNamara traced a lineage that included medieval beliefs about "witches, demons, wizards, fairies, ghosts, elves," as well as the mystery airship sightings in the US in the late nineteenth century and the 1947 Kenneth Arnold sighting, which he dismissed as "mountain top mirages." Despite this long lineage, McNamara concluded that, "throughout the entire course of human history there has never been an authentic case of physical contact with an alien spacecraft or of the recovery of any artifact of clearly extraterrestrial origin."

Having set up what he considered the relevant background to the study, McNamara's article proceeded to "examine the physical and psychological characteristics of the human 'instrument' to try to understand its sources of error and limits of observation." In other words, McNamara found the root of the UFO problem in the unreliability of the human observer. He wrote about the physical limits of the eye and how easily they can lead someone to see a "figment of the imagination." The eye-brain "mechanism" is also faulty, he wrote, in that the brain only receives a fraction of the information the eye processes, confirming the old adage that "the human sees what he wants to see, what he is conditioned to see, and what he expects to see" given that the partial information is filtered through what is familiar and known.

McNamara condemned human psychology for fostering the secret hope "that a wise and benevolent superior civilization is near at hand to help solve the crushing problems of the world." He equally condemned the mass media for their role in deluging the average citizen with information until "the individual loses his capacity for individual reason and follows the flock." McNamara described the feedback loop that media can generate when reporting on a sighting, which encourages others to report their own sightings, again and again, until "the original (erroneous) interpretation of the report as an extraterrestrial spacecraft lives on and may even be quoted and re-quoted throughout the UFO literature as a 'classical unsolved' case."

Having dealt with the question of the human instrument, McNamara finished his analysis by debunking the various natural origin explanations for UFO sightings. These included misidentified sightings of such things as "bright planets and stars, meteors, aircraft landing lights and navigation lights, high altitude balloons, aircraft contrails, sun glints from aircraft, chemical seeding experiments in the ionosphere from rockets, satellite re-entries, unusual cloud formations, birds, insects, power line reflections, reflections from windows and other surfaces, aurora, sundogs, mirages, – the list is almost endless." He added that photographs and radar readings are also unreliable, given their tendency to malfunction and produce anomalous effects.

McNamara likewise dismissed "local effects of UFO landings" as nothing more than, again, misidentified natural phenomena (in cases of broken tree limbs and depressions in the soil) or "the action of the fairy-ring mushroom" (in the case of rings of burnt grass). As for close encounter cases, he was clear: "No such cases have ever been adequately substantiated."

All this is not to say that McNamara was a total unbeliever: "few scientists doubt that there are probably many planets in our galaxy with intelligent life forms." They are just unlikely to be here, on Earth, given the many factors keeping them apart, such as massive interplanetary distances and the time it must take to develop such advanced technology. In his summary, McNamara was unequivocal: "Two thousand years of observations and thirty years of rather intensive collection (15,000 reports in the U.S.A.F. Project Bluebook and 1500 in Canada) and examination of reports have not yielded any positive sighting or artifact of extra-terrestrial origin." About the only thing UFO reports had been good for, he argued, was assisting with the data collection on "meteor research and the recording of rare atmospheric phenomena."[70]

In other words, McNamara's report was a concise summary of views that had been articulated by many people since the early 1950s. Millman had expressed much the same in many letters to colleagues and citizens. It is clear that for the NRC scientists, UFOs were nothing but an intrusion into the daily work of normal science – perhaps useful, in isolated incidents, for providing additional information about known meteorological effects, but otherwise a waste of time.

The timing of this article was not a coincidence. Though undated, the article's bibliography cites other works up to 1975, so it was likely published in the late 1970s. The years around 1980 were another major hinge point for the Canadian UFO investigation. Beginning in that decade, nearly the only documents newly collected or remaining in the archives were sighting reports. Almost no other kind of document was retained, whether an official memo or a letter from a citizen. It is unclear exactly why this is the case, but it was probably a combination of at least two factors. First, the NRC may have continued to receive letters, but simply did not respond to and retain them as they had done with previous correspondence, and so they did not end up in the archives. Second, it is possible that by this point, due to the NRC's passive involvement and clearly unenthusiastic attitude (and the stock responses that every other department sent out), citizens simply stopped sending their reports to the government and turned in greater numbers to independent investigators. As to the NRC's involvement in UFO investigation, McNamara's report likely served as the final nail in the coffin, affording the council the same kind of rationale for ending its active involvement as that which the members of the US Project Blue Book gleaned from the 1969 Condon Report. McNamara's report was the justification for the unofficial termination of the NRC's "investigation" – an investigation the organization never wanted in the first place and a termination it had sought since the DND thrust the responsibility upon them.

THE END OF THE INVESTIGATION

This is not to say that from 1980 to the end of sighting report collection in 1995, the Canadian government did not receive a single citizen letter. There were inevitably a few that trickled in, but compared to previous decades the volume was substantially reduced: during this period the NRC only received about a half dozen unique letters. Considering how many it had received prior to McNamara's report, it was a drastic difference. One of these exchanges was the one outlined above, concerning Mr X's access to RCMP files.

Another was a January 1984 letter that a mathematics professor at Trent University, in Peterborough, Ontario, sent to the minister of defence, only to have it immediately forwarded to the NRC. "Our official science," the professor wrote, "claims that all UFO's can be explained by something originating on Earth, since the distance to the closest star is 4 light years away and since it is believed that Einstein has proved that the speed of light cannot be exceeded." Like others before him, including Wilbert Smith, this mathematics professor claimed to have discovered new physical laws governing the universe. In short, he believed that the speed of light was not always constant, that it varied in other parts of the universe. As such, interstellar travel would actually be possible and therefore, he wrote, "some of the UFO's come from the cosmos and that the illegal immigrants from the cosmos are now citizens of several countries, including Canada." What the professor was apparently trying to explain was a potential security risk: "Since the UFO's avoided official contacts, there is reason to believe that their intentions towards us are not friendly ones and that they might plan the biological deterioration of the Earth's people by radioactive fallouts over the densely populated areas and/or by the sophisticated radiesthesian and ultrasonic equipment used against neighbours by those who have already settled among us."[71] There is no record of a government response to this letter.

In 1986, Gallup again asked Canadians about UFOs and the results, curiously, reverted to previous levels. Almost 70 per cent of the respondents had heard of them, a decline of 10 per cent, and only 36 per cent thought they were real. Then, two years later, the numbers rose again, to their highest values so far: nearly 84 per cent of Canadians had heard of UFOs, almost 11 per cent thought they had seen one, and about 47 per cent thought they were real.

This was again reflected in local media. For example, in 1986 the University of Alberta student newspaper, the *Gateway*, reported on a photographer who had travelled across Canada and the US taking portraits of UFO believers. His photos were collected into a book, with a foreword written by Tom Wolfe, author of the bestselling book *The Right Stuff*. There is no identifiable angle to the piece other than to indicate the breadth of interest in UFOs that still persisted, and that the photographer himself saw his work as "a bid for tolerance."[72]

The 1980s also saw their fair share of Hollywood media, which helped stoke the imaginations and passions of curious ufologists. Two *Star Wars* sequels were released, along with *E.T. the Extra-Terrestrial*, several *Star Trek* films, a sequel to *Aliens*, and the action film *Predator*.[73] Beyond films, a couple of landmark books were published: Whitley Strieber's *Communion*, a best-selling tale of alien abduction which, to many believers, seemed terrifyingly accurate; and *The Roswell Incident*, by William Moore and Charles Berlitz.[74] The story of Roswell is a strange one. The event itself happened in 1947, but interest quickly died off. The public did not really become aware of the story until the publication of Moore and Berlitz's book in 1980. It is likely that the fluctuations in UFO belief among Canadians surveyed in the Gallup polls resulted from a continued increase in UFO media, especially books like *The Roswell Incident* which traced the history back to the late 1940s and insinuated a complex, multidecade cover-up. In effect, the poll data showed a complex process of belief slowly building over time as a result of several factors working in tandem.

However, the only ideas that fluctuated in these polls were positive beliefs. The numbers for those who did not believe that UFOs were real remained steady, at about 19 per cent. Of course, the vehemence of the letters that the government received belied these conservative numbers and gave the somewhat false impression that the public was obsessed with the phenomenon.

Two more letters during this period, for instance, echoed the Trent University professor's concerns about malevolent extraterrestrials and mentioned encounters with actual alien beings. On 12 September 1990, a school principal from Bloodvein, Manitoba, reported "that community members had seen a U.F.O. and little men" over the course of several days. At first, a witness had sighted a big, bright light in the sky, like a falling star. Another witness later that evening was doing dishes in her kitchen when she looked out the window and observed "about 50yds in the bush, the head of a person shaped like an egg, sharp pointed ears, with eyes shut and wrinkled, she could not see a nose or a mouth. This person was about 3ft. tall." Another witness saw, while driving, "someone run across the road in the headlights. The person was 3ft tall, brown in color and was naked. [The witness] could not determine the sex, nor could she see the face of this person." Last, a seven-year old witness "claimed to have been bitten by one of these little men, but upon examination, no injuries could be found nor could he provide a description of these little men." What were the RCMP investigators to make of such accounts? The final line of the report declared: "Police have not recd any further reports of U.F.O. sightings and do not believe the witnesses in this incident to be reliable."[75]

Five years later, a woman reported to the DND that her son had been abducted by aliens. The boy stated that "an alien approx 2½ ft tall entered his room through his second story townhouse window." The report continued with an account which the mother and son jointly provided: "Mother could not verify how he was able to move from the window to the ship. She described the ship as a dovetail shape grey in colour. The ship had pinky, orange cushion walls that smelled similar to paint chemicals. Upon entering the ship he noticed five others. They communicated to him, without moving their lips, ensuring that he would be all right. He described them as being between 2½–4½ ft tall, pointed ears, slanted almond eyes, three fingers (they were wearing five finger medical gloves[)]." The boy stated that the aliens performed some medical tests and examined his chest and brain before returning him to his room and putting him to sleep. At first, the boy thought he must have dreamed the whole encounter and so did not tell his mother for several days. However, he displayed physical evidence in the form of "scabs on his chest, in the shape of a square horseshoe." In the end, the investigator merely suggested to the mother that she take her son to a medical facility and take photographs of his chest.[76] This was the only alien abduction narrative that I found among the documents at LAC, but there was an increase of such stories in the 1990s. This was certainly due in part to recent publications and releases in the genre, such as the aforementioned *Communion* book, but also the now-ubiquitous television series *The X-Files*, which premiered in 1993.[77] I would be remiss not to include a mention of this series in a book such as this.

Lastly, a resident of Sidney, British Columbia, wrote to the NRC in January 1992 about a UFO sighting that he had been "privileged to observe approximately 56 years ago" while based in the Arctic doing aerial mapping. "Having now passed my 81st birthday with time running short," he wrote, "I feel I should try to outline and describe the incredible sighting I was so privileged to see, and to say that I firmly believe I was the only person likely to have observed this phenomenon." The sighting occurred in 1936 in Aylmer Lake, Northwest Territories, on a clear day without cloud cover. The witness happened to look up while doing a flight inspection on his plane, and saw a "completely stationary" vehicle in the sky. "In trying to describe this vehicle I can only say that it was the most magnificent configuration of an airship one could imagine … I can still see this vehicle today in my mind's eye clear as the day of sighting." Its colouration was "light aluminum but without shine," and was made of entirely unknown materials. No outer appendages, portholes, or "propellant medium" were discernable, and there was "no sign of contrails at take off." The vehicle eventually "took off at a fantastic speed going east" and, in a matter of moments, vanished.

"The fact," wrote this witness, "that I have not bothered to mention this sighting officially or otherwise until now undoubtedly seems strange. At the time in question, as a young fellow, I took most happenings for granted. I was fascinated by the beauty of the barren lands and the great solitude it presented. I took the sighting I have described as a point of interest only. From an early age I considered our world to be a mere speck in the vast universe. This possibly explains my lack of excitement concerning the incident I have described. If the foregoing event I have described is considered 'old hat' or 'shear fantasy' [*sic*] no acknowledgement will be expected."[78]

Suffice it to say, this octogenarian witness received no reply. By the early 1990s, the NRC was almost entirely uninterested, its role in the collection of reports as passive and listless as the RCAF's E.W. Greenwood, back in 1967, had feared it would become. It was only

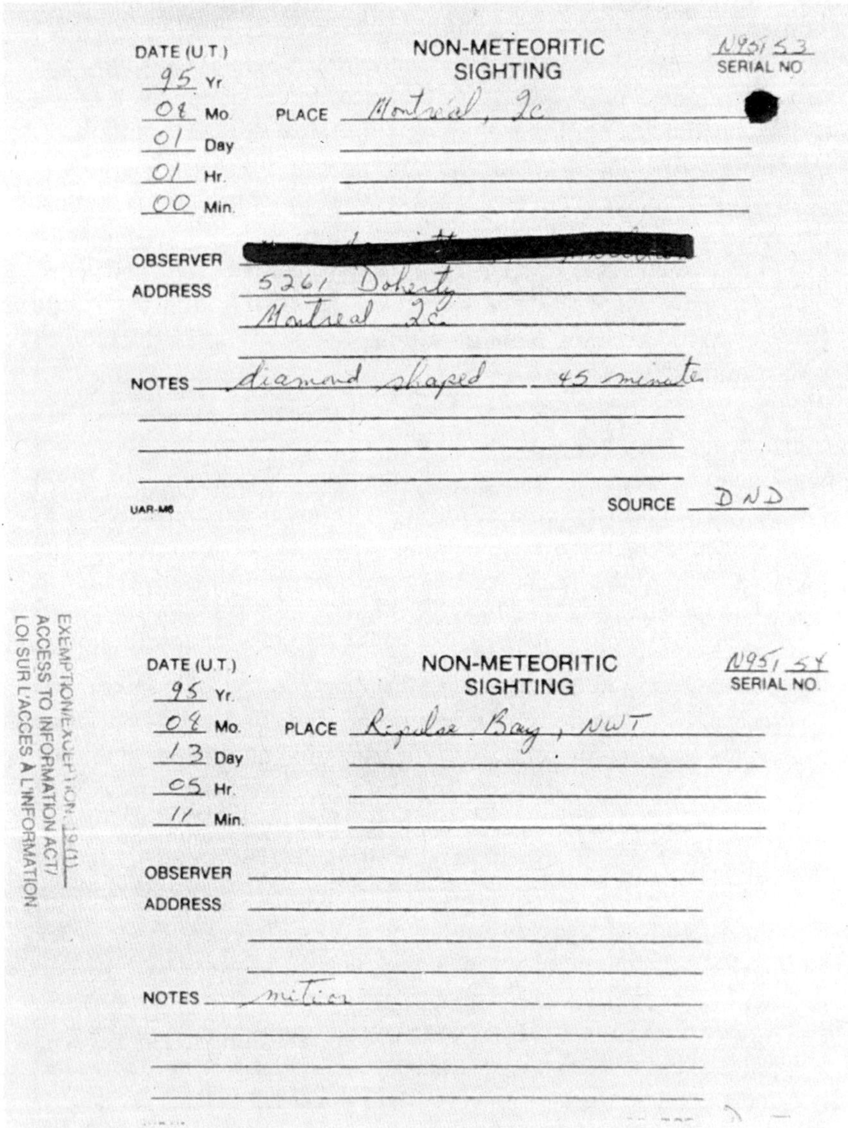

DATE (U.T.)

95 Yr.
08 Mo.
01 Day
01 Hr.
00 Min.

NON-METEORITIC SIGHTING

N95153
SERIAL NO.

PLACE Montréal, Qc

OBSERVER [redacted]
ADDRESS 5261 Doherty
Montreal Qc.

NOTES diamond shaped 45 minute

UAR-M6

SOURCE DND

EXEMPTION/EXCEPTION: 19(1)
ACCESS TO INFORMATION ACT/
LOI SUR L'ACCES À L'INFORMATION

DATE (U.T.)

95 Yr.
08 Mo.
13 Day
05 Hr.
11 Min.

NON-METEORITIC SIGHTING

N95154
SERIAL NO.

PLACE Repulse Bay, NWT

OBSERVER
ADDRESS

NOTES motion

Figure 5.2 | Final sighting report catalogued before official termination of the NRC's UFO sightings program.

three more years before it all came to a close, once and for all. In 1995, the forty-five-year-long investigation was finally terminated in its entirety due to budget cuts and retirements within the department.[79] The very last sighting report that the NRC catalogued came from Repulse Bay, Northwest Territories, on 13 August 1995. The time was given as 5:11 a.m. and the "Notes" section on the reporting card simply said "meteor."[80] No other information was provided. After decades of receiving thousands of UFO reports, rampant citizen speculation, and scientific frustration, Canada's UFO investigation ended not with a bang, but a whimper.

In 1970, Peter Millman wrote to the American astronomer J. Allen Hynek: "I try very hard to keep an open mind in this subject, but I must confess I get more and more disillusioned with what people report they have seen with their eyes."[81] Millman's attitude may help to explain why the government's UFO investigations front in Canada went quiet shortly after. The NRC continued to receive sighting reports, at a rate of several per week and sometimes one per day, but only rarely did an NRC scientist follow up on them. In the cases where a witness did receive a reply, it inevitably attempted to supply a prosaic explanation for the sighting. Peter Millman wrote a number of such replies over the years, but other NRC scientists also did so.

Ian Halliday, who worked in the same NRC section as Millman, sent a typical response in November 1974. A citizen had written in describing "an interesting atmospheric phenomenon" that he had observed while flying over Melville Island in the Arctic. In clear skies, this citizen saw "an orange, yellowish, ballshaped image at the horizon ... similar in size and colour to the moon or sun when hidden behind cloud." Over the next few minutes, the object grew in size and became more diffuse until it finally faded away.[82]

Halliday provided two possible explanations. The object might have been the "moderately bright star Altair," approximately in the position that the citizen had described. It could also have been the "much brighter star Sirius" which, though located in the opposite direction, could perhaps have been reflected through the windows depending on the airplane's configuration. "Neither of these explanations is very convincing," Halliday admitted, "but they appear to be the best ones available for the time of your observation."[83] Even when the attending scientist was unconvinced, no other speculation was ever indulged. It had to be a prosaic explanation or nothing at all. This is clear from the numerous cases in which NRC replies simply stated that no explanation could be provided due to the inadequate information supplied.

In terms of debunking, it is clear that the NRC's favourite explanation was that UFOs were misidentified meteors. This explanation became so common that in August 1977, someone at the NRC began impressing reports with a special stamp: "IDENTIFIED AS A METEOR."[84] The stamp was clearly meant to convey certainty; its wording and the capital letters were unambiguous. What is even more interesting is that about ten months later, the wording changed. A stamped report from June 1978 instead read: "IDENTIFIED AS POSSIBLE METEOR." No document in the archives provides an explanation for this change, or even mentions the use of the stamp.

On the surface, the change in the stamps' wording is a subtle one, but given the attitude toward UFOs within the NRC, and the amount of work put into ignoring the issue, it is interesting to see the agency's official certainty in the prosaic explanation slip a little. Someone must have realized that despite their best efforts, NRC scientists could not know for sure what citizens had seen in the skies. Some margin of error had to be built into their analyses of sightings, even if "analysis" meant simply a four-word stamp.

Nevertheless, for the NRC, the question was moot. Once the transfer of responsibility had taken place and the files had been downgraded to unclassified, the job was presumably done. In his book *The UFO Experience*, J. Allen Hynek wrote that the 1969 report of the Condon Committee from the University of Colorado gave the study of UFOs in the US the "kiss of death."[85] The NRC tried to effect the same death for the Canadian documents, and it seems to have succeeded given how sharply documentation dropped off after 1980. Despite the introduction in Canada, in 1983, of access-to-information legislation, the disclosure that citizen UFO investigators had long called for did not materialize.

This was, as Mark Fenster argues, the ironic result of the flaw in the "transparency fix," that it is unable to deliver on its promise. By putting UFOs to political work, in the 1960s advocates began using the visibility metaphor as part of a broader countercultural movement that saw public trust in government decline. However, Canada's history of secrecy, replicated from Britain's model, prevented any kind of significant disclosure of information, and citizens' frustration with this situation was evident in the letters described in this chapter.

This is not to say, though, that the fault lies entirely with the government. The way in which citizens presented themselves, and unapologetically demanded answers, did not endear them to the government. Citizens rarely looked credible. The conflict that developed between them and the Canadian state as a result of the latter's attempt to educate the public, which hit the wall of citizens' iconoclasm and their refusal to "see the light" of modern science, only strengthened in the years after the National Research Council assumed responsibility for UFO investigation.

Conclusion

In 2005, Library and Archives Canada released a virtual exhibition titled "Canada's UFOs: The Search for the Unknown."[1] This resource allows users to search a selection of UFO documents and offers a short timeline and map featuring some of the more sensational sightings described in the previous chapters. The exhibition was created as part of a broader initiative, begun in the late 1990s, which "utilised the interactive technology of the Web, making digitised images more than just illustrations or pictures at an exhibition."[2] The point was to make as many records as possible accessible to the public.

In the words of Michael Eamon, project manager for "Canada's UFOs," the initiative was meant "to make records known." At LAC, during this wave of digitization, there was no special interest in the UFO material other than that the public generally found the subject intriguing – it was a "hot topic" – and so it lent itself well to a virtual presentation that might draw in more eyes.[3] It certainly worked to draw me in. I stumbled across it one day while idly reading about UFOs. In fact, the site provided the inspiration for what eventually became this book.

Released ten years after the NRC catalogued the final sighting of Canada's UFO investigation, "Canada's UFOs" serves as bookends for the whole project. LAC created the exhibition in the absence of any specific directive to do so, or contact with any other department originally involved such as the DND or the RCMP. They created it simply because of a sustained public interest in UFOs. The government may have worked as hard as it could to ignore the issue, but the public maintains a fascination with this topic, for myriad reasons.

The same year as the release of "Canada's UFOs," new Gallup results showed that 21 per cent of Canadians believed that extraterrestrials have visited the Earth at some point in the past.[4] While this number represents a decline from the 1970s and '80s, the fascination has yet to disappear. Such a belief, and the fact that it was at its highest during the 1970s, squares with an influx of "ancient alien" theories such as those found in *Chariots of the Gods?* and *2001: A Space Odyssey*, both released in the late 1960s. More recently, a 2018 Ipsos/Historica Canada poll included a question about the UFO landing pad constructed in St Paul, Alberta, in 1967: 27 per cent of respondents answered correctly that it was the world's first.[5]

Sightings of UFOs remain steady today, although citizen organizations now perform all the data collection and analysis. This small group of disconnected citizens, which began writing to the government for answers in the early 1960s, still exists today and continues to ask the same questions. A recent edited collection of essays by leading ufologists notes that, some seventy-five years after the Kenneth Arnold sighting and the alleged Roswell crash, we arguably know no more than we did then: "The UFO field has produced thousands of dedicated researchers over the years, and reams of literature; but to what end? What can we claim to know conclusively today about the underlying nature of UFO phenomena that we didn't know in the late-1940s?"[6]

Indeed, the book questions whether "ufology" even exists at all: "If 'ology' refers to a branch of knowledge or learning sprung from organized research, then ufology is a broken twig." This is certainly the position that mainstream scientists within the Canadian government adopted, given that they had argued, as early as the 1950s, that UFOs were nothing but misidentified natural phenomena or the products of delusional minds. It does not change the fact, however, that Canadian citizens took an interest in UFOs, and were dismayed and angered that their government did not respond in kind.

From 1950 to 1995, the Canadian government did its best to ignore UFOs. Failing that, government officials attempted to put UFOs to good use. For much of this time, especially from the early 1960s onward, a small group of disconnected citizens from around the country wrote letters to various government departments to report sightings and to demand answers to the UFO mystery. Frequently, they found themselves the victims of what they called "doublespeak" – the government's attempt to respond to them without giving any actual information. Such non-answers had a direct effect on the way in which citizen ufologists organized. For instance, beginning in the late 1950s, some citizens organized and participated in UFO clubs.

However, citizens requesting information about UFOs were not the only ones who were frustrated. Officials in the government's various departments found it equally disconcerting and annoying that some citizens continued to demand answers when none were available, and that they refused to accept this explanation. In their letters, moreover, some of these citizens were rude and demanding – and even the attempts they made to appear professional sometimes came across as bizarre. This dynamic caused both sides to double down. The government's position on the unreality of UFOs and extraterrestrials hardened, whereas the citizen activists turned to conspiracy theories to explain the state's unwillingness to engage. This dynamic demonstrates how, for these citizens, the UFO phenomenon served to structure their very experience of the state. They came to know at least a part of the state's power through the experience of interacting with state officials.

There were several individuals in the Canadian government, however, who did take UFOs seriously. Chapter 1 told the story of Wilbert Smith, an electrical and radio engineer employed at the Department of Transport. Smith became convinced that UFOs were real, the product of extraterrestrial intelligence. He set about trying to prove this through a series of experiments, conducted between 1950 and 1954 under the banner of Project Magnet at the Department of Transport. Smith's efforts included establishing "weighting factors" to assist in determining the validity of any given UFO observation, a balloon experiment which he conducted in an attempt to ascertain the reliability of witness observations, and the establishment of a UFO observatory on the outskirts of Ottawa. Smith's efforts were largely unsuccessful, as he failed to convince his DoT colleagues of the reality of UFOs. The department terminated Project Magnet in 1954, forcing Smith to continue his work privately.

For scientists like Peter Millman, the NRC astronomer who chaired Project Second Storey (PSS), UFOs never even registered as genuinely real. If they were real at all, they existed for Millman only as misidentified natural phenomena. What the UFO mystery came down to was the problem of stubbornness on the part of citizens, and the need for the state to educate the public. As detailed in Chapter 2, this was the philosophy behind the approach to the PSS committee, and its conclusions followed from this. PSS, which ran from 1952 to 1954, concluded that UFOs neither posed a security threat nor were of scientific interest. More specifically, UFOs simply were not amenable to scientific inquiry – that is, they did not even constitute a type of object that scientists could, or would, study. As such, the committee recommended ending all such investigations and ensuring thereby that any citizens asking for information would be told in no uncertain terms that UFOs were a waste of time. PSS's conclusion had a significant impact on the study of UFOs in Canada for decades to come.

Canadian citizens interested in UFOs began to show their frustration with PSS's attitude in the late 1950s and early 1960s. Chapter 3 provided examples of letters that citizens wrote to the government asking for information on the subject. Citizens like D.M. Spicer and Ken Kaasen were unhappy that the government was not taking a more serious interest in UFOs. They believed that UFOs were indeed real, might constitute a security threat, and were certainly of scientific interest. It quickly became clear, however, that the citizens writing in would not receive the responses they thought they deserved.

This was the result of a combination of factors. The government, in general, simply did not have the information they wanted. There is no evidence of any kind of a cover-up of information. Instead, the more realistic scenario was a cock-up. Given that the Canadian state does not exist as such but rather comprises a multitude of autonomous departments and agencies, it was actually quite uncommon for government officials to communicate with one another about the topic. As a result, citizens sometimes received multiple, contradictory answers, fuelling conspiracy beliefs. Again, this back-and-forth shows how some citizens came to know the state and its bureaucracy. Chapter 3 historicized these beliefs as part of a much broader cultural shift occurring in the 1960s, which saw increasingly anti-authoritarian views and a growing distrust of government.

The fault here did not lie entirely with the government. From the beginning, UFO enthusiasts seemed to be a different breed of correspondent. Often brash and assuming, they demanded information rather than asked for it, and were indignant when they did not receive it. They rarely presented themselves as professional researchers and, when they did, their affiliations often seemed illegitimate.

One of the only aspects of the phenomenon that did attract the government's attention was encounters that left behind physical traces. Chapter 4 recounted three cases from 1967 that defied explanation: Stefan Michalak's UFO encounter at Falcon Lake, Manitoba; the crop circles in a farmer's field at Duhamel, Alberta; and the Shag Harbour crash in Nova Scotia. Each of these three cases provided material that government scientists could actually analyze. That is to say, the cases yielded *tangible evidence*, a necessary ingredient for the kind of investigation that many citizens wanted the government to undertake. Unfortunately, even these exceptional cases failed to convince government officials of the reality of UFOs. Each investigation simply hit a wall, as the evidence failed to yield further clues. Although these cases remain mysteries, however, they also represent the climax of the government's investigation into UFOs.

Chapter 5 covered the remaining years of the UFO investigation, which ran until 1995. The conspiracy theories described in Chapter 3 had evolved by this point. Although citizens were still attempting to elicit information about UFOs, they also came to understand their work as a fight against government secrecy. Linked as it was to the radicalism of the 1960s, this second, related aspect may be understood as a moment of questioning established authority, as a broader idea of what it meant to be a citizen in relation to the state. By the 1970s and '80s, this change manifested concretely in calls for transparency in government and disclosure of information, culminating in the establishment of Canada's Access to Information Agreement in 1983. Unfortunately, this legislation did not solve the problems that UFO enthusiasts had identified. As Mark Fenster argues, the "transparency fix" is ultimately an illusion that obfuscates more than it reveals. Realistically, transparency is just one ideal competing among others, and it simply cannot muster the same level of political clout that secrecy arouses.

As such, Canada's UFO investigation declined rapidly after 1980. The Department of National Defence managed to transfer responsibility for the investigation to an unwilling National Research Council, which in turn took a passive approach to the subject. The government's position on UFOs remained almost unchanged since Project Second Storey's conclusions in the mid-1950s. If anything, the state's attitude only hardened over time in response to citizens' letters and, by the time the NRC catalogued its final UFO sighting in 1995, the agency had long since given up any pretense at serious investigation.

At the heart of this story were the myriad changes taking place during Canada's postwar years. Especially relevant to the UFO investigation was the rise of an anti-authoritarian attitude and a growing distrust of institutions. Citizens made it clear in their letters that they were not afraid to call out the government when they felt they had discovered duplicity, however bizarre their approach may have seemed. The government, for its part, found itself unprepared to handle this new kind of interaction and unwilling to engage with the antagonistic approach on which some citizens insisted.

Zygmunt Bauman explains how, after the French Revolution, states turned from controlling to educating the public. The goal was to inaugurate a new age of reason by ridding the masses of their old, superstitious ways. In the postwar period, as Chandra Mukerji argues, this meant courting the scientific community so that the state might draw on its cultural authority in times of need. The Canadian state – visible through the actions of its officials – attempted to draw on the authority of its scientists to debunk UFOs as a means of ridding citizens of their ignorance.

As Steven Shapin and Simon Schaffer argue, solutions to the problem of knowledge are simultaneously solutions to the problem of social order. So, in its attempts to solve the seemingly scientific questions about UFOs – what are they and what can we know about them? – the state was simultaneously attempting to solve a problem of social order, namely how to make sense of, and deal with, aggressive citizens who refused to acquiesce to institutional authority. Through this attempt, which manifested most often in formal (and formulaic) replies to UFO enthusiasts' letters, some citizens came to know the state in a very specific way, as an institution motivated by a positivistic idea of science that spared no room for alternative explanations for supernatural phenomena.

In one sense, this is an accurate representation of the state and how it approached the topic. In another sense, it is too simplistic. As this book has attempted to show, there was resistance on both sides, state and citizen, whereby each reinforced the other. The attempt here is not to prove one side correct over the other but to describe the rationale behind both sides to understand why, and how, they came into conflict.

This book has traced the history of the state's involvement with UFOs, as well as the reaction of a small, scattered group of citizens to this effort – a reaction underpinned by these citizens' beliefs about authority and expertise during a time of anti-authoritarianism – and how these two directions fed into one another across the postwar decades. At the broadest level, the story of Canada's UFO investigation really came to represent a growing recognition that the value of UFOs lay in putting them to specific kinds of work to achieve certain goals, whether social, political, or psychological.

Since we will likely never know "the truth" about UFOs – whether or not they are extraterrestrial in origin – here is where I believe the most fruitful analysis lies: in looking at the boundaries between expert and non-expert, state and citizen, real and not real. These boundaries indicate to us where conflict occurs – and indeed, these boundaries are usually formed *as a result of* conflict. The boundary between UFO enthusiasts and skeptical scientists does not exist naturally; rather, it is created through histories, just like the one presented here. And since these boundaries tend to become more entrenched as time passes, it is likely that people and states will continue to use, and to perpetuate, the UFO phenomenon for their own ends.

Notes

INTRODUCTION

1 Ken Kaasen, letter to the Defence Research Board, 25 July 1960, Flying Saucers file, Library and Archives Canada, Ottawa, ON (hereafter "LAC"), RG 24, acc. 83–84/167, box 7523, file 3800-10-1, pt. 1.

2 C.A. Pope, letter to Ken Kaasen, 9 August 1960, Flying Saucers file, LAC, RG 24, acc. 83–84/167, box 7523, file 3800-10-1, pt. 1.

3 See: Robbie Graham, ed., *UFOs: Reframing the Debate* (Hove, UK: White Crow Books, 2017). Geppert refers to the anxiety over this situation as a "blind spot" that historians are forced to circumnavigate, lest they "only perpetuate the discursive deadlock between believers and skeptics, proselytizers and debunkers, and amateurs and scientists." See: Alexander C.T. Geppert, "Extraterrestrial Encounters: UFOs, Science and the Quest for Transcendence, 1947–1972," *History and Technology* 28, no. 3 (2012): 337.

4 That is, this history is not evaluative but descriptive and explanatory. See: Steven Shapin and Simon Schaffer, *Leviathan and the Air-Pump: Hobbes, Boyle, and the Experimental Life* (Princeton, NJ: Princeton University Press, 1985), 12. Similarly, D.W. Pasulka, in her book about the UFO phenomenon as a potential new religious movement, argues that "there is no need to consider whether the belief [in UFOs] is justified or not if one is just analyzing its social effects and influence." D.W. Pasulka, *American Cosmic: UFOs, Religion, Technology* (New York: Oxford University Press, 2019), 8–9.

5 In this book, I differentiate between government and state. The word *government* is used whenever a specific department or agency is discussed, such as when a citizen wrote a letter to a specific department like National

Defence. Since the UFO investigation spanned several decades, naturally the government and its departments changed over time, in terms of scope, power, and composition. This means that many citizens were writing to many different government officials throughout this time. Whenever I refer to Canadian government priorities more generally, I refer to the *state*. An example is when, seeking to illustrate broader changes and meanings, I discuss the relationship between citizens and the state in general. This point will be explored in more detail below.

6 See, for instance: Chris Rutkowski and Geoff Dittman, *The Canadian UFO Report: The Best Cases Revealed* (Toronto: Dundurn, 2006); Palmiro Campagna, *The UFO Files: The Canadian Connection Exposed* (Toronto: Stoddart, 1998); Grant Cameron, *Charlie Red Star: True Reports of One of North America's Biggest UFO Sightings* (Toronto: Dundurn, 2017); Chris Styles and Graham Simms, *Impact to Contact: The Shag Harbour Incident* (Halifax: Arcadia House Publishing, 2013); and Matthew Hayes, "'Then the Saucers Do Exist?': UFOs, the Practice of Conspiracy, and the Case of Wilbert Smith," *Journal of Canadian Studies* 51, no. 3 (2018), 665–96.

7 Greg Eghigian, "Suspense and the UFOs" (invited talk, Working Group on the History of Technology, Consortium for the History of Science, Technology and Medicine, Philadelphia, 12 December 2017).

8 Most of this story concerns Canada and the US. However, UFOs are a global phenomenon. Unfortunately, as is the case with writing on Canada's UFO history, the literature on transnational or global histories of UFOs is small. Two starting points are: Geppert, "Extraterrestrial Encounters"; and Greg Eghigian, "'A transatlantic buzz': flying saucers, extraterrestrials and America in postwar Germany," *Journal of Transatlantic Studies* 12, no. 3 (2014), 282–303.

9 Hilary Evans and Dennis Stacy, *UFOs, 1947–1997* (London: John Brown Publishing, 1997), 5. A "modern" era of UFOs implies a "pre-modern era." Unfortunately, the history of aerial sightings prior to 1947 is beyond the scope of this book. For an introduction to pre-1947 reports, see, for instance: Carl Jung, *Flying Saucers: A Modern Myth of Things Seen in the Skies* (1959; Princeton, NJ: Princeton University Press, 1978); Brenda Denzler, *The Lure of the Edge: Scientific Passions, Religious Beliefs, and the Pursuit of UFOs* (Berkeley: University of California Press, 2001), ch. 1; and Jacques Vallee, *Passport to Magonia: From Folklore to Flying Saucers* (1964; Brisbane: Daily Grail Publishing, 2014).

10 Denzler, *Lure of the Edge*, 4.

11 Kathryn Olmsted, *Real Enemies: Conspiracy Theories and American Democracy, World War I to 9/11* (New York: Oxford University Press, 2009), 184.

12 John Lewis Gaddis, *The Cold War: A New History* (New York: Penguin, 2005), 84.

13 See: Susan Lepselter, *The Resonance of Unseen Things: Poetics, Power, Captivity, and UFOs in the American Uncanny* (Ann Arbor: University of Michigan Press, 2016).

14 The ufologist Stephen Bassett has been particularly vocal about this goal. See his website: www.paradigmresearchgroup.org.

15 It was around this time, in the late 1940s or early 1950s, when the term "Unidentified Flying Object" was coined by US Air Force captain Edward Ruppelt, who would later take charge of Project Blue Book. "Ruppelt wanted something that did not imply that 'unidentified objects' seen in the sky were alien spacecraft." David Clarke, *How UFOs Conquered the World* (London: Aurum Press, 2015), 25.

16 Canadian Press, "Area Covered by 'Flying Saucers' is Broadened," *Charlottetown Guardian*, 8 July 1947.

17 Charles Ziegler, "UFOs and the US Intelligence Community," *Intelligence and National Security* 14, no. 2 (1999): 4.

18 Edward Ruppelt, *The Report on Unidentified Flying Objects* (New York: Doubleday, 1956), 65.

19 Ziegler, "UFOs and the US Intelligence Community," 11.

20 Ibid., 13.

21 More recently, it has come to light that the Pentagon has been secretly funding a UFO investigation project, the Advanced Aerospace Threat Identification Program. See: Helene Cooper, Ralph Blumenthal, and Leslie Kean, "Glowing Auras and 'Black Money': The Pentagon's Mysterious U.F.O. Program," *New York Times*, 16 December 2017, https://www.nytimes.com/2017/12/16/us/politics/pentagon-program-ufo-harry-reid.html.

22 A large collection of files specifically about Wilbert Smith, the electrical engineer employed with the Department of Transport discussed in Chapter 1, are found in the University of Ottawa archives. I also consulted files held in the City of Vancouver archives, the archives of Saint Mary's University in Halifax, and those of Acadia University in Wolfville, Nova Scotia. Since the time of this writing, a new, substantial archive of UFO documents has become available at the New Brunswick Provincial Archives, donated by the late Stanton Friedman, one of the best-known

ufologists. However, due to time and space constraints, this material is not included here.

23 There is some discrepancy between the amount of documentation as compared to the number of sightings. A single sighting might generate several pages of documentation: a report might be one to three pages long, or more; it might be accompanied by witness statements on additional pages, including drawings or maps; a covering letter may be attached if the report was forwarded to another official or agency, etc. As such, the volume of documentation outstrips the number of sightings.

24 A number of factors cast the accuracy of this number into doubt. While individual departments often failed to communicate with one another effectively, there were instances where they did exchange reports and so there are a number of duplicated reports in the various files at LAC. Many sighting reports contain only partial information – either because the investigator did not include it all, or it was redacted after the fact for privacy concerns – and many others are now illegible having been poorly microfilmed or photocopied. Some sighting reports that appear to have duplicates in different departments contain key details like dates and locations that do not exactly align, and so it is sometimes difficult to determine whether they relate to the same event. There is also the question of what exactly constituted a UFO sighting, as there are many reports of fireballs and meteorites in the UFO files. As astronomer Martin Beech usefully argues, there is also a distinction to be made between a "report" and an "event." Some UFO sighting events might generate multiple reports – each of which might comprise multiple pages – in cases with more than one witness. However, to count reports rather than unique events would inflate the number of UFO encounters. See: Martin Beech, "The Millman Fireball Archive," *Journal of the Royal Astronomical Society of Canada* 97, no. 2 (2003): 72.

25 Again, several factors compromise the accuracy of these figures. There is no obvious reason why there are such spikes in certain years (such as in 1981, 1985, and 1990). The role of popular culture, especially Hollywood entertainment, is certainly a factor in explaining some spikes throughout the decades. This aspect will be explored throughout the book. However, it must also be kept in mind that the archives themselves are partial. Especially prior to 1965, the documents available are somewhat sketchy. Consistent and accurate reporting procedures were not in place until the mid-1960s, when the RCMP became the primary agency responding to reports on the ground. It was also standard procedure in many departments to destroy documents after a number of years (in some cases as few as three years) if they were no longer considered important. As a result,

there may well have been more sightings from the late 1940s to the mid-1960s, but they were not reported properly or the records have been lost. There is also, of course, the assumption that more sightings are made than are reported. A person might see a UFO and choose not to report, fearing ridicule from family, friends, or government officials, or because it is unclear where to send a report to in the first place. However, as the number of unreported sightings is, by definition, unknown, I only take into account those documented in the archives.

26 Martin Beech found almost identical results in his analysis of the National Research Council's archive of fireball reports in Canada, a separate collection of 3,876 reports corresponding to 2,129 unique events of visually observed fireball meteors, from 1962 to 1989. Similar to the UFO reports, residents of Ontario reported fireball observations most often, followed by residents of Quebec and British Columbia. These reports clustered along lines of population density. Beech, "Millman Fireball Archive," 73.

27 Documentation of UFO sightings prior to 1950 is incredibly slim, with less than ten pages of material. This is most likely due to the fact that the archival record was destroyed, a routine procedure within the government. Also, the Canadian government did not officially collect reports at this time but discovered them instead mostly through newspaper reports. Martine Paquette, LAC archivist, email correspondence with the author, 27 July 2017.

28 Whitley Strieber, *Communion: A True Story* (New York: Avon Books, 1987).

29 Robert MacDougall, "Sympathetic Physics: The Keely Motor and the Laws of Thermodynamics in Nineteenth-Century Culture," *Technology and Culture* 60, no. 2 (2019): 438–66.

30 Ian Milligan, *Rebel Youth: 1960s Labour Unrest, Young Workers, and New Leftists in English Canada* (Vancouver: UBC Press, 2014), 3.

31 Lara Campbell and Dominique Clément, "Introduction: Time, Age, Myth: Towards a History of the Sixties," in *Debating Dissent: Canada and the Sixties*, ed. Lara Campbell, Dominique Clément, and Gregory S. Kealey (Toronto: University of Toronto Press, 2012), 21.

32 Neil Nevitte, *The Decline of Deference: Canadian Value Change in Cross-National Perspective* (Toronto: University of Toronto Press, 1996).

33 Robert Bothwell, *Alliance and Illusion: Canada and the World, 1945–1984* (Vancouver: University of Washington Press, 2008); Robert Teigrob, *Warming Up to the Cold War: Canada and the United States' Coalition of the Willing, from Hiroshima to Korea* (Toronto: University of Toronto Press, 2009).

34 Dimitry Anastakis, *Death in the Peaceable Kingdom: Canadian History since 1867 through Murder, Execution, Assassination, and Suicide* (Toronto: University of Toronto Press, 2015), 182.

35 One more aspect of this large societal change was the increasing secularization of society. A fuller examination of this is beyond the scope of the book, but let it suffice to say that this also played a role in driving a wedge between government and citizen. During the postwar period, Canadians became less religious, or, at the very least, membership in churches and religious organizations declined. At the same time, some Canadians took it upon themselves to articulate and demonstrate visions of a truly secular society by entering into politics. Some UFO enthusiasts echoed the spirit of this shift; while ufologists rarely ran for political office, they certainly engaged with the political sphere in their own way, by taking a new attitude toward the government – that is, as an institution that needs to be pressured into giving up its secrets. And again, at the same time, one possible consequence of this secularization may have been an increasing willingness to look to the stars, rather than to the Church, for extraterrestrial life and the answers to Earth's problems. Ironically, some of the most compelling recent analyses of the UFO phenomenon see it as akin to a new religious movement. The connections between the UFO phenomenon and religious movements and histories is a fascinating area of study that requires more work. For examples, see: David Lyon and Marguerite Van Die, eds., *Rethinking Church, State, and Modernity: Canada Between Europe and America* (Toronto: University of Toronto Press, 2000); Pasulka, *American Cosmic*; Elliot Hanowski, "Activist Unbelief in Canadian History," *Secularism and Nonreligion* 7, no. 10 (2018): 1–9; D. Alistair Hay, "An Investigation into the Swiftness and Intensity of Recent Secularization in Canada: Was Berger Right?" *Sociology of Religion* 75, no. 1 (2014): 136–62; Matthew Hayes and Noah Morritt, "Michael W. Burke-Gaffney and the UFO Debate in Atlantic Canada, 1947–1969," *Scientia Canadensis* 42, no. 1 (2020): 54–74.

36 Joseph E. Uscinski and Joseph M. Parent, *American Conspiracy Theories* (New York: Oxford University Press, 2014); Joseph Uscinski, ed., *Conspiracy Theories and the People Who Believe Them* (New York: Oxford University Press, 2018).

37 Jan-Willem van Prooijen, *The Psychology of Conspiracy Theories* (London: Routledge, 2018). See also: Joseph Heath, *Enlightenment 2.0: Restoring Sanity to Our Politics, Our Economy, and Our Lives* (Toronto: HarperCollins, 2014).

38 Greg Eghigian, "Making UFOs Make Sense: Ufology, Science, and the History of Their Mutual Misunderstanding," *Public Understanding of Science*, 26 (2017): 612–26.

39 Joseph Uscinski, ed., *Conspiracy Theories*, 14.

40 This is a different kind of failure from scientific or technological failure, which comprises the small amount of literature on the topic. See: W. Patrick McCray, "What Makes a Failure? Designing a New National Telescope, 1975–1984," *Technology and Culture* 42, no. 2 (2001): 265–91; and Edward Jones-Imhotep, *The Unreliable Nation: Hostile Nature and Technological Failure in the Cold War* (Cambridge, MA: MIT Press, 2017). Andrew Burtch provides a counterexample in his history of Canada's voluntary civil defence, a nationwide government campaign to convince citizens to prepare for nuclear war. Many citizens refused to cooperate, reflecting a failure on the part of the government to establish its authority and satisfactorily alleviate citizens' concerns. Similarly, the Canadian government failed to convince citizens of its authority when it came to making statements about UFOs. See: Andrew Burtch, *Give Me Shelter: The Failure of Canada's Cold War Civil Defence* (Vancouver: UBC Press, 2012).

41 Margot Canaday, *The Straight State: Sexuality and Citizenship in Twentieth-Century America* (Princeton, NJ: Princeton University Press, 2011), 5.

42 Similarly, Theda Skocpol sees the state, in one definition, as a set of individuals and groups who work toward accomplishing goal-oriented activities, within the bounds of available resources. As a result, "the state certainly does not become everything," but rather becomes one actor among others competing for the power to structure relationships between citizens and authority. Theda Skocpol, "Bringing the State Back In: Strategies of Analysis in Current Research," in *Bringing the State Back In*, ed. Peter B. Evans, Dietrich Rueschemeyer, and Theda Skocpol (Cambridge, UK: Cambridge University Press, 1985).

43 E.A. Heaman, *A Short History of the State in Canada* (Toronto: University of Toronto Press, 2015), 1.

44 Tina Loo, *Moved by the State: Forced Relocation and Making a Good Life in Postwar Canada* (Vancouver: UBC Press, 2019), 6.

45 Mike Larsen and Kevin Walby, "Introduction: On the Politics of Access to Information," in *Brokering Access: Power, Politics, and Freedom of Information Process in Canada*, ed. Mike Larsen and Kevin Walby (Vancouver: UBC Press, 2012), 4.

46 Zygmunt Bauman, "On the Origins of Civilisation: A Historical Note," *Theory, Culture & Society* 2, no. 3 (1985): 7.
47 Tina Loo refers to this process as an expert-driven extension of state power "over ever more peoples and places." Loo, *Moved by the State*, 27.
48 Zygmunt Bauman, *Legislators and Interpreters: On Modernity, Post-Modernity and Intellectuals* (Ithaca, NY: Cornell University Press, 1987), 4.
49 Dipesh Chakrabarty, "The Muddle of Modernity," *American Historical Review* 116, no. 3 (2011): 669.
50 Chandra Mukerji, *A Fragile Power: Scientists and the State* (Princeton, NJ: Princeton University Press, 1989).
51 Edward Jones-Imhotep and Tina Adcock, "Introduction: Science, Technology, and the Modern in Canada," in *Made Modern: Science and Technology in Canadian History*, ed. Edward Jones-Imhotep and Tina Adcock (Vancouver: UBC Press, 2018), 18.
52 Ibid., 12.
53 Shapin and Schaffer, *Leviathan*, 15.
54 Gordon Gauchat, "The cultural authority of science: Public trust and acceptance of organized science," *Public Understanding of Science* 20, no. 6 (2011): 752.

CHAPTER ONE

1 Arthur Bray, *The UFO Connection* (Ottawa: Jupiter Publishing, 1979), 75.
2 "U.B.C. 'Open House' Aired Over CJOR," newspaper clipping, n.d., University of Ottawa Archives (hereafter "UOA"), CA ON0034 30-003-S1-SS3-F1, Wilbert Smith: Biographical Material.
3 "In Memoriam: Wilbert B. Smith," UOA, CA ON0034 30-003-S1-SS3-F1, Wilbert Smith: Biographical Material.
4 Wilbert Smith, memorandum to C.R.R. at the Department of Transport, "Satellite Transmissions – Sputnik I," 19 November 1957, Library and Archives Canada (hereafter "LAC"), RG 97, vol. 182, file 5010-4, pt. 2, Unidentified Flying Objects (Incl. Outer Space Travel) file.
5 Paul Hellyer, former minister of national defence, interview by the author, 16 June 2017.
6 Wilbert Smith, memorandum to the Controller of Telecommunications, Department of Transport, 21 November 1950, LAC, RG 97, vol. 182, file 5010-4, pt. 1, Unidentified Flying Objects File.
7 Wilbert Smith, "notes on interview," 15 September 1950, UOA, CA ON0034 30-003-S1-SS3-F3, Project Magnet, vol. 1.

8 Arthur Bray, *Science, the Public and the* UFO (Ottawa: Bray Book Service, 1967); Bray, *The* UFO *Connection.*

9 Vannevar Bush was an American scientist who served as chairman of the US National Defense Research Committee created during the Second World War. See: Donald Avery, *The Science of War: Canadian Scientists and Allied Military Technology During the Second World War* (Toronto: University of Toronto Press, 1998). For many years, Bush has been connected to the UFO phenomenon as one of the alleged architects of America's UFO cover-up. Smith's memo was instrumental in making this connection.

10 Wilbert Smith, memorandum to the Controller of Telecommunications, Department of Transport, 21 November 1950, LAC, RG 97, vol. 182, file 5010-4, pt. 1, Unidentified Flying Objects File.

11 Wilbert Smith, "Project Magnet Report," n.d., LAC, RG 24, acc. 83–84/167, box 7523, file 3800-10-1, pt. 1, Flying Saucers file.

12 Wilbert Smith, letter to Air Services, Department of Transport, 3 January 1951, UOA, CA ON0034 30-003-S1-SS3-F3, Project Magnet, vol. 1.

13 "Ottawa Constructing Flying Saucer Sighting Station – Just in Case," *Sudbury Daily Star*, 12 November 1953.

14 Wilbert Smith, letter to Air Services, Department of Transport, 3 January 1951, UOA, CA ON0034 30-003-S1-SS3-F3, Project Magnet, vol. 1.

15 Wilbert Smith, "Preliminary Report on Initial Experiment Geo-Magnetic Release," 10 March 1950, UOA, CA ON0034 30-003-S1-SS3-F3, Project Magnet, vol. 1.

16 Wilbert Smith, "Interim Report Project Magnet," 25 June 1952, UOA, CA ON0034 30-003-S1-SS3-F3, Project Magnet, vol. 1.

17 Edward Jones-Imhotep, *The Unreliable Nation: Hostile Nature and Technological Failure in the Cold War* (Cambridge, MA: MIT Press, 2017).

18 Wilbert Smith, "The Establishment of Magnetic Fields," 26 June 1951, UOA, CA ON0034 30-003-S1-SS3-F3, Project Magnet, vol. 1.

19 Wilbert Smith, "Project Magnet Report," 18 January 1952, UOA, CA ON0034 30-003-S1-SS3-F3, Project Magnet, vol. 1.

20 Robert Wise, dir., *The Day the Earth Stood Still* (Los Angeles: 20th Century Fox, 1951).

21 "Flying Saucer Seen North of Didsbury," *Didsbury Pioneer*, 5 April 1950. Also see a second article, four times the length, which appeared later the same month: "Latest Information on 'Flying Saucers,'" *Didsbury Pioneer*, 19 April 1950.

22 Wilbert Smith, "Project Magnet Report," 18 January 1952, UOA, CA ON0034 30-003-S1-SS3-F3, Project Magnet, vol. 1.
23 Wilbert Smith, "Memorandum to Project Second Storey Committee," 16 June 1952, LAC, RG 24, acc. 83–84/167, box 7523, file 3800-10-1, pt. 1, Flying Saucers file.
24 J.H. Thompson, Department of Transport, memorandum to Defence Research Board, 10 September 1952, LAC, RG 24, acc. 83–84/167, box 7523, file 3800-10-1, pt. 1, Flying Saucers file.
25 Wilbert Smith, "Summary of Sightings Reported to and Analysed by Department of Transport During 1952," n.d., UOA, CA ON0034 30-003-S1-SS3-F1, reprint, Project Magnet Report.
26 Wilbert Smith, "Project Magnet Report," 18 January 1952, UOA, CA ON0034 30-003-S1-SS3-F3, Project Magnet, vol. 1.
27 Ibid.
28 See: Susan Lepselter, *The Resonance of Unseen Things: Poetics, Power, Captivity, and UFOs in the American Uncanny* (Ann Arbor: University of Michigan Press, 2016).
29 Mark O'Connell, *The Close Encounters Man: How One Man Made the World Believe in UFOs* (New York: HarperCollins, 2017), 63
30 Ray Pratt, *Projecting Paranoia: Conspiratorial Visions in American Film* (Lawrence: University Press of Kansas, 2002).
31 Don Siegel, dir., *Invasion of the Body Snatchers* (Los Angeles: Allied Artists Pictures, 1956).
32 O'Connell, *The Close Encounters Man*, 108.
33 Richard Dolan, *UFOs and the National Security State: Chronology of a Cover-Up, 1941–1973* (Rochester, NY: Keyhole Publishing, 2013).
34 Reg Whitaker and Gary Marcuse, *Cold War Canada: The Making of a National Insecurity State, 1945–1957* (Toronto: University of Toronto Press, 1996).
35 Dennis Molinaro, "'In the Field of Espionage, There's No Such Thing as Peacetime': The Official Secrets Act and the PICNIC Wiretapping Program," *Canadian Historical Review* 98, no. 3 (2017): 457–82.
36 Reg Whitaker, Gregory S. Kealey, and Andrew Parnaby, *Secret Service: Political Policing in Canada from the Fenians to Fortress America* (Toronto: University of Toronto Press, 2012), 186.
37 Gary Kinsman and Patrizia Gentile, *The Canadian War on Queers: National Security as Sexual Regulation* (Vancouver: UBC Press, 2009).
38 Donald Keyhoe, *The Flying Saucer Conspiracy* (New York: Henry Holt, 1955), 17.

39 Associated Press, "Writer Believes 'Flying Saucers' Real Objects," *Charlottetown Guardian*, 27 December 1949.

40 Keyhoe, *The Flying Saucer Conspiracy*.

41 Donald Keyhoe, *The Flying Saucers Are Real* (1950; New York: Gutter Books, 2011).

42 Joseph Masco, *The Nuclear Borderlands: The Manhattan Project in Post-Cold War New Mexico* (Princeton, NJ: Princeton University Press, 2006), 1.

43 Ibid., 26.

44 Gordon Douglas, dir., *Them!* (Hollywood: Warner Bros. Pictures, 1954).

45 Robert Wise, dir., *The Day the Earth Stood Still* (Los Angeles: 20th Century Fox, 1951); Byron Haskin, dir., *The War of the Worlds* (Hollywood: Paramount Pictures, 1953).

46 Desmond Leslie and George Adamski, *The Flying Saucers Have Landed* (London: Werner Laurie, 1954).

47 Wilbert Smith, letter to Donald Keyhoe, 26 September 1950, UOA, CA ON0034 30-003-S1-SS3-F3, Project Magnet, vol. 1.

48 Donald Keyhoe, *Flying Saucers from Outer Space* (New York: Henry Holt, 1953), 144.

49 "William H.," letter to Wilbert Smith, 22 October 1953, LAC, RG 97, vol. 182, file 5010-4, pt. 1, Unidentified Flying Objects (Incl. Outer Space Travel) file.

50 For instance: Deputy Minister, Department of National Defence, letter to Under Secretary of State of External Affairs, 10 December 1957, LAC, RG 24, vol. 17988, file HQC 940-105, pt. 2, Department of National Defence microfilm reel T-3291.

51 Wilbert Smith, "Memorandum to Mr. van Allen," 8 September 1954, LAC, RG 97, vol. 182, file 5010-4, pt. 1, Unidentified Flying Objects (Incl. Outer Space Travel) file.

52 For instance: Allen Lee Wiseman, letter to Wilbert Smith, 25 June 1955, LAC, RG 97, vol. 182, file 5010-4, pt. 1, Unidentified Flying Objects (Incl. Outer Space Travel) file.

53 Myroslaw Drozda, letter to Wilbert Smith, n.d., LAC, RG 97, vol. 182, file 5010-4, pt. 1, Unidentified Flying Objects (Incl. Outer Space Travel) file.

54 Dwight A. Myer, letter to Wilbert Smith, 9 August 1954, UOA, CA ON0034 30-003-S1-SS3-F3, Project Magnet, vol. 1.

55 Joseph P. Neville, letter to Wilbert Smith, 4 January 1955, LAC, RG 97, vol. 182, file 5010-4, pt. 1, Unidentified Flying Objects (Incl. Outer Space Travel) file.

56 Keyhoe, *Flying Saucers from Outer Space*, 131.

57 J.-C. Lessard, "Memorandum to the Minister," 17 November 1953, LAC, RG 97, vol. 182, file 5010-4, pt. 1, Unidentified Flying Objects (Incl. Outer Space Travel) file.
58 Draft report, 1953, LAC, RG 97, vol. 182, file 5010-4, pt. 1, Unidentified Flying Objects (Incl. Outer Space Travel) file.
59 "'Interplanetary Visitors' Subject of Research," *Vancouver Daily Province*, 13 November 1953.
60 "Ottawa Constructing Flying Saucer Sighting Station – Just in Case," *Sudbury Daily Star*, 12 November 1953.
61 "Laboratory to Probe Flying Saucers," newspaper clipping, n.d., LAC, RG 97, vol. 182, file 5010-4, pt. 1, Unidentified Flying Objects (Incl. Outer Space Travel) file.
62 "Clipping from the Canadian Edition of Time Magazine 14 November, 1953," LAC, RG 24, acc. 83–84/167, box 7523, file 3800-10-1, pt. 1, Flying Saucers file.
63 Bruce MacDonald, "Maze of Instruments in Tiny Shack Hunts for Saucers – Ottawa," *Toronto Daily Star*, 14 November 1953.
64 G.S. Pope, memorandum to Mr Oatway, 16 September 1965, LAC, RG 24, acc. 83–84/167, box 7523, file 3800-10-1, pt. 1, Flying Saucers file.
65 Jonathan Turner, "The Defence Research Board of Canada, 1947 to 1977" (PhD diss., University of Toronto, 2012), 164.
66 G.C.W. Browne, "Memorandum to Supt. Of Radio Regulations," 25 June 1954, LAC, RG 97, vol. 182, file 5010-4, pt. 1, Unidentified Flying Objects (Incl. Outer Space Travel) file.
67 W.H. van Allen, letter to Mr Bantey, 18 December 1953, LAC, RG 97, vol. 182, file 5010-4, pt. 1, Unidentified Flying Objects (Incl. Outer Space Travel) file.
68 A number of correspondents misspelled Smith's name, likely because Donald Keyhoe did so in his book. Keyhoe eventually realized the mistake and apologized to Smith. See: Donald Keyhoe, letter to Wilbert Smith, 9 January 1954, UOA, CA ON0034 30-003-S1-SS3-F3, Project Magnet, vol. 1.
69 Alexander Barrie, letter to W.H. van Allen, 18 June 1954, LAC, RG 97, vol. 182, file 5010-4, pt. 1, Unidentified Flying Objects (Incl. Outer Space Travel) file.
70 W.H. van Allen, letter to Alexander Barrie, 29 June 1954, LAC, RG 97, vol. 182, file 5010-4, pt. 1, Unidentified Flying Objects (Incl. Outer Space Travel) file.
71 O'Connell, *The Close Encounters Man*, 50.
72 "Flying-Saucer Men," *Time*, 27 October 1952, 48–9.

73 R.S. Lambert, "Flying Saucers – their lurid past," *Saturday Night*, 17 May 1952, 18.

74 W.H. van Allen, letter to Alexander Barrie, 23 July 1954, LAC, RG 97, vol. 182, file 5010-4, pt. 1, Unidentified Flying Objects (Incl. Outer Space Travel) file.

75 "Memorandum to the Deputy Minister," 17 May 1955, LAC, RG 97, vol. 182, file 5010-4, pt. 1, Unidentified Flying Objects (Incl. Outer Space Travel) file.

76 "Machine 'Records Saucer,'" *Vancouver Province*, 10 August 1954.

77 "'Thing Trips Saucer Alarm at Shirley Bay Sighting Post," *Ottawa Journal*, 9 August 1954.

78 The American astronomer J. Allen Hynek experienced the same problem after travelling all the way to Iran to view an eclipse. See: O'Connell, *The Close Encounters Man*, 114.

79 G.C.W. Browne, "Memorandum to Supt. Of Radio Regulations," 25 June 1954, LAC, RG 97, vol. 182, file 5010-4, pt. 1, Unidentified Flying Objects (Incl. Outer Space Travel) file.

80 W.H. van Allen, draft form letter to unidentified recipient, n.d., LAC, RG 97, vol. 182, file 5010-4, pt. 1, Unidentified Flying Objects (Incl. Outer Space Travel) file.

81 A.R. Bray, letter to the Department of Transport, 16 November 1964, LAC, RG 97, vol. 182, file 5010-4, pt. 2, Unidentified Flying Objects (Incl. Outer Space Travel) file.

82 F.G. Nixon, letter to A.R. Bray, 20 November 1964, LAC, RG 97, vol. 182, file 5010-4, pt. 2, Unidentified Flying Objects (Incl. Outer Space Travel) file.

83 J.A. Connolly, letter to Julian Hennessey, 8 June 1964, LAC, RG 97, vol. 182, file 5010-4, pt. 2, Unidentified Flying Objects (Incl. Outer Space Travel) file.

84 Letter (author's name redacted) to Bob Ward, 5 July 1978, LAC, RG 12, vol. 3930, file 2-1-33, pt. 1, Department of Transport Minister's Office file.

85 Wilbert Smith, "Memorandum to Superintendent of Radio Regulations," 10 June 1954, LAC, RG 97, vol. 182, file 5010-4, pt. 1, Unidentified Flying Objects (Incl. Outer Space Travel) file.

86 Wilbert Smith, "Memorandum to Mr. van Allen," 8 September 1954, LAC, RG 97, vol. 182, file 5010-4, pt. 1, Unidentified Flying Objects (Incl. Outer Space Travel) file.

87 W.H. van Allen, "Memorandum to Deputy Minister," 4 March 1955, LAC, RG 97, vol. 182, file 5010-4, pt. 1, Unidentified Flying Objects (Incl. Outer Space Travel) file.

88 J.R. Baldwin, memorandum to W.H. van Allen, 8 March 1955, LAC, RG 97, vol. 182, file 5010-4, pt. 1, Unidentified Flying Objects (Incl. Outer Space Travel) file.

89 Wilbert Smith, "Memorandum to Superintendent of Radio Regulations," 10 June 1954, LAC, RG 97, vol. 182, file 5010-4, pt. 1, Unidentified Flying Objects (Incl. Outer Space Travel) file.

90 A.S. Shore, letter to Chairman, Defence Research Board, 20 November 1957, LAC, RG 24, acc. 83–84/167, box 7523, file 3800-10-1, pt. 1, Flying Saucers file.

91 Wilbert Smith, letter to "George," 12 June 1955, UOA, CA ON0034 30-003-S1-SS1-F15, Project Magnet: Correspondence file.

92 For example: Wilbert Smith, letter to Donald Keyhoe, 6 August 1952, UOA, CA ON0034 30-003-S1-SS3-F3, Project Magnet, vol. 1.

93 W.W. Stewart, letter to Wilbert Smith, 20 May 1955, LAC, RG 97, vol. 182, file 5010-4, pt. 1, Unidentified Flying Objects (Incl. Outer Space Travel) file.

94 Keyhoe, *The Flying Saucer Conspiracy*, 196.

95 Wilbert Smith, draft form letter, n.d., LAC, RG 97, vol. 182, file 5010-4, pt. 1, Unidentified Flying Objects (Incl. Outer Space Travel) file.

96 Geoffrey C. Bowker and Susan Leigh Star, *Sorting Things Out: Classification and Its Consequences* (Cambridge, MA: MIT Press, 2000).

97 Bruno Latour, *We Have Never Been Modern* (Cambridge, MA: Harvard University Press, 1993).

98 Tina Loo, "High Modernism, Conflict, and the Nature of Change in Canada: A Look at *Seeing Like a State*," *Canadian Historical Review* 97, no. 1 (2016): 46.

99 Wilbert Smith, letter to Mr Fry, 24 January 1956, UOA, CA ON0034 30-003-S1-SS1-F15, Project Magnet: Correspondence file.

100 Wilbert Smith, letter to John Diefenbaker, 10 April 1959, UOA, CA ON0034 30-003-S3-F5, Federal Government of Canada, pt. 1 of 2.

101 Wilbert Smith, letter to "Bill," 2 February 1959, UOA, CA ON0034 30-003-S1-SS1-F15, Project Magnet: Correspondence file.

CHAPTER TWO

1 J. Allen Hynek, *The UFO Experience: A Scientific Inquiry* (Chicago: Henry Regnery, 1972), 67–8.

2 Ibid., 70.

3 Directorate of Scientific Intelligence, letter to Secretary, Joint Intelligence Committee, 6 April 1950, LAC, RG 24, acc. 83–84/167, box 7523, file 3800-10-1, pt. 1, Flying Saucers file.

4 "Minutes of the 220th meeting of the Joint Intelligence Committee," 12 April 1950, LAC, RG 24, vol. 17984, file HQ 940-5, pt. 1, microfilm reel T-3291.

5 W.B. Millar, letter to RCAF Air Traffic Control, 17 March 1950, LAC, RG 24, vol. 17988, file HQ 940-105, pt. 1, microfilm reel T-3291.

6 Jack W. Saunders, letter to Air Commodore H.H. Hendrick, 21 April 1950, LAC, RG 24, vol. 17984, file HQ 940-5, pt. 1, microfilm reel T-3291.

7 G.S. Austin, letter to Group Captain Birchall, Canadian Joint Staff, Washington, DC, 3 July 1950, LAC. RG 24, vol. 17984, file HQ 940-5, pt. 1, microfilm reel T-3291.

8 W.W. Bean, memorandum to the Directorate of Scientific Intelligence, 29 June 1950, LAC, RG 24, acc. 83–84/167, box 7523, file 3800-10-1, pt. 1, Flying Saucers file.

9 H. Williamson, memorandum to the Directorate of Air Intelligence, 20 April 1950, LAC, RG 24, vol. 17988, file HQ 940-105, pt. 1, microfilm reel T-3291.

10 A.J.G. Langley, letter to G.S. Austin, Directorate of Air Intelligence, 19 April 1950, LAC, RG 24, vol. 17984, file HQ 940-5, pt. 1, microfilm reel T-3291.

11 M. Weller, letter to O.M. Solandt, 21 April 1952, LAC, RG 24, acc. 83–84/167, box 7523, file 3800-10-1, pt. 1, Flying Saucers file.

12 Letter (author's name redacted) to O.M. Solandt, 18 April 1952, LAC, RG 24, vol. 17984, file HQ 940-5, pt. 1, microfilm reel T-3291.

13 G. Davies, letter to O.M. Solandt, 16 April 1953, LAC, RG 24, acc. 83–84/167, box 7523, file 3800-10-1, pt. 1, Flying Saucers file.

14 Tom Eastham, letter to O.M. Solandt, 2 February 1955, LAC, RG 24, acc. 83–84/167, box 7523, file 3800-10-1, pt. 1, Flying Saucers file.

15 Jason Ridler, *Maestro of Science: Omond McKillop Solandt and Government Science in War and Hostile Peace, 1939–1956* (Toronto: University of Toronto Press, 2015), 181.

16 Ibid., 197.

17 O.M. Solandt, letter to Tom Eastham, 8 February 1955, LAC, RG 24, acc. 83–84/167, box 7523, file 3800-10-1, pt. 1, Flying Saucers file.

18 Ridler, *Maestro of Science*, 197.

19 Christian Nyby, dir., *The Thing from Another World* (Winchester Pictures Corporation, 1951); Rudolph Maté, dir., *When Worlds Collide* (Hollywood: Paramount Pictures, 1951); Harry Horner, dir., *Red Planet Mars* (Melaby Pictures, 1952); Lee Sholem, dir., *Superman and the Mole Men* (Lippert Pictures, 1951).

20 For example, Paul Hellyer, minister of national defence from 1963 to 1967, recalled that during his tenure he received no communications from other departments regarding UFOs. Interview by the author, 16 June 2017.

21 G.C.W. Browne, letter to W.D. McLeod, Officer-in-Charge, Baker Lake Ionosphere Station, 18 April 1952, LAC, RG 97, vol. 115, file 5010-4, pt. 1, Sightings of Unidentified Aerial Objects, "Project Second Storey" file.

22 The meeting minutes stated: "It was agreed that CONFIDENTIAL was sufficient, but that members should be cleared to SECRET to facilitate any exchange of information from international sources." Except for the odd memo that Wilbert Smith marked "Top Secret," at no point during Canada's involvement with UFOs was this security classification increased. In fact, it was later removed altogether. The National Research Council would eventually take over responsibility for collecting UFO reports, but one of the conditions for agreeing to do so was that all reports were to be unclassified.

23 "Minutes of the First Meeting of the Committee Set Up to Deal with 'Flying Saucers' Sightings," 24 April 1952, LAC, RG 24, vol. 17988, file HQ 940-105, pt. 1, microfilm reel T-3291.

24 H.C. Oatway, memorandum to Project Second Storey committee members, 30 April 1952, LAC, RG 97, vol. 115, file 5010-4, pt. 1, Sightings of Unidentified Aerial Objects, "Project Second Storey" file.

25 "Not Chasing Saucers," *Charlottetown Guardian*, 6 May 1952.

26 This was because, as Secretary Oatway explained, "Theta" was not appropriate since the word had "not been assigned to Canada under tripartite agreements," and, "if a single word name were used, it as well as the Committee deliberations, would be classed as Confidential and could not appear on interrogation forms which would be used to obtain data from the public." "Minutes of the 2/52 Meeting of Project Second Storey," 19 May 1952, UOA, CA ON0034 30-003-S1-SS2-F2, Project Second Storey: Defence Research Board Meeting Minutes.

27 Donald H. Menzel, "The Truth About Flying Saucers," *Look Magazine*, 17 June 1952, http://www.project1947.com/fig/look61752.htm.

28 Peter M. Millman, letter to Captain S.B. Goddard, 17 April 1968, LAC, RG 77, vol. 306, file UAR/N68 001-058, microfilm reel T-1741.

29 "Minutes of the 2/52 Meeting of Project Second Storey," 19 May 1952, UOA, CA ON0034 30-003-S1-SS2-F2, Project Second Storey: Defence Research Board Meeting Minutes.

30 Andrew Richter, *Avoiding Armageddon: Canadian Military Strategy and Nuclear Weapons, 1950–1963* (Vancouver, UBC Press, 2002), 5.

31 Andrew Godefroy, *In Peace Prepared: Innovation and Adaptation in Canada's Cold War Army* (Vancouver: UBC Press, 2014), 11.

32 The minutes state: "It was pointed out that the business of the Committee is not to undertake the actual interrogation of persons who have seen unidentified flying objects. Therefore, in so far as the Committee was concerned, there could be no direct action taken to follow up a promising sighting." That is, the committee decided it would act only as an advisory, not an investigative, body. "Minutes of the 3/52 Meeting of Project Second Storey," 31 July 1952, UOA, CA ON0034 30-003-S1-SS2-F2, Project Second Storey: Defence Research Board Meeting Minutes.

33 This is an early example of the kinds of UFO clubs and organizations that concerned citizens would begin establishing in earnest in the 1960s. These clubs will be explored in more detail in Chapter 3.

34 "Minutes of the 3/52 Meeting of Project Second Storey," 31 July 1952, UOA, CA ON0034 30-003-S1-SS2-F2, Project Second Storey: Defence Research Board Meeting Minutes.

35 Wilbert Smith, letter to Donald Keyhoe, 6 August 1952, UOA, CA ON0034 30-003-S1-SS2-F3, Project Magnet, vol. 1.

36 Including the witness's name, address, age group, "occupation and previous relevant experience," and whether the observer was wearing glasses, or had seen "flying objects" before, "and if so, briefly, when, where, and [under what] circumstances." LAC, RG 24, vol. 22349, file NBC-9150-4, Intelligence Reports.

37 Including the date and time, the position of the observer, the number of objects seen, the length of time they were visible, their position in the sky at the beginning versus the end of the sighting, changes in the direction of motion, the object's shape, colour, size, and brightness, whether any exhaust or vapour trails were visible, or noise heard, and the weather conditions during the sighting, including whether the object flew above, behind, or in and out of cloud cover.

38 "Project Second Storey Sighting Report," n.d., UOA, CA ON0034 30-003-S1-SS1-F1, reprint of Project Magnet Report.

39 Theodore Porter, *Trust in Numbers: The Pursuit of Objectivity in Science and Public Life* (Princeton, NJ: Princeton University Press, 1996).

40 J.R. Robertson, letter to the District Controller of Air Services, Edmonton, AB, 21 February 1953, LAC, RG 97, vol. 115, file 5010-4, pt. 1, Sightings of Unidentified Aerial Objects file.

41 These factors corresponded to the questions on the sighting form. Analysts were to assign scores based on things like the level of the observer's relevant training (a trained observer in "sky work" would score higher than a trained observer in "other fields"), how many objects the observer had seen previously (significantly, a higher score was given to someone who had never seen an object before), and how detailed the observer's description was (the more specific and consistent, the higher the score). The weighting factors were meant to assist in the use of "extreme care" so that the interrogator could "avoid influencing the score by any prejudice regarding reliability or confirmation." "Project Magnet," n.d., UOA, CA ON0034 30-003-S1-SS1-F5, Project Magnet: Supplemental Documents.

42 The total list included: balloons, aircraft, the effects of viewing objects through screens and glass, "nacreous or mother of pearl clouds," noctilucent clouds, cloud reflections, optical phenomena, meteors, stars and planets, and the aurora. Each of these objects had a description that outlined what they would generally look like to an observer on the ground, preparing the interrogator to identify a potential match in the observer's description. Several of the descriptions stated that the average person should not be likely to misidentify the object for a UFO. In the case of optical phenomena, for instance, the description stated that rainbows might at times "give the appearance of a small object in the sky," but "because rainbows are [a] fairly common occurrence, they are unlikely to deceive anyone." However, the committee obviously felt it necessary to include such examples, just in case.

43 "Flying Saucer Seen by Ancient Monks," *Gleichen Call*, 11 March 1953.

44 RCMP reports commonly described UFO sightings as a "complaint" and, as such, to be filed through the Criminal Investigation Branch, indicating a legalistic approach to the problem. The NRC, on the other hand, was interested – if at all – in whether or not the sighting might provide information about a misidentified meteor or fireball, and therefore processed UFO reports through the Meteorite Section of the Upper Atmosphere Division. These reports focused on weather conditions and descriptions of the object that would help determine what kind of natural phenomenon it might have been.

45 Edward Ruppelt, *The Report on Unidentified Flying Objects* (New York: Doubleday, 1956), 28.

46 Hynek, *The UFO Experience*, 175.
47 "Flying Saucers, Canada's Sighting Station," *Charlottetown Guardian*, 8 February 1954.
48 Steve Hewitt, *Spying 101: The RCMP's Secret Activities at Canadian Universities, 1917–1997* (Toronto: University of Toronto Press, 2002), 138.
49 Rudolf Goy, letter to the Air Vice Commander, RCAF, 6 October 1952, LAC, RG 24, acc. 83–84/167, box 7523, file 3800-10-1, pt. 1, Flying Saucers file.
50 R.G. Gooding, memorandum to G.C.W. Browne, Controller of Telecommunications, Department of Transport, 22 September 1952, LAC, RG 97, vol. 115, file 5010-4, pt. 1, Sightings of Unidentified Aerial Objects file.
51 T.E. Morrison, memorandum to the Director of Marine Services, Department of Transport, 8 August 1952, LAC, RG 97, vol. 115, file 5010-4, pt. 1, Sightings of Unidentified Aerial Objects file.
52 Letter (author's name redacted) to Department of National Defence, 6 December 1952, LAC, RG 24, vol. 17988, file HQC 940-105, pt. 1, microfilm reel T-3291.
53 Andrew Thomson, memorandum to W.R. Fryers, Aviation Forecast Office, Regina, 21 January 1953, LAC, RG 97, vol. 115, file 5010-4, pt. 1, Sightings of Unidentified Aerial Objects file.
54 H.V. Anderson, "Sighting of Unidentified Flying Objects Circular Letter M.S. 476," 19 January 1953, LAC, RG 97, vol. 115, file 5010-4, pt. 1, Sightings of Unidentified Aerial Objects file.
55 "Minutes of the 4/52 Meeting of Project Second Storey," 17 November 1952, UOA, CA ON0034 30-003-S1-SS2-F2, Project Second Storey: Defence Research Board Meeting Minutes.
56 "Minutes of the 5/53 Meeting of Project Second Storey," 9 March 1953, UOA, CA ON0034 30-003-S1-SS2-F2, Project Second Storey: Defence Research Board Meeting Minutes.
57 G.C. Campbell, letter to the Chief of the Air Staff, RCAF, 25 May 1953, LAC, RG 24, vol. 17988, file HQC 940-105, pt. 1, microfilm reel T-3291.
58 Leonard H. Stringfield, letter to Project Magnet, 30 September 1953, LAC, RG 24, acc. 83–84/167, box 7523, file 3800-10-1, pt. 1, Flying Saucers file.
59 Byron Haskin, dir., *The War of the Worlds* (Hollywood: Paramount Pictures, 1953).
60 Elmore Philpott, letter to Wilbert Smith, 17 November 1953, LAC, RG 97, vol. 182, file 5010-4, pt. 1, Unidentified Flying Objects (Incl. Outer Space Travel) file.

61 Millman was referring to this book: Desmond Leslie and George Adamski, *The Flying Saucers Have Landed* (London: Werner Laurie, 1954).
62 "Minutes of the Sixth Meeting of Project Second Storey," 22 February 1954, LAC, RG 24, acc. 83–84/167, box 7523, file 3800-10-1, pt. 1, Flying Saucers file.
63 Peter M. Millman, "Project Second Storey Summary Report," 21 November 1953, UOA, CA ON0034 30-003-S1-SS2-F1, Project Second Storey Information and Spacecraft Witness Interview Instructions.
64 Hynek, *The UFO Experience*, 169.
65 G.C.W. Browne, letter to Andrew Thomson, Controller of Meteorological Services, Department of Transport, 17 July 1952, LAC, RG 97, vol. 115, file 5010-4, pt. 1, Sightings of Unidentified Aerial Objects file.
66 Hynek, *The UFO Experience*, 22.
67 Letter (author's name redacted) to APRO, 25 August 1968, LAC, RG 77, vol. 306, file UAR/N69 01-030, microfilm reel T-1741.

CHAPTER THREE

1 Jan-Willem van Prooijen, *The Psychology of Conspiracy Theories* (New York: Routledge, 2018), viii.
2 Tom Eastham, letter to O.M. Solandt, 2 February 1955, LAC, RG 24, acc. 83–84/167, box 7523, file 3800-10-1, pt. 1, Flying Saucers file.
3 O.M. Solandt, letter to Tom Eastham, 8 February 1955, LAC, RG 24, acc. 83–84/167, box 7523, file 3800-10-1, part 1.
4 Daniel Kamman, letter to the Defence Research Board, 6 February 1956, LAC, RG 24, acc. 83–84/167, box 7523, file 3800-10-1, pt. 1, Flying Saucers file.
5 R.S. Thain, letter to Daniel Kamman, 14 February 1956, LAC, RG 24, acc. 83–84/167, box 7523, file 3800-10-1, pt. 1, Flying Saucers file.
6 "Saucers come from outer space," *Weekend Magazine*, vol. 7, no. 25, 1957.
7 Robert Bothwell, *Alliance and Illusion: Canada and the World, 1945–1984* (Vancouver: UBC Press, 2007), 12; J.L. Granatstein, *Canada's War: The Politics of the Mackenzie King Government, 1939–1945* (1975; Toronto: University of Toronto Press, 1990), xi.
8 Ibid.
9 J.L. Granatstein, *The Ottawa Men: The Civil Service Mandarins, 1935–1957* (Toronto: Oxford University Press, 1982), 92.

10 H.E.J. Holloway, telegram to Wilbert Smith, 2 August 1957, LAC, RG 97, vol. 182, file 5010-4, pt. 2, Unidentified Flying Objects (Incl. Outer Space Travel) file.

11 J.C. Lovelace, letter to Mr and Mrs McGovern, 21 May 1957, LAC, RG 24, vol. 17984, file HQ 940-5, pt. 1, microfilm reel T-3291.

12 W.L. Gillespie, memorandum to Directorate of Operations, Department of National Defence, 9 December 1957, LAC, RG 24, vol. 17988, file HQC 940-105, pt. 2, microfilm reel T-3291.

13 For example: J.D. Harvey, letter to Julian Hennessey, 7 April 1964, LAC, RG 97, vol. 182, file 5010-4, pt. 2, Unidentified Flying Objects (Incl. Outer Space Travel) file.

14 Zuoyue Wang, *In Sputnik's Shadow: The President's Science Advisory Committee and Cold War America* (New Brunswick, NJ: Rutgers University Press, 2009), 77.

15 C.M. Brant, "Satellite Transmissions" memorandum to "S.T.," 4 November 1957, LAC, RG 97, vol. 182, file 5010-4, pt. 2, Unidentified Flying Objects (Incl. Outer Space Travel) file.

16 L.G. Cope, memorandum to Wilbert Smith, 6 November 1957, LAC, RG 97, vol. 182, file 5010-4, pt. 2, Unidentified Flying Objects (Incl. Outer Space Travel) file.

17 *Earth vs. the Flying Saucers* was loosely based on events depicted in Donald Keyhoe's book *Flying Saucers from Outer Space*. *Forbidden Planet* and *Invasion of the Body Snatchers* were both eventually selected for preservation by the US Library of Congress National Film Registry, in recognition of their cultural, historical, and aesthetic significance. Fred F. Sears, dir., *Earth vs. the Flying Saucers* (Clover Productions, 1956); Fred M. Wilcox, dir., *Forbidden Planet* (Beverley Hills: Metro-Goldwyn-Mayer, 1956); Don Siegel, dir., *Invasion of the Body Snatchers* (Los Angeles: Allied Artists Pictures, 1956).

18 Donald Keyhoe, letter to the Defence Research Board, 14 August 1958, LAC, RG 24, acc. 83–84/167, box 7523, file 3800-10-1, pt. 1, Flying Saucers file.

19 C.A. Pope, letter to Donald Keyhoe, 8 October 1958, LAC, RG 24, acc. 83–84/167, box 7523, file 3800-10-1, pt. 1, Flying Saucers file.

20 Donald Keyhoe, letter to Charles Pope, 17 October 1958, LAC, RG 24, acc. 83–84/167, box 7523, file 3800-10-1, pt. 1, Flying Saucers file.

21 C.A. Pope, letter to Donald Keyhoe, 29 October 1958, LAC, RG 24, acc. 83–84/167, box 7523, file 3800-10-1, pt. 1, Flying Saucers file.

22 E.P. Wood, letter to the Chief of the Air Staff, RCAF, 5 May 1959, LAC, RG 24, vol. 17984, file HQ 940-5, pt. 1, microfilm reel T-3291.

23 Irvin Yeaworth, dir., *The Blob* (Los Angeles: Fairview Productions, 1958); Edward L. Cahn, dir., *It! The Terror from Beyond Space* (Hollywood: Vogue Pictures, 1958).

24 *The Twilight Zone*, created by Rod Serling (New York: CBS Productions, 1959–64).

25 D.M. Spicer, letter to the Department of Transport, Saskatoon, 13 December 1959, LAC, RG 97, vol. 182, file 5010-4, pt. 2, Unidentified Flying Objects (Incl. Outer Space Travel) file.

26 S.L. Young, memorandum ("Another Letter from D.M. Spicer") to the Regional Director of Air Services, Winnipeg, 23 December 1959, LAC, RG 97, vol. 182, file 5010-4, pt. 2, Unidentified Flying Objects (Incl. Outer Space Travel) file.

27 C.R. Brereton, letter to D.M. Spicer, 29 December 1959, LAC, RG 97, vol. 182, file 5010-4, pt. 2, Unidentified Flying Objects (Incl. Outer Space Travel) file.

28 D.M. Spicer, letter to the Department of Transport, Winnipeg, 31 December 1959, LAC, RG 97, vol. 182, file 5010-4, pt. 2, Unidentified Flying Objects (Incl. Outer Space Travel) file.

29 Regional Superintendent, Air Traffic Control, Winnipeg, memorandum to the Director General, Air Services, Ottawa, 6 January 1960, LAC, RG 97, vol. 182, file 5010-4, pt. 2, Unidentified Flying Objects (Incl. Outer Space Travel) file.

30 R.W. Goodwin, memorandum ("Inquiries from D.M. Spicer – Saskatoon"), 19 February 1960, LAC, RG 97, vol. 182, file 5010-4, pt. 2, Unidentified Flying Objects (Incl. Outer Space Travel) file.

31 Joseph E. Uscinski and Joseph M. Parent, *American Conspiracy Theories* (New York: Oxford University Press, 2014), 17.

32 Christopher Dummitt, *Unbuttoned: A History of Mackenzie King's Secret Life* (Montreal: McGill-Queen's University Press, 2017), xiv.

33 Marshall Berman, *All That Is Solid Melts into Air: The Experience of Modernity* (New York: Simon & Schuster, 1982), 24.

34 van Prooijen, *Psychology of Conspiracy Theories*, 5.

35 Ibid., 26.

36 Ibid., 40.

37 Frank Scully, *Behind the Flying Saucers* (New York: Henry Holt, 1950), 3. This is the same Frank Scully that was mentioned in Wilbert Smith's memo about his alleged meeting with the physicist Robert Sarbacher.

38 John Dunlop, "Egmont Eye: Outer Limits," *Sechelt Peninsula Times*, 18 August 1965.

39 Kenneth Kaasen, letter to the Chief of the Air Staff, RCAF, 14 February 1960, LAC, RG 24, vol. 17984, file HQ 940-5, pt. 1, microfilm reel T-3291.

40 J.S.D. Francis, letter to Kenneth Kaasen, 23 February 1960, LAC, RG 24, vol. 17984, file HQ 940-5, pt. 1, microfilm reel T-3291.

41 Brenda Denzler, *The Lure of the Edge: Scientific Passions, Religious Beliefs, and the Pursuit of UFOs* (Berkeley: University of California Press, 2003), 14.

42 Donald Keyhoe, *The Flying Saucer Conspiracy* (New York: Henry Holt, 1955), 24.

43 Ken Kaasen, letter to the Commanding Officer, RCAF Station Edmonton, 21 April 1960, LAC, RG 24, vol. 17984, file HQ 940-5, pt. 1, microfilm reel T-3291.

44 L.C. Dilworth, letter to the Air Officer Commanding, RCAF Station Trenton, ON, 23 June 1960, LAC, RG 24, vol. 17984, file HQ 940-5, pt. 1, microfilm reel T-3291; G.A. Woolley, letter to the Chief of the Air Staff, RCAF, 13 May 1960, LAC, RG 24, vol. 17984, file HQ 940-5, pt. 1, microfilm reel T-3291.

45 L.C. Dilworth, letter to Kenneth Kaasen, 23 June 1960, LAC, RG 24, vol. 17984, file HQ 940-5, pt. 1, microfilm reel T-3291.

46 Ken Kaasen, letter to the Defence Research Board, 25 July 1960, LAC, RG 24, acc. 83–84/167, box 7523, file 3800-10-1, pt. 1, Flying Saucers file.

47 C.A. Pope, letter to Ken Kaasen, 9 August 1960, LAC, RG 24, acc. 83–84/167, box 7523, file 3800-10-1, pt. 1, Flying Saucers file.

48 Ken Kaasen, letter to Patricia Larkin, for the Public Relations Officer, Defence Research Board, 11 August 1960, LAC, RG 24, acc. 83–84/167, box 7523, file 3800-10-1, pt. 1, Flying Saucers file.

49 Ken Kaasen, letter to "UFO Investigations," RCAF, Ottawa, 23 October 1960, LAC, RG 24, vol. 17984, file HQ 940-5, pt. 1, microfilm reel T-3291.

50 Ken Kaasen, letter to Douglas S. Harkness, 4 March 1962, LAC, RG 24, vol. 17984, file HQ 940-5, pt. 1, microfilm reel T-3291.

51 Douglas S. Harkness, letter to Ken Kaasen, 8 March 1962, LAC, RG 24, vol. 17984, file HQ 940-5, pt. 1, microfilm reel T-3291.

52 Robert MacDougall, "Sympathetic Physics: The Keely Motor and the Laws of Thermodynamics in Nineteenth-Century Culture," *Technology and Culture* 60, no. 2 (2019): 438–66.

53 Robert MacDougall, "Why Do People Believe in Pseudoscience?", *Gizmodo*, 11 March 2019, https://gizmodo.com/why-do-people-believe-in-pseudoscience-1833193811; see also: Robert MacDougall, "Convention of Cranks: Why the Nineteenth Century's Golden Age of Pseudoscience May Be a Precursor of Our Own," *SCOPE Magazine*, Spring 2011, http://www.scope-mag.com/about/issues/spring-2011/convention-of-cranks.

54 Bryant and Helen Reeve, *Flying Saucer Pilgrimage* (Mundelein, IL: Palmer Publications, 1965), 114.

55 Ibid., 200.

56 Ken Kaasen, letter to Douglas S. Harkness, 12 March 1962, LAC, RG 24, vol. 17984, file HQ 940-5, pt. 1, microfilm reel T-3291.

57 W.H. Muncy, memorandum ("Unidentified Flying Objects – Mr. Ken Kaasen"), 22 March 1962, LAC, RG 24, vol. 17984, file HQ 940-5, pt. 1, microfilm reel T-3291.

58 Douglas S. Harkness, letter to Ken Kaasen, n.d., LAC, RG 24, vol. 17984, file HQ 940-5, pt. 1, microfilm reel T-3291.

59 Douglas S. Harkness, letter to Ken Kaasen, April 1962, LAC, RG 24, vol. 17984, file HQ 940-5, pt. 1, microfilm reel T-3291.

60 Richard Hofstadter, *The Paranoid Style in American Politics: and Other Essays* (New York: Knopf, 1965), 14.

61 Michael Butter and Peter Knight, "The History of Conspiracy Theory Research: A Review and Commentary," *Conspiracy Theories and the People Who Believe Them*, ed. Joseph Uscinski (New York: Oxford University Press, 2019), 35.

62 A. de Niverville, "Vital Intelligence Sightings – CIRVIS Reporting Procedures," 10 March 1960, LAC, RG 12, acc. 1980–81/303, box 14, file 700-20, pt. 2, Reporting of Vital Intelligence Sightings (CIRVIS/MERINT) file.

63 In total, there are about 250 images of UFOs in the files at LAC. These range from the smallest drawings of a flash of light on a sighting report (these are most common) to full-page spreads depicting spacecraft (least common). There is but a very small handful of photographs, all of them invariably too dark or blurry to make out any significant detail. All of the drawings and illustrations were done in black and white – or, had any been created in colour originally, the colours did not survive the copying process over the years. I do not think much can be said about the drawings. In general, they are quite mundane. Despite their allure, they do not offer as much as they seem to promise. They are often too vague or poorly rendered to pick out detail. David Clarke, a journalism professor at Sheffield Hallam University, also encountered images in the UK's UFO files: scores of drawings and

illustrations of UFOs, sent to the government by concerned citizens. These became the basis for Clarke's book, *UFO Drawings from the National Archives*, a beautiful history of UFO art in the UK. Clarke has this to say about the images: "Most of the illustrations in this book lack the sophistication of drawings produced by professional artists for use in newspapers and magazines. Viewed from a purely aesthetic viewpoint, sketches of UFOs made by schoolchildren or policemen might appear naïve or worthless. But as visual evidence of unusual sightings that are deeply meaningful and significant to those individuals who see UFOs, they are uniquely valuable historical documents in their own right, and shed light on how the events and popular culture of the age imprinted on people's imaginations." The drawings Clarke found are of a different nature than those in Canada's UFO files. The UK drawings are colourful, full of life and energy, and communicate their creators' feelings (fear, concern, anxiety, joy, hope) much more clearly than do their Canadian counterparts. Perhaps Clarke is able to see the UK images as deeply meaningful, but I think it would be overstating the case to say the same for the Canadian ones. They are certainly interesting and provide a small window into the minds of those people claiming to have seen UFOs in Canada. In the end, however, I think they serve more as accompaniments to the sighting reports rather than standalone pieces for analysis. See: David Clarke, *UFO Drawings from the National Archives* (London: Four Corners Irregulars, 2017), 17.

64 Department of National Defence, CERVIS-MERINT Reporting Procedure poster, n.d., LAC, RG 12, acc. 1980–81/303, box 14, file 700-20, pt. 2, Reporting of Vital Intelligence Sightings (CIRVIS/MERINT) file.

65 H. Raynes, memorandum to "A.D.M.A.," Ottawa, 22 February 1962, LAC, RG 12, acc. 1980–81/303, box 14, file 700-20, pt. 2, Reporting of Vital Intelligence Sightings (CIRVIS/MERINT) file.

66 F.T. Wright, "Report of Strange Object Striking Clan Lake, N.W.T.," 19 July 1960, LAC, RG 18, vol. 3779, file HQ-400-Q-5, pt. 1, Unidentified Flying Objects (Sighting Of) file.

67 L.J. Matheson, "Report of Strange Object Striking Clan Lake, N.W.T.," 25 July 1960, LAC, RG 18, vol. 3779, file HQ-400-Q-5, pt. 1, Unidentified Flying Objects (Sighting Of) file.

68 H.F. Price, message form to RCMP Fort Smith, NT, 9 August 1960, LAC, RG 18, vol. 3779, file HQ-400-Q-5, pt. 1, Unidentified Flying Objects (Sighting Of) file.

69 H.F. Price, letter to the Officer Commanding, RCMP Fort Smith, NT, 10 August 1960, LAC, RG 18, vol. 3779, file HQ-400-Q-5, pt. 1, Unidentified Flying Objects (Sighting Of) file.

70 W.H. Kelly, letter to the Officer Commanding, "G" Division, RCMP, 16 August 1960, LAC, RG 18, vol. 3779, file HQ-400-Q-5, pt. 1, Unidentified Flying Objects (Sighting Of) file.

71 J.T. Parsons, letter to the RCMP Commissioner, 18 August 1960, LAC, RG 18, vol. 3779, file HQ-400-Q-5, pt. 1, Unidentified Flying Objects (Sighting Of) file.

72 L.C. Dilworth, letter to W.H. Kelly, Assistant Director of Security and Intelligence, RCMP, 23 September 1960, LAC, RG 18, vol. 3779, file HQ-400-Q-5, pt. 1, Unidentified Flying Objects (Sighting Of) file.

73 J.T. Parsons, letter to the RCMP Commissioner, 16 May 1961, LAC, RG 18, vol. 3779, file HQ-400-Q-5, pt. 1, Unidentified Flying Objects (Sighting Of) file.

74 B.H.B. Moffit, memorandum to J.K. Brown, 30 September 1965, LAC, RG 77, vol. 310, file DND/UAR (1965–66) 1–10, microfilm reel T-1743.

75 J.S.R. Francis, memorandum ("Policy – Unidentified Flying Objects"), 16 June 1959, LAC, RG 24, vol. 17988, file HQC 940-105, pt. 2, microfilm reel T-3291.

76 Letter (author's name redacted) to the Office of the Prime Minister, 8 April 1966, LAC, RG 24-G-1, BAN 2003-00412-2, box 1, file 2000-4, Intelligence – General: Unknown Flying Objects file.

77 Wilfrid Daniels, letter to the Chief of Information Services, Department of Transport, 2 April 1964, LAC, RG 97, vol. 182, file 5010-4, pt. 2, Unidentified Flying Objects (Incl. Outer Space Travel) file.

78 J.J.A. Hennessey, letter to the Chief of the Air Staff, RCAF, 1 October 1964, LAC, RG 97, vol. 182, file 5010-4, pt. 2, Unidentified Flying Objects (Incl. Outer Space Travel) file.

79 This figure may seem small, but even in 1966, 5 per cent of the population comprised nearly ten million people!

80 Polls from the 1970s and 1980s show a significant difference: Canadians tended to believe less strongly than Americans in the reality of UFOs. These polls are discussed in more detail in Chapter 5.

81 Douglas Marshall, "Look, Ma! It's Flying Saucer Time Again," *Maclean's*, 2 May 1966, 47.

82 R.J. Childerhose, "Flying Saucers: Does Somebody Up There Like Us?", *Weekend Magazine*, no. 46 (1966), 34–9.

83 *The Outer Limits*, created by Leslie Stevens (Daystar Productions, 1963–65).

84 *Star Trek*, created by Gene Roddenberry (Los Angeles: Desilu Productions, 1966).

85 John R. Kohr, letter to Charles Pope, 18 January 1966, LAC, RG 24, acc. 83–84/167, box 7523, file 3800-10-1, pt. 1, Flying Saucers file.
86 See: Lee McIntyre, *Post-Truth* (Cambridge, MA: MIT Press, 2018).
87 van Prooijen, *Psychology of Conspiracy Theories*, 38.
88 Letter (author's name redacted) to F.B. Caldwell, Department of National Defence, 23 June 1966, LAC, RG 24-G-1, BAN 2003-00412-2, box 1, file 2000-4, Intelligence – General: Unknown Flying Objects file.
89 Ibid.
90 Letter (author's name redacted) to the Department of National Defence, 5 July 1966, LAC, RG 24-G-1, BAN 2003-00412-2, box 1, file 2000-4, Intelligence – General: Unknown Flying Objects file.
91 J.C. Arnell, memorandum ("Unidentified Flying Objects – Follow-Up Action on Reports"), 22 August 1966, LAC, RG 24-G-1, BAN 2003-00412-2, box 1, file 2000-4, Intelligence – General: Unknown Flying Objects file.
92 F.B. Caldwell, letter (recipient's name redacted), 23 August 1966, LAC, RG 24-G-1, BAN 2003-00412-2, box 1, file 2000-4, Intelligence – General: Unknown Flying Objects file.
93 Ibid.
94 Frederic Jameson, *Postmodernism, or, The Cultural Logic of Late Capitalism* (Durham, NC: Duke University Press, 1991).
95 Jonathan Kay, *Among the Truthers: A Journey into the Growing Conspiracist Underground of 9/11 Truthers, Birthers, Armageddonites, Vaccine Hysterics, Hollywood Know-Nothings and Internet Addicts* (Toronto: HarperCollins, 2011), 106.
96 Carlo Ginzburg, *The Night Battles: Witchcraft and Agrarian Cults in the Sixteenth and Seventeenth Centuries* (1966; Baltimore: Johns Hopkins University Press, 1983), 18.
97 Jacques Vallee, *Passport to Magonia: From Folklore to Flying Saucers* (1969; Brisbane: Daily Grail Publishing, 2014), 8.
98 Ibid., 11.
99 Carl Jung, *Flying Saucers: A Modern Myth of Things Seen in the Skies* (1964; Princeton, NJ: Princeton University Press, 1978), 16–17.
100 Ibid., 22.
101 James Smith, interview by the author, 17 July 2018.
102 Wilbert Smith, letter to Donald Keyhoe, 6 August 1952, UOA, CA ON0034 30-003-S1-SS3-F3, Project Magnet: vol. 1.
103 Denzler, *Lure of the Edge*, 16.
104 See: Grant Cameron, *Charlie Red Star: True Reports of One of North American's Biggest UFO Sightings* (Toronto: Dundurn Press, 2017).

105 "UFOs sighted," *Coast News*, 31 August 1967.

106 Reeve and Reeve, *Flying Saucer Pilgrimage*, 17.

107 Robert D. Putnam, *Bowling Alone: The Collapse and Revival of American Community* (New York: Simon & Schuster, 2000), 27. Also see the discussion of "belief communities," in the context of UFOs, in: D.W. Pasulka, *American Cosmic: UFOs, Religion, Technology* (New York: Oxford University Press, 2019), 12–13.

108 Putnam, *Bowling Alone*, 16.

109 Vancouver Area Flying Saucer Club newsletter, January–February 1957, City of Vancouver Archives, Pamphlet Collection, PAM 1957-172.

110 Ra McGuire, blog post, 2 April 2016, http://www.ramcguire.com/blog/2016/4/2/ufo.

111 Vancouver Area Flying Saucer Club, poster announcing a public lecture, 7 May 1964, City of Vancouver Archives, Pamphlet Collection, PAM 1964-148.

112 Letter (author's name redacted) to the Department of National Defence, 21 August 1958, LAC, RG 24, vol. 17984, file HQ 940-5, pt. 1, microfilm reel T-3291.

113 UFO Sighting Report, Vancouver, 19 July 1965, LAC, RG 77, vol. 306, file UAR/N65 001-036, microfilm reel T-1741.

114 Debbie Meldrum, letter to the RCMP, 23 June 1989, LAC, RG 10, acc. 1990–91/073, box 1, file N89-1-70, National Research Council Non-Meteoritic Sighting file.

115 K.D. Smith, letter to Commanding Officer, "G" Division, RCMP, 31 January 1967, LAC, RG 18, vol. 3779, file HQ-400-Q-5, pt. 1, Unidentified Flying Objects (Sighting Of) file.

116 L.A. Bourgeois, letter to the Office of Information, Department of National Defence, 4 March 1965, LAC, RG 24, vol. 17988, file HQC 940-105, pt. 2, microfilm reel T-3291.

117 "Now we have undersea UFO's," *Peninsula Times*, 5 June 1968.

118 Mark O'Connell, *The Close Encounters Man: How One Man Made the World Believe in UFOs* (New York: HarperCollins, 2017), 189–90.

119 Keyhoe, *Flying Saucer Conspiracy*, 258.

120 Edward Ruppelt, *The Report on Unidentified Flying Objects* (New York: Doubleday, 1956), 242. There is, in fact, a scholarly literature on "prematurity" in science that analyzes why some objects are "discovered" more quickly than others. See, for instance: Ernest B. Hook, ed., *Prematurity in Scientific Discovery: On Resistance and Neglect* (Berkeley: University of California Press, 2002).

121 Desmond Leslie and George Adamski, *The Flying Saucers Have Landed* (London: Werner Laurie, 1954), 50.
122 Ibid., 66.
123 J. Allen Hynek, foreword to *Challenge to Science: The UFO Enigma*, by Jacques and Janine Vallee (New York: Ballantine, 1966).
124 Reeve and Reeve, *Flying Saucer Pilgrimage*, 23.
125 Leslie and Adamski, *The Flying Saucers Have Landed*, 11.
126 In fact, the historians on the podcast *BackStory* make the claim that much, or at least some, of the current doubt about scientific reliability and accuracy originated specifically in these early conflicts over UFOs. See: Ed Ayers, Brian Balogh, and Nathan Connolly, "Close Encounters: UFOs in American History," no. 0218, 21 September 2018, *BackStory*, podcast, https://www.backstoryradio.org/shows/close-encounters.
127 Lara Campbell and Dominique Clément, "Introduction: Time, Age, Myth: Towards a History of the Sixties," in *Debating Dissent: Canada and the Sixties*, ed. Lara Campbell, Dominique Clément, and Gregory S. Kealey (Toronto: University of Toronto Press, 2012), 10–11.

CHAPTER FOUR

1 J. Allen Hynek, *The UFO Experience: A Scientific Inquiry* (Chicago: Henry Regnery, 1972), 25–7.
2 Tom Hawthorn, *The Year Canadians Lost Their Minds and Found Their Country: The Centennial of 1967* (Madeira Park, BC: Douglas and McIntyre, 2017), v.
3 Ibid., 5.
4 Paul Hellyer, "Speech by the Honourable Paul T. Hellyer, PC MP Minister of National Defence at a Banquet, St. Paul, Alberta," 3 June 1967, LAC, MG 32, B-33, vol. 3, file 1, Speeches file.
5 John A. Keel, *The Mothman Prophecies* (New York: Tor, 1975).
6 See: Loren Coleman, *Bigfoot! The True Story of Apes in America* (New York: Paraview, 2003), ch. 7; Brian Regal, *Searching for Sasquatch: Crackpots, Eggheads, and Cryptozoology* (London: Palgrave Macmillan, 2011); Joshua Blu Buhs, *Bigfoot: The Life and Times of a Legend* (Chicago: University of Chicago Press, 2009).
7 J. Ruddy, "Look – there's a flying saucer!", *Maclean's*, November 1967, 34–6, 92–4.
8 Hynek, *The UFO Experience*, 111.

9 Leo Cadieux, letter to C.M. Drury, November 1967, LAC, RG 24-G-1, BAN 2003-00412-2, box 1, file 2000-4, Intelligence – General: Unknown Flying Objects file.
10 Hynek, *The UFO Experience*, 112.
11 Nearly every book that discusses UFOs in Canada has a section on the case. See, for example: Palmiro Campagna, *The UFO Files: The Canadian Connection Exposed* (Toronto: Stoddart, 1998), ch. 8; and John Robert Colombo, *True Canadian UFO Stories* (Toronto: Prospero Books, 2004), 144.
12 Stan Michalak and Chris Rutkowski, *When They Appeared: Falcon Lake 1967: The Inside Story of a Close Encounter* (Winnipeg: McNally-Robinson, 2017).
13 Stephen Michalak, *My Encounter with the UFO* (Winnipeg: Osnova Publications, 1967). See: LAC, RG 77, vol. 311, file DND/UAR (1967) 200, microfilm reel T-1744.
14 C.J. Davis, UFO Sighting Report, Falcon Lake, MB, 26 May 1967, LAC, RG 24, acc. 83–84/167, box 7523, file 3800-10-1, pt. 1, Flying Saucers file.
15 Michalak and Rutkowski, *When They Appeared*, 50.
16 C.J. Davis, UFO Sighting Report, Falcon Lake, MB, 26 May 1967, LAC, RG 24, acc. 83–84/167, box 7523, file 3800-10-1, pt. 1, Flying Saucers file.
17 In addition to APRO's Mr Thompson, another citizen, Gerald Hart, also showed up to "aid" the investigation. It is clear that nobody, apart from Michalak himself, trusted Hart; his motives were always unclear.
18 "UFO Report: Falcon Lake, Man.," n.d., LAC, RG 24, acc. 83–84/167, box 7523, file 3800-10-1, pt. 1, Flying Saucers file.
19 Brenda Denzler, *The Lure of the Edge: Scientific Passions, Religious Beliefs, and the Pursuit of UFOs* (Berkeley: University of California Press, 2003), 27.
20 Crop circles have even become commercialized: in 2014, the tech company Nvidia created a crop circle in a California field in the shape of their new microchip, to help promote the release of the company's new mobile processor. See: https://blogs.nvidia.com/blog/2014/01/05/salinas-crop-circle-and-project-192/, accessed 2 October 2018.
21 See, for instance: Mark Pilkington, *Mirage Men: A Journey in Disinformation, Paranoia and UFOs* (London: Constable, 2010), 9.
22 David Clarke, *How UFOs Conquered the World: The History of a Modern Myth* (London: Aurum Press, 2015), 92.

23 Charles Maxwell, dir., *A Field Full of Secrets* (Cleveland: Gravitas Ventures, 2014).
24 As such, it is possible that the marks appeared days before Schielke found them.
25 G.H.S. Jones, "Onsite Inspection of Reputed UFO Landing Marks at Duhamel, Alberta," n.d., LAC, RG 24, acc. 83–84/167, box 7523, file 3800-10-1, pt. 1, Flying Saucers file. Emphasis in original.
26 Ibid.
27 UFO Sighting Report, Camrose, AB, 8 August 1967, LAC, RG 77, vol. 310, file DND/UAR (1967) 91–100, microfilm reel T-1744.
28 G.H.S. Jones, "Onsite Inspection of Reputed UFO Landing Marks at Duhamel, Alberta," n.d., LAC, RG 24, acc. 83–84/167, box 7523, file 3800-10-1, pt. 1, Flying Saucers file. Emphasis in original.
29 Ibid.
30 F.M. Caldwell, memorandum ("Ministerial Inquiry"), 25 August 1967, LAC, RG 77, vol. 310, file DND/UAR (1967) 91–100, microfilm reel T-1744.
31 T.R. Overton, "Soil Samples Received in DRB, Originating from a Supposed 'UFO' Site at Duhamel (Alberta)," 17 October 1967, LAC, RG 77, vol. 310, file DND/UAR (1967) 91-100, microfilm reel T-1744.
32 F.M. Caldwell, memorandum ("Ministerial Inquiry"), 25 August 1967, LAC, RG 77, vol. 310, file DND/UAR (1967) 91–100, microfilm reel T-1744.
33 UFO Sighting Report, Barrington Passage, NS, 5 October 1967, LAC, RG 77, vol. 311, file DND/UAR (1967) 201–14, microfilm reel T-1744.
34 Chris Styles and Graham Simms, *Impact to Contact: The Shag Harbour Incident* (Halifax: Arcadia House Publishing, 2013), 14–15.
35 Telex message, "Provide helo to airlift three divers," 7 October 1967, LAC, RG 77, vol. 310, file DND/UAR (1967) 116–25, microfilm reel T-1744.
36 Telex message, "Two days of underwater search by divers," 8 October 1967, LAC, RG 77, vol. 310, file DND/UAR (1967) 116–25, microfilm reel T-1744.
37 Letter (author's name redacted) to RCMP, 12 October 1967, LAC, RG 18, vol. 3779, file HQ-400-Q-5, pt. 2, Flying Saucers file; letter (author's name redacted) to RCMP Headquarters, 7 October 1967, LAC, RG 18, vol. 3779, file HQ-400-Q-5, pt. 2, Flying Saucers file.
38 Ray MacLeod, "Something Concrete in Harbor UFO – RCAF," *Chronicle Herald* (Halifax), 7 October 1967, LAC, RG 77, vol. 310, file DND/UAR (1967) 116–25, microfilm reel T-1744.

39 Telex message, "Search continued 08 Oct negative results," 9 October 1967, LAC RG 77, vol. 310, file DND/UAR (1967) 116–25, microfilm reel T-1744.

40 W.W. Turner, memorandum ("UFO Report: Lower Wood Harbour, N.S."), 25 October 1967, LAC, RG 77, vol. 310, file DND/UAR (1967) 116–25, microfilm reel T-1744.

41 Styles and Simms, *Impact to Contact*.

CHAPTER FIVE

1 D. Davies, letter ("Unidentified Flying Objects"), 20 June 1968, LAC, RG 77, vol. 306, UAR/N68 001-058, microfilm reel T-1741. Davies likely got this idea from John Wyndham's novel *The Midwich Cuckoos* (London: Michael Joseph, 1957) and/or Wolf Rilla's movie adaptation, *Village of the Damned* (Beverley Hills: Metro-Goldwyn-Mayer, 1960).

2 H.H.A. Parker, memorandum ("Canadian Aerial Phenomena Investigations Committee"), 10 July 1967, LAC, RG 24-G-1, BAN 2003-00412-2, box 1, file 2000-4, Unknown Flying Objects file.

3 John H. Hodgson, letter to R.J. Uffen, 23 June 1967, LAC, RG 24, acc. 83–84/167, box 7523, file 3800-10-1, pt. 1, Flying Saucers file.

4 R.M. Aldwinckle, memorandum ("Unidentified Flying Objects (UFO's) – DND Interest"), 5 July 1967, LAC, RG 24, acc. 83–84/167, box 7523, file 3800-10-1, pt. 1, Flying Saucers file.

5 H. Sheffer, memorandum ("UFOs – Comments on paper for defence council"), 26 July 1967, LAC, RG 24, acc. 83–84/167, box 7523, file 3800-10-1, pt. 1, Flying Saucers file.

6 W.G. Schneider, letter to H. Sheffer, 28 August 1967, LAC, RG 24-G-1, BAN 2003-00412-2, box 1, file 2000-4, Unknown Flying Objects file.

7 Draft letter (unsigned) to C.M. Drury, September 1967, LAC, RG 24, acc. 83–84/167, box 7523, file 3800-10-1, pt. 1, Flying Saucers file.

8 C.M. Drury, letter to L. Cadieux, 23 October 1967, LAC, RG 24, acc. 83–84/167, box 7523, file 3800-10-1, pt. 1, Flying Saucers file.

9 Boilerplate response letter (unsigned), January 1968, LAC, RG 24, vol. 24031, file 3800-10-1, pt. 2, Flying Saucers file.

10 E.W. Greenwood, memorandum ("Investigation – UFO Reports"), 8 November 1967, LAC, RG 24, acc. 83–84/167, box 7523, file 3800-10-1, pt. 1, Flying Saucers file.

11 N.H. Ross, memorandum ("Investigation – UFO Reports"), November 1967, LAC, RG 24-G-1, BAN 2003-00412-2, box 1, file 2000-4, Unknown Flying Objects file.

12 Allan K. Vezina, letter to Leo Cadieux, 5 January 1968, LAC, RG 24, vol. 24031, file 3800-10-1, pt. 2, Flying Saucers file.
13 Allan K. Vezina, letter to Paul T. Hellyer, 9 June 1967, LAC, RG 24-G-1, BAN 2003-00412-2, box 1, file 2000-4, Unknown Flying Objects file.
14 Leo Cadieux, letter to Allan K. Vezina, 13 June 1967, LAC, RG 24-G-1, BAN 2003-00412-2, box 1, file 2000-4, Unknown Flying Objects file.
15 Allan K. Vezina, letter to Leo Cadieux, 15 June 1967, LAC, RG 24-G-1, BAN 2003-00412-2, box 1, file 2000-4, Unknown Flying Objects file.
16 Leo Cadieux, letter to Allan K. Vezina, 19 June 1967; and Allan K. Vezina, letter to Leo Cadieux, 15 June 1967, both LAC RG 24-G-1, BAN 2003-00412-2, box 1, file 2000-4, Unknown Flying Objects file.
17 Draft letter (unsigned) to C.M. Drury, September 1967, LAC, RG 24, acc. 83–84/167, box 7523, file 3800-10-1, pt. 1, Flying Saucers file.
18 Telex message ("Mr William Albert Small)," 14 November 1967, LAC, RG 77, vol. 311, file DND/UAR (1967) 164–76, microfilm reel T-1744.
19 "Pupils hear UFO talk," *Newmarket Era*, 7 November 1973, 30.
20 Franklin J. Schaffner, dir., *Planet of the Apes* (APJAC Productions, 1968).
21 Stanley Kubrick, dir., *2001: A Space Odyssey* (Stanley Kubrick Productions, 1968).
22 Erich von Däniken, *Chariots of the Gods?* (New York: Putnam, 1968).
23 C.M. Drury, letter to L. Cadieux, 16 February 1968, LAC, RG 24, acc. 83–84/167, box 7523, file 3800-10-1, pt. 1, Flying Saucers file.
24 Peter M. Millman, letter to A.F. McQuarrie, 22 March 1968, LAC, RG 77, vol. 306, file UAR/N68 001-058, microfilm reel T-1741.
25 Peter M. Millman, letter to Captain S.B. Goddard, 17 April 1968, LAC, RG 77, vol. 306, file UAR/N68 001-058., microfilm reel T-1741.
26 Brian Wilks, *Browsing Science Research at the Federal Level in Canada: History, Research Activities, and Publications* (Toronto: University of Toronto Press, 2004), 118.
27 National Research Council Proceedings of the Twelfth Meeting of the Associate Committee on Meteorites, 5 April 1968, LAC, RG 77, acc. 1997–98/094, vol. 34.
28 Edward Leith, letter to Peter Millman, 11 April 1968, LAC, RG 77, vol. 311, file DND/UAR (1967) 200, microfilm reel T-1744.
29 Peter M. Millman, letter to the RCMP Commissioner, 22 March 1968, LAC, RG 18, vol. 3779, file HQ-400-Q-5, pt. 1, Unidentified Flying Objects (Sighting Of) file.
30 Greg Eghigian, "Suspense and the UFOs" (invited talk, Working Group on the History of Technology, Consortium for the History of Science, Technology and Medicine, Philadelphia, 12 December 2017).

31 Donald Keyhoe, *The Flying Saucer Conspiracy* (New York: Henry Holt, 1955), 79. See also: Donald Keyhoe, *Flying Saucers: Top Secret* (New York: G.P. Putnam's Sons, 1960), 10.

32 N.H. Ross, memorandum ("Policy – Release DND UFO Information"), 21 November 1967, LAC, RG 77, vol. 311, file DND/UAR (1967) 164–76, microfilm reel T-1744.

33 H.C. Oatway, memorandum ("Project Second Storey Material"), 28 March 1968, LAC, RG 24, vol. 24031, file 3800-10-1, pt. 2, Flying Saucers file.

34 L.J. L'Heureux, letter to Peter Millman, 16 April 1968, LAC, RG 24, acc. 83–84/167, box 7523, file 3800-10-1, pt. 1, Flying Saucers file.

35 Ann Rees, "Sustaining Secrecy: Executive Branch Resistance to Access to Information in Canada," in *Brokering Access: Power, Politics, and Freedom of Information Process in Canada*, ed. Mike Larsen and Kevin Walby (Vancouver: UBC Press, 2012), 43.

36 Ibid., 55.

37 Vivienne Monty, "Due North: Issues in Access to Government Information, A View from Canada," *Journal of Government Information* 23, no. 4 (1996): 492.

38 Rees, "Sustaining Secrecy," 47.

39 W.W. Turner, memorandum ("Unidentified Flying Objects (UFOs) – DND Files"), 13 June 1968, LAC, RG 24-G-1, BAN 2003-00412-2, box 1, file 2000-4, Unknown Flying Objects file.

40 J.W. Quinn, UFO Sighting Report, Fort Resolution, NT, 19 July 1968, LAC,
RG 18, vol. 3779, file HQ-400-Q-5, pt. 2, Flying Objects (Sighting Of) file.

41 V.K. Weys, UFO Sighting Report, Fort Smith, NT, 26 July 1968, LAC, RG 18, vol. 3779, file HQ-400-Q-5, pt. 2, Flying Objects (Sighting Of) file.

42 J.G.W.R. Monier, UFO Sighting Report, Amos, QC, 29 July 1968, LAC, RG 18, vol, 3779, file HQ-400-Q-5, pt. 2, Flying Objects (Sighting Of) file.

43 Letter (author's name redacted) to Colonel L.A. Bourgeois, 5 August 1968, LAC, RG 24, vol. 24031, file 3800-10-1, pt. 2, Flying Saucers file.

44 Donald W. Golding, letter to the Chief of the Defence Staff, Department of National Defence, 2 October 1968, LAC, RG 77, vol. 306, file UAR/N68 116-170, microfilm reel T-1741.

45 Donald Golding, "Unidentified Flying Objects Report: 3 Year Study," 1968, LAC, RG 24, vol. 24031, file 3800-10-1, pt. 2, Flying Saucers file.

46 Canadian Aerial Phenomena Research Organization UFO Sighting Report, Ste. Ross, MB, 2 February 1969, LAC, RG 77, vol. 306, file UAR/N69 031-049, microfilm reel T-1741.

47 Brian C. Cannon, letter to Peter Millman, 5 March 1969, LAC, RG 77, vol. 306, file UAR/N69 031-049, microfilm reel T-1741.
48 Thomas James Cameron, letter to the Office of the Prime Minister, 19 March 1969, LAC, MG 32, B-33, vol. 90.
49 G.J. Cook, letter to Thomas James Cameron, 29 April 1969, LAC, MG 32, B-33, vol. 90.
50 B.C. Cannon, letter to the Commanding Officer, CFB Esquimault, 15 April 1969, LAC, RG 24-G-1, BAN 2003-00412-2, box 1, file 2000-4, Unknown Flying Objects file.
51 B.A. McIntosh, "UFO Sighting Report on 23 April 1969," n.d., LAC, RG 77, vol. 306, file UAR/N69 050-100, microfilm reel T-1741.
52 Arthur Bray, letter to Bruce McIntosh, 27 April 1969, LAC, RG 77, vol, 306, file UAR/N69 050-100, microfilm reel T-1741.
53 B.C. Cannon, letter to Canadian Forces Headquarters, 27 May 1969, LAC, RG 24-G-1, BAN 2003-00412-2, box 1, file 2000-4, Unknown Flying Objects file.
54 The poll did not elaborate on what "real" meant in this context, whether of extraterrestrial origin or otherwise. See: Canadian Institute of Public Opinion (CIPO), Gallup Poll, May 1974, #365 (data set), Gallup Canada Inc.
55 Roper Center for Public Opinion Research, Gallup Poll, November 1973, #883.Q05A (data set).
56 CIPO, Gallup Poll, February 1978, #409 (data set), Gallup Canada Inc.
57 CIPO, Gallup Poll, January 1979, #420 (data set), Gallup Canada Inc.
58 "Children's Writing Contest: Mr. Smith Reads Up on Flying Saucers," *Winnipeg Tribune*, 25 March 1978.
59 Steven Spielberg, dir., *Close Encounters of the Third Kind* (London: EMI Films, 1977).
60 George Lucas, dir., *Star Wars: A New Hope* (San Francisco: Lucasfilm, 1977); Robert Wise, dir., *The Andromeda Strain* (New York: Universal Pictures, 1971); Peter Hyams, dir., *Capricorn One* (London: ITC Entertainment, 1978); Ridley Scott, dir., *Alien* (Los Angeles: 20th Century Fox, 1979); *In Search Of…* , created by Alan Landsburg (Universal TV Alternative Studios, 1977–82).
61 For example: Mr X, "Res Bureaux Bulletin No. 47," May 1979, LAC, RG 18, vol. 3779, file HQ-400-Q-5, part 1, Unidentified Flying Objects (Sighting Of) file. *Fortean* refers to anomalous phenomena that cannot be explained by modern science. The term derives from the pioneering studies of American researcher and writer Charles Fort, whose best-known work is *The Book of the Damned* (1919).

62 Mr X, letter to the RCMP Commissioner, 30 May 1979, LAC, RG 18, vol. 3779, file HQ-400-Q-5, pt. 1, Unidentified Flying Objects (Sighting Of) file.
63 Corporal Ford, memo to the Federal Police Branch, 13 June 1979, LAC, RG 18, vol. 3779, file HQ-400-Q-5, pt. 1, Unidentified Flying Objects (Sighting Of) file.
64 D. Chiarot, letter to Mr X, 27 June 1979, LAC, RG 18, vol. 3779, file HQ-400-Q-5, pt. 1, Unidentified Flying Objects (Sighting Of) file.
65 Mr X, letter to D. Chiarot, 3 July 1979, LAC, RG 18, vol. 3779, file HQ-400-Q-5, pt. 1, Unidentified Flying Objects (Sighting Of) file.
66 D. Chiarot, letter to Mr X, 27 July 1979, LAC, RG 18, vol. 3779, file HQ-400-Q-5, pt. 1, Unidentified Flying Objects (Sighting Of) file.
67 Mark Fenster, *The Transparency Fix: Secrets, Leaks, and Uncomfortable Government Information* (Stanford, CA: Stanford University Press, 2017), 3.
68 Ibid., 11.
69 A.G. McNamara, "UFO's: What Are They?," n.d., LAC, RG 12, vol. 3930, file 2-1-33, pt. 1, Unidentified Flying Objects file.
70 Ibid.
71 Letter (author's name redacted) to the Minister of Defence, 10 January 1984, LAC, RG 77, acc. 1985–86/179, file N84-1-29, Non-Meteoritic Sighting file. *Radiesthesia* refers to the ability to sense radiation but has its origins in the better-known process of dowsing.
72 Suzanne Lundrigan, "In search of our space brothers," *Gateway* (University of Alberta), 25 March 1986.
73 Irvin Kershner, dir., *The Empire Strikes Back* (San Francisco: Lucasfilm, 1980); Richard Marquand, dir., *Return of the Jedi* (San Francisco: Lucasfilm, 1983); Steven Spielberg, dir., *E.T. the Extra-Terrestrial* (Universal City, CA: Amblin Productions, 1982); Nicholas Meyer, dir., *Star Trek II: The Wrath of Khan* (Hollywood: Paramount Pictures, 1982); Leonard Nimoy, dir., *Star Trek III: The Search for Spock* (Hollywood: Paramount Pictures, 1984); James Cameron, dir., *Aliens* (Los Angeles: 20th Century Fox, 1986); John McTiernan, dir., *Predator* (Lawrence Gordon Productions, 1987).
74 Whitley Strieber, *Communion: A True Story* (New York: Avon Books, 1987); William Moore and Charles Berlitz, *The Roswell Incident* (New York: Grosset & Dunlap, 1980).
75 UFO Sighting Report, Bloodvein Indian Reserve, MB, 10 October 1990, LAC, RG 10, acc.1991–92/022, box 1, file N89 71–117, Non-Meteoric Sighting file.

76 Caprice Brunelle, letter to Denise Cardinal, 19 March 1995, LAC, RG 77, acc. 1997–98/046, box 1, file N95 1–54, Non-Meteoritic Sightings file.
77 *The X-Files*, created by Chris Carter (Los Angeles, 20th Century Fox Television, 1993).
78 Letter (author's name redacted) to the National Research Council, 17 January 1992, LAC, RG 77, acc. 1992–93/308, vol. 1, file N92-1-83, Non-Meteoritic Sighting file.
79 Martin Beech, "The Millman Fireball Archive," *Journal of the Royal Astronomical Society of Canada* 97 (April 2003): 72; Chris Rutkowski and Geoff Dittman, *The Canadian UFO Report: The Best Cases Revealed* (Toronto: Dundurn Press, 2006), 237.
80 Non-Meteoritic Sighting (UFO Sighting Report), Repulse Bay, NT, 13 August 1995, LAC, RG 77, acc. 1997–98/046, box 1, file N95 1–54, Non-Meteoritic Sighting file.
81 Peter M. Millman, letter to J. Allen Hynek, 2 July 1970, LAC, RG 77, vol. 310, file DND/UAR (1967) 71–80, microfilm reel T-1744.
82 R.E. Thom, letter to the Meteor Centre, National Research Council, 21 November 1974, LAC, RG 77, vol. 307, file UAR/N74 063-117, microfilm reel T-1742.
83 Ian Halliday, letter to R.E. Thom, 29 November 1974, LAC, RG 77, vol. 307, file UAR/N74 063-117, microfilm reel T-1742.
84 E.P. DeBalinnard, letter to W.R. Danner, 15 August 1977, LAC, RG 77, vol. 309, file UAR/N80 001-050, microfilm reel T-1743.
85 J. Allen Hynek, *The UFO Experience: A Scientific Inquiry* (Chicago: Henry Regnery, 1972).

CONCLUSION

1 "Canada's UFOs: The Search for the Unknown," online resource, LAC, last modified 29 January 2018, https://www.bac-lac.gc.ca/eng/discover/unusual/ufo/Pages/default.aspx.
2 Michael Eamon, "A 'Genuine Relationship with the Actual': New Perspectives on Primary Sources, History and the Internet in the Classroom," *History Teacher* 39, no. 3 (2006): 305.
3 Michael Eamon, interview by the author, 5 July 2017.
4 Linda Lyons, "Paranormal Beliefs Come (Super)Naturally to Some," *Gallup News*, 1 November 2005, https://news.gallup.com/poll/19558/paranormal-beliefs-come-supernaturally-some.aspx.
5 "Most Canadians (79%) Can Tell You We're a Maple Syrup Power House, Only a Quarter (27%) Know We're a UFO Destination," *IPSOS News*,

27 June 2018, https://www.ipsos.com/en-ca/news-polls/Historica-Canada-Canada-Day-Poll-June-27-2018.

6 Robbie Graham, introduction to *UFOs: Reframing the Debate*, ed. Robbie Graham (London: White Crow Books, 2017), xxiii.

Index

access to information: legislation, 17, 126, 137–9, 150, 160, 166; need for secrecy, 67, 93, 139, 150, 166. *See also* citizen: concerns about government secrecy
Aerial Phenomena Research Organization (APRO), 110, 112–13, 198n17
Arnold, Kenneth, 5, 18, 119, 151
associate committees. *See under* National Research Council
atomic bomb, 32, 103

boundary formation (real vs not real), 46–7, 168
Bray, Arthur, 22, 42–3, 140–1, 144
Bush, Vannevar, 22, 177n9

Canadian Aerial Phenomena Investigations Committee (CAPIC), 131–2
Canadian Aerial Phenomena Research Organization (CAPRO), 143–5
Canadian UFO Research (CUFOR), 142
Central Intelligence Agency (CIA), 68
Chuvalo, George, 92
citizen: antagonism, 93, 126, 131, 134, 164, 167; concerns about government secrecy, 16, 32, 83–5, 103, 126, 137; distrust of government, 11, 13, 50, 80, 92–3, 104, 134, 167; distrust of science, 84–5, 98, 101, 103, 197n126; frustration with government replies, 62, 78, 91, 93, 145; "iconoclast" skeptics, 84, 105, 161; investigation, 4, 132, 140, 142–4; organizing, 11, 97–9, 163–4; privacy, 77
Civilian Saucer Investigations (Los Angeles UFO club), 58
Clan Lake incident, 89–90
Cold War, 6, 30–1, 80
Condon Report, 8, 128, 154
conspiracy theory: of government cover-up, 31–2, 45, 92; theoretical explanation, 12–13, 15, 72, 79–80, 86, 93, 104
cranks, 34, 43–4, 64, 95, 134
crop circles, 113–19, 198n20

Defence Research Board, 39, 49, 52, 54, 74, 76, 83, 138
distrust: mutual mistrust, 13, 18, 26, 93, 96, 164. *See also under* citizen
doubletalk, 71, 81, 91, 145, 163

evidence for UFOs: and belief, 12, 94; importance of physical, 23, 59, 90, 107, 123; lack of, 53, 57, 63, 122, 124
extraterrestrials: contact with, 5, 52, 108–9, 156; hypotheses for, 24, 33, 40, 54, 94; offers of technology by, 26; public belief in, 12, 25, 137; varieties of, 10, 32, 154

failure: of government inaction, 13, 99; of technology, 24, 175n40
Falcon Lake incident, 108–13, 118, 123. *See also* Michalak, Stephen
flying saucer (moniker), 5, 35, 171n15. *See also* UFOs
form letters, 42, 44, 145, 148
Fort, Charles, 203n61

Gallup polls, 91, 98, 145, 155, 163
"go-around," the. *See* doubletalk
Golding, Donald, 142–3
government (Canada): disbelief in UFOs, 48, 55, 62, 96, 100, 125, 151–3; foreign affairs, 73–4; internal confusion, 87, 126; listless approach, 34, 45, 130; miscommunication, 48, 54, 72–5, 93, 165, 184n20; transparency, 11, 84, 150–1, 160, 166; unwanted publicity, 8, 15, 35, 37, 39–40, 51, 65, 95; vs the state, 169n5

Hellyer, Paul, 19, 46, 106, 134, 184n20
Hollywood. *See* UFOs: in the media
Hynek, J. Allen, 49, 68, 102, 106–7

"iconoclast" citizen skeptics. *See under* citizen
investigation of UFOs: deference to America, 11, 67; responsibility for, 54, 62, 124, 145, 154. *See also* citizen: investigation; United States of America: early UFO investigations
ionosphere, 24–5, 54; "boys from topside," 98

Joint Army-Navy-Air Force Publication (JANAP) 146 (D), 82, 95

Kaasen, Ken, 3–4, 81–6
Keyhoe, Donald, 31, 45, 76, 82, 102, 137–8

Library and Archives Canada (LAC), 8, 22, 138, 162, 173n27

McGuire, Ramon (of rock band Trooper), 100
McNamara, A.G., 151–3
Menzel, Donald Howard, 56
Michalak, Stephen, 108–13, 123, 136, 143
Millman, Peter, 55–6, 65, 67–8, 136, 138
Montreal UFO Study Group (MUFOSG), 143–4

National Aeronautics and Space Administration (NASA), 75, 142

National Defence, Department of: avoiding publicity, 95, 101, 138; interest in UFOs, 89, 114, 130; internal confusion, 87, 140; limits of investigation, 89–90, 118, 121, 128; responsibility for investigation, 82, 107, 126–7, 185n32
National Investigations Committee on Aerial Phenomena (NICAP), 74, 82–3
National Research Council: associate committees, 136; final report, 151–3; opinion on citizen expertise, 134, 142, 160; passive role, 140, 153, 157, 159; responsibility for investigation, 128–30, 135
North American Aerospace Defense Command (NORAD), 140

Oatway, H.C., 53, 55, 76, 184n24
Ottawa Flying Saucer Club (OFSC), 97–9

Project Magnet: declassification of, 138; publicity, 35, 49, 66, 144; purpose, 16, 18, 23, 24; security classification, 34, 184n22; termination, 41, 42, 46, 48
Project Second Storey: as advisory body, 62, 65; distrust of, 58; documentation, 76, 138; official stance on UFOs, 16, 68, 70, 73, 165; sighting report form, 60–1
publicity, unwanted. *See under* government (Canada)

reliability of UFO witness reports, 51, 59, 61, 89, 122, 141, 156, 186n41
Robertson Panel (CIA), 68–9
Roswell incident, 5, 18, 155, 163
Royal Canadian Air Force (RCAF): correspondence with citizens, 77, 83; internal confusion, 51, 85–6, 127; response to extraterrestrial contact claims, 52; response to physical evidence, 112, 116; responsibility for investigation, 66, 74, 82, 90
Royal Canadian Mounted Police (RCMP): correspondence with citizens, 148; investigation, 90, 110, 140; officer disbelief, 101, 156; reporting procedure, 9, 63, 123, 140–1, 172n25, 186n44; sighting report, 61
Ruppelt, Edward, 57, 62, 67, 102, 171n15

Sarbacher, Robert, 19–22
secularization of society, 174n35
Shag Harbour incident, 119–23
sighting reports: accuracy of, 172n24; declassification of, 138; Department of National Defence questionnaire, 51, 54, 58–9; drawings, 192n63; reporting procedures, 77, 87, 186n44; volume of, 4, 9–10, 60, 63
Smith, Wilbert: balloon experiment, 28–9, 58; belief in extraterrestrials, 15, 22, 30, 54; biography, 19; and cranks, 34, 43; criticism from colleagues, 34, 37, 43, 45; frustration with government, 18, 26, 45, 47, 58, 60, 85; in Keyhoe's books, 33; meeting with Sarbacher, 19–22; and Ottawa Flying Saucer Club, 97,

98; search for advanced technology, 24, 27; UFO observatory, 37, 41, 73
Solandt, Omond, 39, 52–3, 55, 72–3
Soviet Union, 6, 30, 84, 90
Spicer, D.M., 77–8
state, Canadian: and citizen experience, 12, 32, 48, 85, 164, 167; foreign affairs, 57; relationship with science, 14–15, 18, 46, 161; theoretical explanation, 13–14, 96, 169n5, 175n42; use of UFOs by the, 11, 13, 60, 86, 105. *See also* government (Canada)
Strategic Air Command (SAC). *See* United States Strategic Air Command

transparency. *See* government (Canada)
Transport, Department of: correspondence with citizens, 43, 74, 102; distancing from Wilbert Smith, 35, 74–5; mandate, 46. *See also* government (Canada): unwanted publicity

UFOs: archival documents, 9, 137–8, 184n22; clubs, 97–9, 135; continuity with fairy tales, 97; drawings, 192n63; global history of, 170n8; as hoax, 56, 113, 118; as intrusion into science, 129, 153; landing pad for, 106; in the media, 10, 25, 30, 53, 77, 92, 135, 146, 152, 155, 172n25; as misidentification, 23, 56, 60, 70, 152, 159, 186n42; modern era of, 5, 170n9; as scientific opportunity, 128; as security threat, 4, 6; tangibility of, 114; as "work," 11, 59, 84, 105, 168
United States of America: early UFO investigations, 8, 57; influence on Canada, 5–6, 11, 57–8, 67, 82
United States Strategic Air Command (SAC), 78

Vancouver Area Flying Saucer Club (VAFSC), 99
Vezina, Allan K., 131–4

X, Mr, 146–50